Business Statistics

Business Statistics

Telsa Floyd

Larsen & Keller
www.larsen-keller.com

Business Statistics
Telsa Floyd
ISBN: 978-1-64172-083-0 (Hardback)

Larsen & Keller
Published by Larsen and Keller Education,
5 Penn Plaza,
19th Floor,
New York, NY 10001, USA

Cataloging-in-Publication Data

Business statistics / Telsa Floyd.
p. cm.
Includes bibliographical references and index.
ISBN 978-1-64172-083-0
1. Commercial statistics. 2. Business. 3. Statistics. I. Floyd, Telsa.
HF1017 .B87 2019
519.5--dc23

Printed and bound in China.

For more information regarding Larsen and Keller Education and its products, please visit the publisher's website www.larsen-keller.com

Table of Contents

Preface

The field of business statistics is concerned with making effective and good decisions in the face of uncertainty. It is useful in the areas of econometrics, financial analysis, marketing research and services improvement. It is a branch of applied statistics that uses the data collected from business and government agencies. Time series is an important aspect of business statistics. A comprehension of descriptive statistics, probability, binomial and normal distributions, linear regressions and correlation, etc. are vital to the study of business statistics. This textbook unfolds the innovative aspects of business statistics, which will be crucial for the holistic understanding of the subject matter. It presents the complex subject of business statistics in the most comprehensible and easy to understand language. This book, with its detailed analyses and data, will prove immensely beneficial to professionals and students involved in this area at various levels.

A detailed account of the significant topics covered in this book is provided below:

Chapter 1, Business statistics is a science concerned with good decision-making under uncertain circumstances. It is applied in many disciplines like econometrics, financial analysis, auditing, marketing research and services improvement. Economic statistics is concerned with the processing, collection, compilation and analysis of economic data. This is an introductory chapter, which will delve into all the significant aspects of statistical thinking, economic data, business intelligence, data collection, etc. **Chapter 2**, Data analysis is the process of transforming, cleansing and modeling data with the objective of deriving useful information, forming conclusions and for supporting good decision-making. This chapter has been carefully written to provide an easy understanding of the varied aspects of data description and analysis, such as measures of dispersion, data distribution, data visualization and predictive analytics with respect to business statistics. **Chapter 3**, Probability refers to the measurement of the likelihood of occurrence of an event. The estimation of characteristics of a population is based on an analysis of a selection of a statistical sample. The aim of this chapter is to explore the concepts of probability, sampling and statistical distributions for business. It includes topics such as set theory, probability distribution, interval estimation, inference, sampling, large sample theory, sampling distribution, point estimation, etc. **Chapter 4**, A hypothesis test in statistics is a method of statistical inference. In this method, two sets of statistical data are compared or a sample data set is compared with a data set obtained from an idealized model. The topics elaborated in this chapter, such as null hypothesis, test statistic, Welch's t-test, Type I, II and III errors, etc., will help in developing a better perspective of hypothesis testing and its application in the varied areas of business. **Chapter 5**, Econometrics is a branch of economics that applies statistical methods to economic data and ascribes empirical content to economic relations. All the diverse principles of econometrics have been carefully analyzed in this chapter, such as econometric model, endogeneity and panel data, for a comprehensive understanding of the subject.

I would like to make a special mention of my publisher who considered me worthy of this opportunity and also supported me throughout the process. I would also like to thank the editing team at the back-end who extended their help whenever required.

Telsa Floyd

1

Business and Economic Statistics

Business statistics is a science concerned with good decision-making under uncertain circumstances. It is applied in many disciplines like econometrics, financial analysis, auditing, marketing research and services improvement. Economic statistics is concerned with the processing, collection, compilation and analysis of economic data. This is an introductory chapter, which will delve into all the significant aspects of statistical thinking, economic data, business intelligence, data collection, etc.

Statistical Thinking

Understanding statistics is important for anyone running an organization of any scale. There are many common misconceptions in the field that can be very harmful to the performance of a company, and a good leader must invest the time to train themselves to think in the right way.

Statistical thinking is the ability to align one's thoughts with the fundamental ideas of statistics, allowing the person to make better decisions in any given situation. There is a lot we can learn from the structured, rigid nature of statistics, and a surprising amount of that carries over to areas of life that we wouldn't normally associate with statistical analysis.

Important Principles

The fundamental principle of statistical thinking is that the world around us is one large network of systems, all connected in ways that are rigidly (although not always clearly) defined. Realizing this, if we can measure this system, we can apply statistics to everyday life to a large extent, analyzing everything that happens around us, which will help us look for a root cause or sources of variation in the system much more effectively.

In addition, statistical thinking also allows one to avoid falling for some of the most common traps in analyzing data. For example, understanding how deviations work, and what they indicate about the validity of statistical results, is an important principle for anyone working with large amounts of data. The risk of making a decision that looks like an improvement on the chart, but is not supported by statistical analysis, can not only be damaging or costly to a company, but can reduce confidence in your skills.

Another critical point from those with good statistical thinking is that variation is inevitable in any kind of process. What this means is that it's often impossible to predict a certain outcome with 100% accuracy, and knowing where to expect those variations can be of great benefit.

Anyone who's had to work with statistical analysis should already have some intuition for this, and it can only grow stronger the more you apply your knowledge to real-world situations.

Lacking good statistical thinking often leads to many problems in an organization. It's hard to define the exact scope of a given problem in many cases without having access to statistical data about that problem, and as a result, if the problem statement is not clear, identifying the root cause or sources of variation can be nearly impossible.

This carries over to the management style of a person without strong statistical thinking. They would not be able to understand the complex processes that govern the work of their organization properly, and as a result, they can't be expected to make accurate decisions from their leadership position.

It also limits their ability to coach and mentor their employees on what statistical analysis to perform.

Effects on Development Pace

What this ultimately leads to is a slowed pace of development, and improvements that could have been realized much earlier end up going undiscovered. Even worse, these problems can compound in the long run, further decreasing the productivity of the company and causing stagnation.

Last but not least, a leader who doesn't understand statistical thinking properly is not prone to taking calculated risks. This can have one of two outcomes – either the leader will be reluctant to take any risks at all, or they will leap at every opportunity, no matter how much danger it might pose to the company as a whole. Risk-taking is an important part of any business, but it must be done in a way that minimizes the potential negative impact for everyone, especially those that have no say in the decision. Statistical thinking helps better quantify risks.

The good news is, statistical thinking is a skill that can be honed with practice. A good leader must identify their shortcomings in this area and take steps to improve the way they analyze every situation. There are specific routines that can be followed to improve one's understanding of statistical thinking, and as long as you keep moving in the right direction, you're going to see positive results in the long run.

Economic Data

Economic data refer to the Economic Census of establishments and various surveys and data for establishments and firms. With very few exceptions, the public use versions for these files are limited to data presented in aggregate form. Access to these data will only be granted to qualified researchers on approved projects with authorization to use specific data sets.

Types of Economic Data

It is obvious that the content of economic data is undergoing profound change and that at the present time we are in the middle of these changes. Nevertheless, it will be useful to identify what are the main types of economic data currently available and to discuss the ways these bodies of data are changing.

National Income Accounts

Within the past decade national income accounts have come to be recognized as one of the most basic types of information about a nation's economic activity. In a number of countries the government is required to present, along with its budget, a forecast of the national income accounts for the coming period, showing how the proposed government budget relates to anticipated economic developments.

National income accounts today generally cover five sectors of the economy:

- The gross national income and product account shows who purchases the final output of the economy and how the income generated by such economic activity flows to individuals as income, to governments as taxes, or to corporations as profits.
- The personal income account shows the income received by individuals, whether in their role as participants in the productive process or as recipients of social security benefits or other transfers from government. The personal income account also shows how people dispose of their income, i.e., how much of their income goes for consumer expenditures and personal taxes and how much is saved.
- The public sector account, which has become considerably more important in recent years, shows, on the receipts side, what the government receives from taxes on individuals or on businesses and how much it receives as property income, such as the surplus of government enterprises. The expenditure side of the government account shows the outlays of the government in terms of the functions which it undertakes, such as education, health, defense, general administration, and economic development.
- The balance of payments account shows the foreign trade of an economy in terms of imports and exports and transfers to and from abroad. This account shows whether a nation is running down its reserves of foreign exchange or acquiring a surplus.
- The final account, the saving and investment account, on one side brings together the excess of income over expenditure in each of the other sectors, and on the other side shows the capital formation by government and by public and private enterprises.

These five sector accounts are so set up that an expenditure in one account corresponds to a receipt in some other account. Thus, for example, the amount of consumer expenditures in the personal income account corresponds exactly to the sale of goods to consumers appearing in the gross national product account.

Flow of Funds Data

The national income accounts cover only current income and expenditure transactions; they exclude those financial transactions that merely alter the assets and liabilities of the various sectors of the economy. Because this type of financial information is important in any analysis of fiscal and monetary policy, sets of information on the sources and uses of funds by the different sectors of the economy have been developed in many countries. In the United States information on the flow of funds is published by the Federal Reserve Board. This information is generally consistent with the national income accounting data, but the two sets of data are not fully integrated. In some other countries—for example, Canada, the Netherlands, and France—the flow-of-funds data have been integrated with national income data to produce one consistent set of data interrelating the income accounts with the financial transactions of each sector.

Input Output Data

Input-output data showing the purchase of inputs and sale of outputs by industrial sectors of the economy are also becoming available for many countries, but unlike national income and flow-of-funds data, this information rarely appears on an annual basis. The statistical requirements of a complete input-output system are very considerable, and it is usually possible to obtain such a body of data only for periods for which economic censuses are available. Again, however, there is an increasing tendency toward integration of national income accounting data and input-output data. For example, the gross product originating by industrial sector has come to be a common breakdown in the national income accounts, and this often matches the industrial breakdown provided in the input-output matrix.

National Wealth

The development of flow-of-funds accounts and input-output matrices has fostered increased interest in balance sheets for various sectors of the economy. Data on the financial transactions of each sector and on capital formation make possible, via a perpetual-inventory approach, the development of national wealth and sector balance sheets. This work, however, is still in its early stages, and few countries at present publish official current data on national wealth.

Data Coverage, Collection and Processing

One of the major characteristics of economic data systems at the present time is increasing detail, both in terms of time coverage and in terms of disaggregation. For example, today most of the industrial economies publish quarterly data on national income accounts; and for some components, such as personal income, they may even publish monthly data. There is also increasing interest in regional breakdowns of information within nations. In large part this is due to the fact that the different regions of a nation develop differently, and economic development must recognize differences in regional patterns, for the consideration of problems of location of new industries and for dealing explicitly with problems of regional poverty.

In developing these new bodies of data, governments have made use of two new tools which have made possible the development of much more reliable data at lower cost:

(1) the use of sample surveys and

(2) the development of electronic data processing.

Since World War ii there has been a considerable increase in the use of sample surveys that are specifically designed to obtain desired information. Many of these sample surveys have been very successful in providing data which heretofore were completely unavailable. Private groups as well as governments have been able to develop important bodies of data. For example, in the United States the Survey Research Center at the University of Michigan has developed an important body of information on consumer expenditures, and the McGraw-Hill Publishing Company has developed an interesting and useful survey of investment plans of industrial firms.

The development of electronic data processing techniques has permitted governments to make use of existing bodies of information in ways which were previously impossible because of the extremely high cost of processing. The increased use of high-speed computers to process and edit data has meant that major bodies of data that are collected for other purposes, e.g., income taxes and social security, can be utilized for statistical purposes. Furthermore, bodies of information, such as census data, can be made available in a space of a few months rather than the several years which used to be required before final tabulations were available.

Economic Data Issues

Good economic data are a precondition to effective macroeconomic management. With the complexity of modern economies and the lags inherent in macroeconomic policy instruments, a country must have the capacity to promptly identify any adverse trends in its economy and to apply the appropriate corrective measure. This cannot be done without economic data that is complete, accurate and timely.

Increasingly, the availability of good economic data is coming to be seen by international markets as an indicator of a country that is a promising destination for foreign investment. International investors are aware that good economic data is necessary for a country to effectively manage its affairs and, other things being equal, will tend to avoid countries that do not publish such data.

The public availability of reliable and up-to-date economic data also reassures international investors by allowing them to monitor economic developments and to manage their investment risk. The severity of the Mexican and Asian financial crises was made worse by the realization by investors that the authorities had hidden a deteriorating economic situation by slow and incomplete reporting of critical economic data. Being unsure of exactly how bad the economic situation was, they tried to withdraw their assets quickly and in the process caused further damage to the economies in question. It was the realization that data issues lay behind much of the damage done by these international financial crises that led to the creation of international data quality standards, such as the International Monetary Fund (IMF) General Data Dissemination System (GDDS).

Inside a country, the public availability of good quality economic data allows firms and individuals to make their business decisions with confidence that they understand the overall macroeconomic environment. As with international investors, local business people are less likely to overreact to a piece of bad news if they understand the economic context.

Tax data can be a source of economic data. In the United States, the IRS provides tax statistics, but the data are limited by statutory limitations and confidentiality concerns.

Economic Statistics

One of the major functions of economic statistics is to develop concepts, definitions, classifications and methods that can be used to produce statistical information that describes the state of and movements in economic phenomena, both in time and space. This information is then used to analyse the behaviour of economic operators, forecast likely movements of the economy as a whole, make economic policy and business decisions, weigh the pros and cons of alternative investments, etc.

In the world of business, medium-to-large companies are interested in receiving timely information not only about national and international macroeconomic developments, but also on various aspects concerning the sectors in which they operate, at a meaningful level of territorial detail. By contrast, small businesses want information more limited in scope, possibly relating to the local market in which they work, or to their own sector of economic activity. Then there are research centres, either public or private, whose needs for information go in all directions, depending on the subject matter. Lastly, households mainly want information that is quite general (or "curious"), expressed in a form they can understand, almost exclusively "consumed" via the different media (television, the press, Internet, etc.).

Looking to the future, it is possible to identify certain trends in the demand for economic statistics that will presumably strengthen in the years to come. In the first place, demand will focus more and more on the services sector (which already accounts for over 70% of GDP in many developed countries), with new forms of production playing a more important part. The measurement of "intangible" activities will take on increased importance and this should bring about greater integration of economic statistics with social statistics: concepts such as those of human and social capital are already generating interest and becoming the subject of quantification, albeit still in embryonic form.

While the international dimension of various phenomena is set to increase with the integration of production activities dispersed over several countries, this will make it more and more difficult to measure the results of individual national economies. This will require a rethinking of the way in which economic statistics are currently compiled, especially with regard to the exchange of data between national statistical institutes in order to make national statistics more representative and consistent.

Thanks to the development of microeconometric models for the design and evaluation of public policy, there will presumably also be an increase in the demand for access to databases containing statistical information on single units (microdata). Such a trend, which is already apparent at the national and international levels, will inevitably present national statistical institutes as well as international organisations with new regulatory and organisational challenges (especially in terms of the protection of privacy). Finally, it is to be assumed that demand for greater integration of economic, social and environmental statistics will lead to new integrated accounting frameworks capable of bringing together these three main themes, mainly to enable policies that make economic growth socially and environmentally sustainable.

Demand for better integration of economic, social and environmental dimensions is also fostering the development of composite indicators, i.e. indicators that aggregate data covering specific phenomena into a single aggregated index, to be used to rank countries (regions, cities, etc.). These indices, very much appreciated by the media, are often used to advocate particular policies or to call public attention to issues not well covered by official statistics (corruption, human rights, etc.). Although the development of composite indicators is criticised by some statisticians and should require the use of an extensive set of statistical methodologies, it is putting pressure on the more traditional statistical sources to move towards new areas of work, including subjective well-being and happiness (or life satisfaction).

Additionally, the increasing role of large emerging countries, such as China, Russia, Brazil, is putting pressure on international organisations to produce more comparable statistics. The limited availability of national statistics adhering to international standards, as well as the high speed with which these countries' economies and societies evolve, make the measurement of key statistics – including population, GDP, employment and international trade – difficult. Therefore, uncertainties still exist on the dimensions of some global phenomena, such as unbalances in the international financial system or migration flows.

A large degree of uncertainty also exists about the condition of several developing countries, especially the poorest, where the availability and quality of key statistics is low. Notwithstanding the efforts made by the international community to support statistical capacity in these countries, several of them do not have basic figures, or they are produced under the control of political authorities, and thus considered unreliable.

Of course, even if statistical data and metadata are available, the capacity to transform this statistical information into knowledge to be used in decision-making by individuals, households, businesses and political institutions largely depends on the users' degree of statistical education, and this in turn depends on the country's level of economic development and also on purely cultural factors. Taking as an example the countries in the OECD, major differences can be observed: in the countries with an English-speaking culture (the United States, Canada, the United Kingdom, Australia, etc.) and in the countries of Northern Europe (Sweden, Finland, Norway, etc.) statistics play a fundamental role in political and cultural life, while in other countries the situation is much more nuanced. In the former, the greater degree of commitment to a culture of statistics is reflected not only in the greater levels of public funds devoted to the production of "official statistics", but also in greater levels of investment in applied economic research by academic institutions, foundations and major private sector companies, as well as training that is more geared to scientific disciplines and to quantitative aspects (including statistics) right down to the primary school level. By contrast, in some other countries there is less public investment in official statistics, a lower level of ability to distinguish between reliable statistical information and opinion polls, and political debate is mostly abstract and less likely to be based on statistically measured "facts".

A greater investment in statistical culture not only tends to improve the capacity to benefit from statistical data, but also creates the means by which information is communicated more accurately, a factor that is all the more important in an era of information oversupply. Naturally, this does not altogether prevent statistics being used for partisan purposes, or errors being made in interpretation. However, in countries with higher levels of statistical culture, there is a clear perception of official statistical information as a "public good", the production of which must be freed from any political influences. This consideration has led some countries to recognize the public function of statistics either in their constitutions or in laws that protect the independence of institutions producing official statistics. The inevitable effect of such recognition is to enhance the credibility of official statistics, and thus increase the demand for them.

That said, field studies have shown that even in the more statistically advanced countries, the proportion of people who know little or nothing about the country in which they are living and working is still high. As an example, a survey carried out in 2003 on a sample of citizens in the United States showed that the ability to correctly indicate the dimensions of key variables such as the public deficit or the tax burden, the level of the minimum wage or benefits under the social welfare system is quite limited, especially among people with the lowest levels of income or education, whose main source of information is television (or speeches by political and religious leaders), and who have no particular political leanings and no wish to be better informed about what is happening in their country.

In conclusion, the role played by statistics in orientating public policies and private decisions seems destined to grow in the near future, as will the difficulty users have in distinguishing reliable statistics from those of a lesser quality. Thus, the main challenge in the years to come for the producers of economic statistics will be based not on their capacity to provide quality statistics, but to offer a product whose quality will be clearly evident to the user. Fundamental to this challenge will be the growth in the statistical culture at every user level, with special attention to the world of the media. Following the principles of national accounting, the value of a service should be measured in terms of the change in the status of the consumer. In the case of statistics (a non-market service), we expect the consumer to experience an increase in his/her knowledge of the real world, enabling better choices for the individual and collective well-being. Until now, little attention has been paid to measuring the actual impact of official statistics. Instead, the focus has been limited to measuring the quantity of data published or the annual gathering of data, in other words the processes of production and not the outcome of the statistical function. One of the future challenges will be how to measure the impact of official statistics on the decision-making processes, both of individuals and of those responsible for political decisions.

Business Data

Business data refers to the information about people, places, things, business rules, and events in relation to operating a business.

Serious businesses need to consider setting up business intelligence and data warehouses. In pursuing these capabilities, they need to adopt a holistic view coupled with wise investment and careful execution. For a business to really grow, it should consider interrelated areas involving people, strategy, process, applications, metrics, data and architecture.

It is very important to gather business data and base an organization's decision on the statistical report to get precise decisions on how to more the company forward for sustainability.

Knowing things about people and their buying behaviors can make a company generate very important business data. For instance, statisticians and market researches know that certain age groups have unique buying habits. Races and people from different demographics locations also have buying patterns of their own so gathering these information in one business database can be a good way to future target marketing.

In terms of production, business data about where to get raw materials, how much the cost is, what are the customs and importation policies of the raw materials' country of origin and other information are also very important.

There are many software applications that manage business data for easy statistical reporting and spotting of trends and patterns.

The Business Data Catalog functionality in some applications allows users to present line-of-business data. It can search and retrieve information from back end systems such as Enterprise Resource Planning (ERP), Customer Resource Management (CRM), Advance Planner and Optimizer (APO) and Supply Chain Management (SCM).

In many companies, they maintain a business data warehouse where data from several are collected and integrate every few minutes. These repositories of business data may supply needed information to generate reports and recommendations in an intelligent manner. Hence the term Business Intelligence is already widely used in the business industry today.

Business intelligence generally refers to technologies and software applications that are used to gather, integrate and analyze business data and other information pertaining to the operation of the company. It can help companies gain more comprehensive and in depth knowledge of the many factors that can affect their business. These knowledge may include metrics on sales, internal operations and production. With recommendations from business intelligence, companies can make better decisions for the business.

For processing billions of business data in the data warehouse for business intelligence, companies use high powered and secure computer systems that are installed with different levels of security access.

Several software applications and tools have been developed to gather and analyze large amounts of unstructured business data ranging from sales statistics, production metrics to employee attendance and customer relations. Business intelligence software applications very depending on the vendor but the common attribute in most of them is that they can be customized based on the needs and requirements of the business company. Many companies have in-house developers to take care of business data as the company continues to evolve.

Some example of business intelligence tools to process business data include Score carding, Business activity monitoring, Business Performance Management and Performance Measurement, Enterprise Management systems and Supply Chain Management/Demand Chain Management. Free Business Intelligence and open source products include Pentaho, RapidMiner, SpagoBI and Palo, an OLAP database.

Business data is the core of the science of Analytics. Analytics is the study of business data that uses statistical analysis in knowing and understanding patterns and trends in order to foresee or predict business performance. Analytics is commonly associated with data mining and statistical analysis although it is more leaned towards physics-like modeling which involves extensive computation.

Examples of Business Data

- Leads & Opportunities: Lists of potential customers.
- Customer: Customer details such as name and address.

- Transactions: Records of commercial transactions such as customer purchases.
- Interactions: Records of interactions with customers and other stakeholders such as investors, employees and the media. For example, records of visits to your website.
- Social Media: Data regarding your target markets or reputation that is collected from social media sources.
- Product: A product catalog that captures the specifications of your products.
- Employee: Employee data such as skill inventories, salary and performance management data.
- Knowledge: Information created by employees and partners that is stored as documents and media.
- Communications: Communications such as business emails and records of customer inquiries.
- Process: Information that pertains to business processes such as manufacturing products, fulfilling orders and supporting customers.
- Supply Chain: Supply chain data such as tracking your inventory in storage and transport.
- Partner: Partner information such as data that is used to monitor the performance of suppliers.
- Risk: Data that is used to identify, analyze and manage risk such as a database of historical construction projects that is used to estimateconstruction project risk.
- Market: Market data such as information about prices offered by competitors.
- Industry: Industry data such as market size and market share data for a product category.

Business Statistics

Business statistics takes the data analysis tools from elementary statistics and applies them to business. For example, estimating the probability of a defect coming off a factory line, or seeing where sales are headed in the future. Many of the tools used in business statistics are built on ones you've probably already come across in basic math: mean, mode and median, bar graphs and the bell curve, and basic probability. Hypothesis testing (where you test out an idea) and regression analysis (fitting data to an equation) builds on this foundation.

There are three major functions in any business enterprise in which the statistical methods are useful. These are as follows:

(i) The planning of operations: This may relate to either special projects or to the recurring activities of a firm over a specified period.

(ii) The setting up of standards: This may relate to the size of employment, volume of sales, fixation of quality norms for the manufactured product, norms for the daily output, and so forth.

(iii) The function of control: This involves comparison of actual production achieved against the norm or target set earlier. In case the production has fallen short of the target, it gives remedial measures so that such a deficiency does not occur again.

A worth noting point is that although these three functions-planning of operations, setting standards, and control-are separate, but in practice they are very much interrelated.

Statistical problems arising in the course of business operations are multitudinous. As such, one may do no more than highlight some of the more important ones to emphasis the relevance of statistics to the business world. In the sphere of production, for example, statistics can be useful in various ways.

Statistical quality control methods are used to ensure the production of quality goods. Identifying and rejecting defective or substandard goods achieve this. The sale targets can be fixed on the basis of sale forecasts, which are done by using varying methods of forecasting. Analysis of sales affected against the targets set earlier would indicate the deficiency in achievement, which may be on account of several causes: (i) targets were too high and unrealistic (ii) salesmen's performance has been poor (iii) emergence of increase in competition (iv) poor quality of company's product, and so on. These factors can be further investigated.

Another sphere in business where statistical methods can be used is personnel management. Here, one is concerned with the fixation of wage rates, incentive norms and performance appraisal of individual employee. The concept of productivity is very relevant here. On the basis of measurement of productivity, the productivity bonus is awarded to the workers. Comparisons of wages and productivity are undertaken in order to ensure increases in industrial productivity.

Statistical methods could also be used to ascertain the efficacy of a certain product, say, medicine. For example, a pharmaceutical company has developed a new medicine in the treatment of bronchial asthma. Before launching it on commercial basis, it wants to ascertain the effectiveness of this medicine. It undertakes an experimentation involving the formation of two comparable groups of asthma patients. One group is given this new medicine for a specified period and the other one is treated with the usual medicines. Records are maintained for the two groups for the specified period. This record is then analysed to ascertain if there is any significant difference in the recovery of the two groups. If the difference is really significant statistically, the new medicine is commercially launched.

Data Collection

Data has become a major priority for businesses of all sizes. As technologies that capture and analyze data proliferate, so too do businesses' abilities to contextualize data and draw new insights from it. The internet of things and artificial intelligence are two critical tools for companies in data capture and analysis, from better understanding day-to-day operations, making business decisions and learning about their customers.

Customer data is a focus area all its own. From consumer behavior to predictive analytics, companies regularly capture, store and analyze large amounts of data on their consumer base every day. Some companies have even built an entire business model around consumer data, whether they create targeted ads or sell to a third party. Customer data is big business.

Data collection for marketing research is a detailed process where a planned search for all relevant data is made by a researcher. The success of marketing research is contingent on the integrity and relevance of the data. And to a high degree, the quality of the data depends on the methods of data collection used. The selection and use of methods for conducting marketing research requires a great deal of experience and expertise in order to correctly gage suitability.

These methods fall into two types of research categories, which are Qualitative Research and Quantitative Research. Qualitative Research is generally used to develop an initial understanding of the problem. It is non statistical in nature and the answers are derived from the data itself. It is used in exploratory and descriptive research designs. Qualitative data can be procured through a variety of forms like interview transcripts; documents, diaries and notes made while observing. Quantitative Research on the other hand, quantifies the data and generalizes the results from the sample to the population.

There are two types of data:

1. Primary Data – Data that is collected first hand by the researcher. This data is specifically collected for the purpose of the study and addresses the current problem. This is original data that is collected by the researcher first hand.

2. Secondary Data – Data from other sources that has been already collected and is readily available. This data is less expensive and more quickly attainable from various published sources. Secondary data is extremely useful when primary data cannot be obtained at all.

The challenge lies in the case of method selection for collecting primary data. The method has to be relevant and appropriate. This will be the most important decision prior to beginning market research.

The market research process consists of 6 distinct steps:

- Step 1 - Determine the research problem and objectives
- Step 2 - Cultivate the overall research plan
- Step 3 – Collect the data
- Step 4 – Analyze the data
- Step 5 – Present or publish the findings
- Step 6 – Use the findings to make an informed decision.

Methods of Data Collection

1. Telephone Interviews

   The biggest advantage of telephone interviews is that is saves cost and time. Today, accessing people via telephone is so much easier because almost everyone has one. Another advantage is fewer interviewers are required in order to conduct telephone interviews than face-to-face interviews.

2. Online Surveys

   Given the current myriad of technological developments, the use of online surveys has rapidly increased. It may well be the least expensive way to reach the greatest amount of people – all over the world. Once an online survey has been designed, it can be stored easily, revised and reused as needed from time to time. The key is in the design and layout of the survey so that respondents don't overlook a survey in their crowded inboxes. The response time is quick so online surveys have become the preferred method of data collection for many consumer satisfaction surveys and product and service feedback. It is easy to track respondents, non-respondents and results through the data collection process. Electronic reminders can be sent easily at a very low cost. Respondents have the option to begin the survey, stop, save the responses at a later more convenient time. Research shows that respondents tend to answer questions more truthfully than when engaged through other methods.

3. Face to Face Interviews

   This method is one of the most flexible ways to gather data and gain trust and cooperation from the respondents. Besides that, interviewing respondents in person means their non-verbal language can be observed as well. It is especially useful to detect discomfort when respondents are discussing sensitive issues. Respondents have more time to consider their answers and the interviewer can gain a deeper understanding of the validity of a response. It is also easier to maintain their interest and focus for a longer period. Focus Group Interviewsentail more respondents at one time.

   Face to face interviews can also take place via Intercept Interviews as well. These interviews can take place on the spot at shopping malls, street corners or even at the threshold of people's homes. It is understandable why these types of interviews must be brief, to the point and free of from distasteful questions as there is a strong risk of the potential respondent leaving. These face to face interactions can be time consuming so enlist a trusted company like Dattel Asia to provide the data needed with unprecedented levels of transparency. Dattel Asia is ASEAN's leading data collection company that utilizes tablets, digital tools and artificial machine learning systems for data collection. A reliable face-to-face data collection service provider that has over 250 skilled Field Data Associates and more than 310,000 unique and verified respondents in their data repository.

Turning Data into Knowledge

Capturing large amounts of data creates the problem of how to sort through and analyze all that data. No human can reasonably sit down and read through line after line of customer data all day long, and even if they could, they probably wouldn't make much of a dent. Luckily, computers are much better at this type of work than humans, and they can operate 24/7/365 without taking a break.

As machine learning algorithms and other forms of AI proliferate and improve, data analytics becomes an even more powerful field for breaking down the sea of data into manageable tidbits of actionable insights. Some AI programs will flag anomalies or offer recommendations to decision-makers within an organization based on the contextualized data.

Without programs like these, all the data capture in the world would be utterly useless.

Data usage by Businesses

There are several ways companies use the consumer data they collect and the insights they draw from that data:

Improving Customer Experience

For many companies, consumer data offers a way to better understand and meet their customers' demands. By analyzing customer behavior, as well as vast troves of reviews and feedback, companies can nimbly modify their digital presence, goods or services to better suit the current marketplace.

Not only do companies use consumer data to improve consumer experiences as a whole, but they also use data to make decisions on an individualized level, said Brandon Chopp, digital manager for iHeartRaves.

"Our most important source of marketing intelligence comes from understanding customer data and using it to improve our website functionality," Chopp said. "Our team has improved the customer experience by creating customized promotions and special offers based on customer data. Since each customer is going to have their own individual preferences, personalization is key."

Refining Marketing Strategy

Contextualized data can help companies understand how consumers are engaging with and responding to their marketing campaigns, and adjust accordingly. This highly predictive use case gives businesses an idea of what consumers will want based on what they have already done. Like other aspects of consumer data analysis, marketing is becoming more about personalization as a result, said Brett Downes, SEO manager at Traffic Jam Media.

"Mapping users' journeys and personalizing their journey, not just through your website but further onto platforms like YouTube, LinkedIn, Facebook or on to any other website is now essential," Downes said. "Segmenting data effectively allows you to market to only the people you know are most likely to engage. These have opened up new opportunities in industries previously very hard to market to."

Turning Data into Cash-flow

Companies that capture data also stand to profit from it. Data brokers, or companies that buy and sell information on customers, have risen as a new industry alongside big data. For businesses that are capturing large amounts of data, this represents an opportunity for a new stream of revenue.

For advertisers, having this information available for purchase is immensely valuable, so the demand for more and more data is ever increasing. That means the more disparate data sources data brokers can pull from to package more thorough data profiles, the more money they can make by selling this information to one another and advertisers.

Using Data to Secure Data

Some businesses even use consumer data as a means of securing more sensitive information. For example, banking institutions will sometimes use voice recognition data to authorize a user to access their financial information or protect them for fraudulent attempts to steal their information.

These systems work by marrying data from a customer's interaction with a call center and machine learning algorithms that can identify and flag potentially fraudulent attempts to access a customer's account. This takes some of the guesswork and human error out of catching a con.

As data capture and analytics technologies become more sophisticated, companies will find new and more effective ways to collect and contextualize data on everything, including consumers. For businesses, doing so is essential to remaining competitive well into the future; failing to do so, on the other hand, is like running a race with your legs tied together. Insight is king, and insight in the modern business environment is gleaned from contextualized data.

Data Privacy Regulations

So much consumer data has been captured and analyzed that governments are crafting strict data privacy regulations designed to give individuals a modicum of control over how their data is used. The European Union's General Data Protection Requirements (GDPR) lays out the rules of data capture, storage, usage, and sharing for companies, and stiff penalties for those that fail to comply. Companies that fail to abide by the rules set out within the GDPR face 20 million Euro fines or up to 4 percent of annual revenue, whichever is higher.

Data privacy has even made it to the U.S. in the form of the California Consumer Privacy Act (CCPA). The CCPA is, in some ways, similar to GDPR but differs in that it requires consumers to opt-out of data collection and names the state as the entity to develop guidelines, rather than the company's internal decision makers.

Data privacy regulations are changing the way businesses capture, store, share and analyze consumer data. Businesses that are so far untouched by data privacy regulations can expect these types of laws to proliferate as more consumers demand privacy rights. Data collection by private companies, though, is unlikely to go away; it will merely change in form as businesses adapt to new laws and regulations.

Data Handling

Data handling is the process of ensuring that research data is stored, archived or disposed off in a safe and secure manner during and after the conclusion of a research project. This includes the development of policies and procedures to manage data handled electronically as well as through non-electronic means.

Data handling is important in ensuring the integrity of research data since it addresses concerns related to confidentially, security, and preservation/retention of research data. Proper planning for data handling can also result in efficient and economical storage, retrieval, and disposal of data. In the case of data handled electronically, data integrity is a primary concern to ensure that recorded data is not altered, erased, lost or accessed by unauthorized users.

Data handling issues encompass both electronic as well as non-electronic systems, such as paper files, journals, and laboratory notebooks. Electronic systems include computer workstations and laptops, personal digital assistants (PDA), storage media such as videotape, diskette, CD, DVD, memory cards, and other electronic instrumentation. These systems may be used for storage, archival, sharing, and disposing off data, and therefore, require adequate planning at the start of a research project so that issues related to data integrity can be analyzed and addressed early on.

Considerations/Issues in Data Handling

Issues that should be considered in ensuring integrity of data handled include the following:

- Type of data handled and its impact on the environment (especially if it is on a toxic media).
- Type of media containing data and its storage capacity, handling and storage requirements, reliability, longevity (in the case of degradable medium), retrieval effectiveness, and ease of upgrade to newer media.
- Data handling responsibilities/privileges, that is, who can handle which portion of data, at what point during the project, for what purpose, etc.
- Data handling procedures that describe how long the data should be kept, and when, how, and who should handle data for storage, sharing, archival, retrieval and disposal purposes.

Deciding how long research data should be kept may depend on the nature of the project, sponsoring agency's guidelines, ongoing interest in or need for the data, cost of maintaining the data in the long run, and other relevant considerations. Under current Health and Human Services requirements, research records must be maintained for at least three years after the last expenditure report. Federal regulations or institutional guidelines may require that data be retained for longer periods.

In the case of data stored electronically, the potential for altering, erasing, losing, or unauthorized access is high. Several years of valuable research data can be compromised or lost as it happned in April 2001, when an intruder broke into a server used by a group of Univeristy of Washington graduate students and deleted the entire file system (UoW website, 2003). Although some aspects of protection from these threats are the responsibility of IT professionals, researchers are ultimately responsible for ensuring the security of their data.

In the " Data Management Guidelines Issued by British Medical Research Council" published on the ORI website (2003) it states that:

" If the data are recorded electronically, the data should be regularly backed up on disc; a hard copy should be made of particularly important data; relevant software must be retained to ensure future access, and special attention should be given to guaranteeing the security of electronic data".

Creating a secure environment for electronic data usually involves all members of a project, which can include an IT Manager, system administrator, support personnel, and several end- users. Some issues to consider when handling data electronically include the following:

- Protect systems' and individual files with login and passwords
- Manage access rights (in the case of computer system administrators not involved in the project their access rights could be limited)
- Regularly update virus protection to prevent vulnerability of data
- Limit physical access to equipment and storage media (for example, in the case of data stored on a computer using a stand-alone computer may be secure than a networked, computer)
- Accurate data removal from old hardware and certification that the data was removed
- Ensure data recoverability in case of emergencies
- Regularly update electronic storage media to avoid outdated storage/retrieval devices
- Backup multiple copies in secured multiple locations
- Encrypt files when wireless devices are used, and keep track of wireless connectivity to prevent accidental file sharing
- Record date and time when a piece of electronic data was originally recorded to prevent alteration or manipulation at a future date

In the article entiled "Preventing data theft", Lynn Greiner quotes Paul Hyde, CEO of Kasten Chase (a company that develops high-assurance data security systems) that:

" It's important to have a level of security that is adequate if the machine is stolen. Everyone who is in the position where they could be separated from the device needs security. I think the best way to look at it, is to look at the criticality of what you're doing, (and) of its importance to the business environment. You have to determine what the value of the information is, and match up security accordingly".

One of the key issues to consider in storing or archiving data manually or electronically is "configuration management." This involves keeping track of data on different media or format during different stages of the project by different users. For example, in a research effort raw data could be recorded in a laboratory notebook, then transferred to an electronic data file for analysis, which could result in output data. The output data then could be converted to plots or graphs. Configuration management will involve keeping track of all these and upgrading the data to newer media or formats as necessary during the life of a particular project. Effective configuration management will not only ensure data integrity but also simplify the use of data.

Disposing research data requires adequate plans, procedures, and impact analysis to ensure that the appropriate data is discarded in a safe and secure manner. Retaining data on paper files and electronic media when not needed after a project is over can lead to unauthorized access to confidential data. The likelihood of this is very high especially when principal investigators retire, leave the project, or die without establishing proper data management procedures on which data should be kept, disposed off, shared, etc.

Disposing of data containing confidential information on human subjects or national security requires additional care to ensure that the information could not be reconstructed from the disposed media. When disposing electronically data stored on computer disks, the disks will have to be erased several times and certified that data could not be recovered from them. Some federal and state agencies have guidelines on how many times a computer disk should be erased to ensure the disk is free of recoverable data. In the case of data stored on film or other toxic media, care should be taken to ensure that the disposal process does not pollute the environment.

Research organizations often contract to commercial data disposing companies to dispose of data stored on non-electronic media such as laboratory notebooks, paper files, etc., and it is the responsibility of the research organization to ensure the commercial company will dispose off the data in a safe and non-recoverable manner.

Data handling requires adequate planning, development of procedures, and training and supervision of research staff to ensure that data is stored, archived or disposed off in a safe and secure manner that preserves the integrity of research data as well as simplifies data management.

Business Intelligence

Business intelligence (BI) leverages software and services to transform data into actionable intelligence that informs an organization's strategic and tactical business decisions. BI tools access and analyze data sets and present analytical findings in reports, summaries, dashboards, graphs, charts and maps to provide users with detailed intelligence about the state of the business.

Working of Business Intelligence

Although business intelligence does not tell business users what to do or what will happen if they take a certain course, neither is BI only about generating reports. Rather, BI offers a way for people to examine data to understand trends and derive insights.

"So many people in the business need data to do their jobs better," says Chris Hagans, vice president of operations for WCI Consulting, a consultancy focused on BI.

Hagans points out that business intelligence tools streamline the effort people need to search for, merge and query data to obtain information they need to make good business decisions.

For example, a company that wants to better manage its supply chain needs BI capabilities to determine where delays are happening and where variabilities exist within the shipping process,

Hagans says. That company could also use its BI capabilities to discover which products are most commonly delayed or which modes of transportation are most often involved in delays.

The potential use cases for BI extend beyond the typical business performance metrics of improved sales and reduced costs, saysCindi Howson, research vice president at Gartner, an IT research and advisory firm. She points to the Columbus, Ohio, school system and its success using BI tools to examine numerous data points — from attendance rates to student performance — to improve student learning and high school graduate rates.

Business Intelligence Tools

Organizations today can choose from a robust list of vendors offering BI tools. Gartner identifies nearly two dozen BI and analytics vendors in its 2017 Magic Quadrant report, listing Microsoft, Qlik and Tableau as leaders. Other BI tools vendors include Information Builders, Sisense and Zoomdata.

Organizations chose a BI platform based on various factors, including the size and complexity of their operations as well as what type of technology they already have (i.e. IBM, Oracle, SAS, SAP — all of which offer BI tools), Hagans says.

Business Intelligence in Action

In the past, IT professionals had been the primary users of BI applications. However, BI tools have evolved to be more intuitive and user-friendly, enabling a large number of users across a variety of organizational domains to tap the tools.

Gartner's Howson differentiates two types of BI. The first is traditional or classic BI, where IT professionals use in-house transactional data to generate reports. The second is modern BI, where business users interact with agile, intuitive systems to analyze data more quickly.

Howson explains that organizations generally opt for classic BI for certain types of reporting, such as regulatory or financial reports, where accuracy is paramount and the questions and data sets used are standard and predicable. Organizations typically use modern BI tools when business users need insight into quickly changing dynamics, such as marketing events, in which being fast is valued over getting the data 100 percent right.

But while solid business intelligence is essential to making strategic business decisions, many organizations struggle to implement effective BI strategies, thanks to poor data practices, tactical mistakes and more.

The Value of Business Intelligence

Although much of today's hype is around big data and advanced analytics (as well as the next step up: artificial intelligence and machine learning), BI is still relevant for multiple reasons.

First, experts say that many organizations still struggle with how to wrangle their data and leverage BI tools to their full potential. As a result, University of Dayton's Gorman says most organizations tend to have pockets of BI capabilities rather than an enterprise-wide platform.

"You might have an executive dashboard that gives something like prices by region and another executive using a BI tool that gives vendor performance," he says.

So these organizations remain focused on fine-tuning and then maximizing their BI initiatives before moving up to more advanced analytics capabilities.

Gorman says that's one reason why the market for BI tools is still growing, as organizations continue to add capabilities in different functional areas to meet growing demand.

According to its Global Business Intelligence Market 2016-2020 report, published in January 2016, global technology research and advisory company Technavio forecast the global BI market to post a compound annual growth rate (CAGR) of more than 10 percent by 2020.

The research study says increasing adoption of data analytics, data availability and implementation of cloud BI as the three major factors driving the market.

Second, organizations will continue to need an accurate understanding of past events and current states. That's why, experts say, that even as organizations increasingly use advanced analytics to forecast the future, they continue to invest in their BI operations.

"You need both, because you need to know what's going on," Howson says. "It doesn't matter if I can predict the future if I don't know what's going on right now."

Additionally, organizations will continue to need BI capabilities to help them validate the analyses produced by more advanced analytics functions as they add those capabilities.

"If we black-box BA tools and say don't look at the reports, just change your price to this or increase your inventory there, we're putting way too much trust into these BA tools," Gorman says. "We have to sanity-check them, and I think the BI tools are a great tool to keep humans in the loop."

References

- Giovanini, Enrico Understanding Economic Statistics, OECD Publishing, 2008, ISBN 978-92-64-03312-2
- What-is-business-data, business-intelligence, data-warehouse: learn.geekinterview.com, Retrieved 21 May 2018
- Business-data-examples: simplicable.com, Retrieved 31 March 2018
- Business-statistics: statisticshowto.com, Retrieved 21 July 2018
- 10625-businesses-collecting-data: businessnewsdaily.com, Retrieved 11 June 2018
- 3-effective-methods-of-data-collection-for-market-research: bigdata-madesimple.com, Retrieved 30 March 2018
- Businesses-collecting-data-10625: businessnewsdaily.com, Retrieved 08 May 2018

2

Data Description and Analysis

Data analysis is the process of transforming, cleansing and modeling data with the objective of deriving useful information, forming conclusions and for supporting good decision-making. This chapter has been carefully written to provide an easy understanding of the varied aspects of data description and analysis, such as measures of dispersion, data distribution, data visualization and predictive analytics with respect to business statistics.

Descriptive Statistics

Descriptive statistics are brief descriptive coefficients that summarize a given data set, which can be either a representation of the entire or a sample of a population. Descriptive statistics are broken down into measures of central tendency and measures of variability (spread). Measures of central tendency include the mean, median, and mode, while measures of variability include the standard deviation, variance, the minimum and maximum variables, and the kurtosis and skewness.

Descriptive statistics, in short, help describe and understand the features of a specific data set by giving short summaries about the sample and measures of the data. The most recognized types of descriptive statistics are the mean, median, and mode, which are used at almost all levels of math and statistics. However, there are less-common types of descriptive statistics that are still very important.

People use descriptive statistics to repurpose hard-to-understand quantitative insights across a large data set into bite-sized descriptions. A student's grade point average (GPA), for example, provides a good understanding of descriptive statistics. The idea of a GPA is that it takes data points from a wide range of exams, classes, and grades, and averages them together to provide a general understanding of a student's overall academic abilities. A student's personal GPA reflects his mean academic performance.

Normal Distribution

The normal distribution is one of the most important concepts in statistics since nearly all statistical tests require normally distributed data. It basically describes how large samples of data look like when they are plotted. It is sometimes called the "bell curve" or the "Gaussian curve".

Inferential statistics and the calculation of probabilities require that a normal distribution is given. This basically means, that if your data is not normally distributed, you need to be very careful what statistical tests you apply to it since they could lead to wrong conclusions.

A normal Distribution is given if your data is symmetrical, bell-shaped, centered and unimodal.

In a perfect normal distribution, each side is an exact mirror of the other. It should look like the distribution on the picture below:

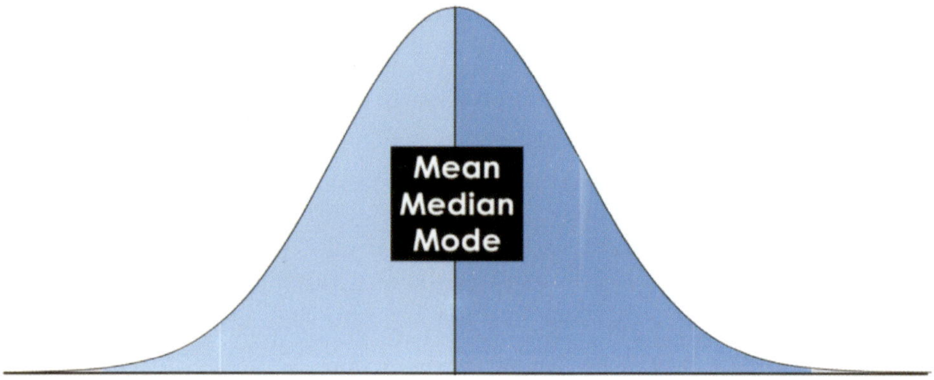

You can see on the picture that the distribution is bell-shaped, which simply means that it is not heavily peaked. Unimodal means that there is only one peak.

Central Tendency

In statistics we have to deal with the mean, mode and the median. These are also called the "Central Tendency". These are just three different kinds of "averages" and certainly the most popular ones.

The mean is simply the average and considered the most reliable measure of central tendency for making assumptions about a population from a single sample. Central tendency determines the tendency for the values of your data to cluster around its mean, mode, or median. The mean is computed by the sum of all values, divided by the number of values.

The mode is the value or category that occurs most often within the data. Therefore a dataset has no mode, if no number is repeated or if no category is the same. The mode is also the only measure of central tendency that can be used for categorical variables since you can't compute for example the average for the variable "gender". You simply report categorical variables as numbers and percentages.

The median is the "middle" value or midpoint in your data and is also called the "50th percentile". Note that the median is much less affected by outliers and skewed data than the mean. I will explain this with an example: Imagine you have a dataset of housing prizes that range mostly from $100,000 to $300,000 but contains a few houses that are worth more than 3 million Dollars. These expensive houses will heavily effect then mean since it is the sum of all values, divided by the number of values. The median will not be heavily affected by these outliers since it is only the "middle" value of all data points. Therefore the median is a much more suited statistic, to report about your data.

In a normal distribution, these measures all fall at the same midline point. This means that the mean, mode and median are all equal.

Measures of Variability

The most popular variability measures are the range, interquartile range (IQR), variance, and standard deviation. These are used to measure the amount of spread or variability within your data.

The range describes the difference between the largest and the smallest points in your data.

The interquartile range (IQR) is a measure of statistical dispersion between upper (75th) and lower (25th) quartiles.

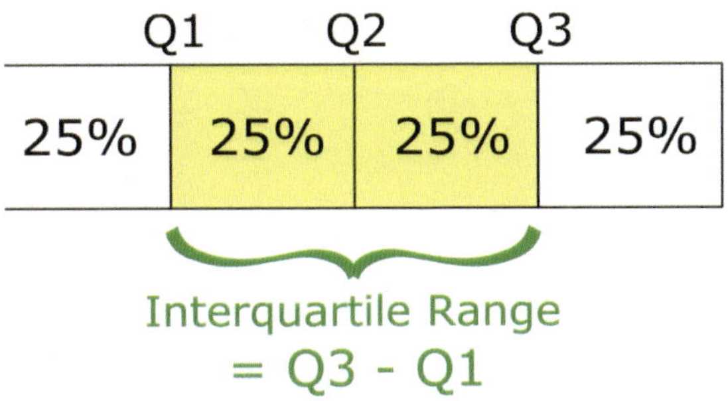

While the range measures where the beginning and end of your datapoint are, the interquartile range is a measure of where the majority of the values lie.

The difference between the standard deviation and the variance is often a little bit hard to grasp for beginners, but we will explain it thoroughly.

Variance and Standard Deviation

The Standard Deviation and the Variance also measure, like the Range and IQR, how spread apart our data is (e.g the dispersion). Therefore they are both derived from the mean.

The variance is computed by finding the difference between every data point and the mean, squaring them, summing them up and then taking the average of those numbers.

The squares are used during the calculation because they weight outliers more heavily than points that are near to the mean. This prevents that differences above the mean neutralize those below the mean.

The problem with Variance is that because of the squaring, it is not in the same unit of measurement as the original data.

Let's say you are dealing with a dataset that contains centimeter values. Your variance would be in squared centimeters and therefore not the best measurement.

This is why the Standard Deviation is used more often because it is in the original unit. It is simply the square root of the variance and because of that, it is returned to the original unit of measurement.

Let's look at an example that illustrates the difference between variance and standard deviation:

Imagine a data set that contains centimeter values between 1 and 15, which results in a mean of 8. Squaring the difference between each data point and the mean and averaging the squares renders a variance of 18.67 (squared centimeters), while the standard deviation is 4.3 centimeters.

When you have a low standard deviation, your data points tend to be close to the mean. A high standard deviation means that your data points are spread out over a wide range.

Standard deviation is best used when data is unimodal. In a normal distribution, approximately 34% of the data points are lying between the mean and one standard deviation above or below the mean. Since a normal distribution is symmetrical, 68% of the data points fall between one standard deviation above and one standard deviation below the mean. Approximately 95% fall between two standard deviations below the mean and two standard deviations above the mean. And approximately 99.7% fall between three standard deviations above and three standard deviations below the mean.

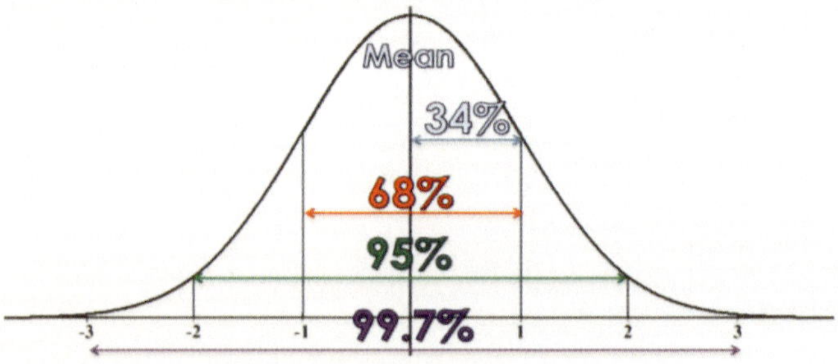

With the so-called "Z-Score", you can check how many standard deviations below (or above) the mean, a specific data point lies. With pandas you can just use the "std()" function. To better understand the concept of a normal distribution, we will now discuss the concepts of modality, symmetry and peakedness.

Modality

The modality of a distribution is determined by the number of peaks it contains. Most distributions have only one peak but it is possible that you encounter distributions with two or more peaks.

The picture below shows visual examples of the three types of modality:

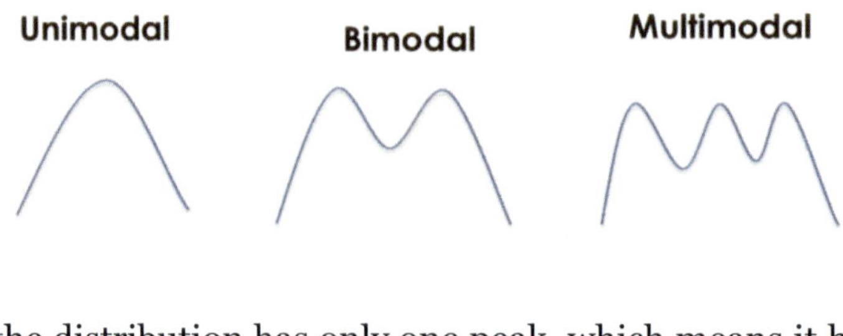

Unimodal means that the distribution has only one peak, which means it has only one frequently occurring score, clustered at the top. A bimodal distribution has two values that occur frequently (two peaks) and a multimodal has two or several frequently occurring values.

Skewness

Skewness is a measurement of the symmetry of a distribution.

Therefore it describes how much a distribution differs from a normal distribution, either to the left or to the right. The skewness value can be either positive, negative or zero. Note that a perfect normal distribution would have a skewness of zero because the mean equals the median.

Below you can see an illustration of the different types of skewness:

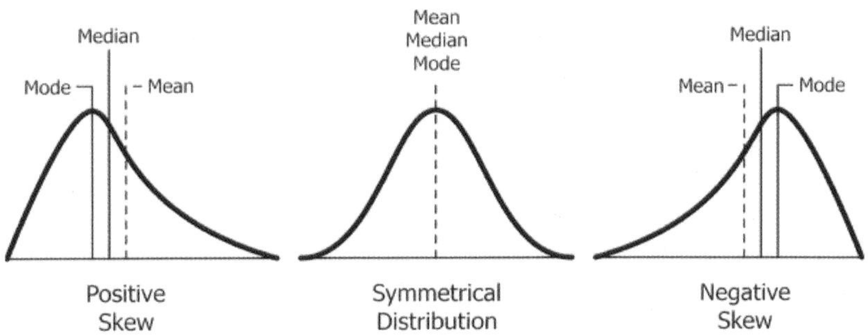

We speak of a positives skew if the data is piled up to the left, which leaves the tail pointing to the right.

A negative skew occurs if the data is piled up to the right, which leaves the tail pointing to the left. Note that positive skews are more frequent than negative ones.

Data Description

In all accountancy, management and consultancy areas, a large volume of data is subject to analysis, interpretation and description. The methods and techniques used can distort the description of the data and ultimately the decision made. Characteristics of a data set may contain the most frequent score, the variability in the score, the 'shape' of the data, the highest and lowest scores, and whether or not the data set contains any unusual data. Interpreting or extracting data visually is, at a minimum, difficult since it may not be possible for us to comprehend large volumes of information. Some formal methods for summarising and characterising the information in a data set are essential. Most populations are large data sets. Therefore, methods for describing such data sets are also essential for statistical inference. There are two key methods used for describing data – one graphical and the other numerical. Both play an important role in statistics and both methods can be used for describing both qualitative and quantitative data.

Describing Qualitative Data

When data is grouped into non-numerical categories, the resulting table is a categorical or qualitative distribution. Therefore the value of a qualitative variable can be classified into categories called classes. Such data can be summarized numerically in two ways – by computing the class frequency, that is, the number of observations in the data set that fall into each class or by computing the class relative frequency, that is, the proportion of the total number of observations falling into each class. (The class relative frequency may also be used, that is, the class frequency divided by the total number of observations in the data set). Although a summary table of the data may be drawn up, a graphical presentation of the data may be required to clearly demonstrate the features of the data. Two of the most widely used graphical methods for describing qualitative data are bar graphs and pie charts. The bar graph plots the class frequency against the class where the height of the 'bar' is equal to the class frequency. A pie chart shows the relative frequencies of the classes where the size of the 'slice' apportioned to each class is proportional to the class relative frequency.

Describing Quantitative Data

When data are grouped according to numerical size, the resulting table is a categorical or quantitative distribution. For describing, summarising and detecting patterns in such data the most common graphical methods for describing frequency distributions are histograms, frequency curves (such as polygons or ogives) and scattergrams.

Histograms

Histograms can be used to display either the frequency or relative frequencies (frequency of each class divided by the total frequency) of the measurements falling into specified intervals known as measurement classes. By looking at a histogram two important facts are apparent. The proportion of the total area above the interval is equal to the relative frequency of measurements falling in the interval. As the number of elements in the data set increase, a better description of the data set can be obtained by decreasing the width of the class intervals. When the class intervals become small enough a relative frequency histogram will appear as a smooth curve. While histograms provide good visual descriptions of data sets they do not allow the identification of individual measurements.

Another form of presentation is the frequency polygon. The frequencies are plotted at the class marks and the successive points are connected. Applying a similar technique to a cumulative distribution (usually a 'less than' distribution) an ogive can be obtained. This is where the cumulative frequencies are plotted at the class boundaries.

x	less than	Frequency	Cumulative frequency	Mid Point
100 < 110	110	1	1	105
110 < 120	120	4	5	115
120 < 130	130	7	12	125
130 < 140	140	13	25	135
140 < 150	150	7	32	145
150 < 160	160	3	35	155
160 or more	180	1	36	170

Fig: for examples of above presentations.

Frequency Polygon

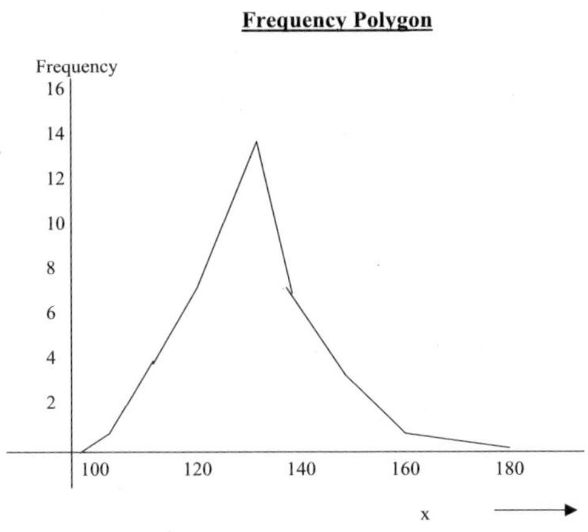

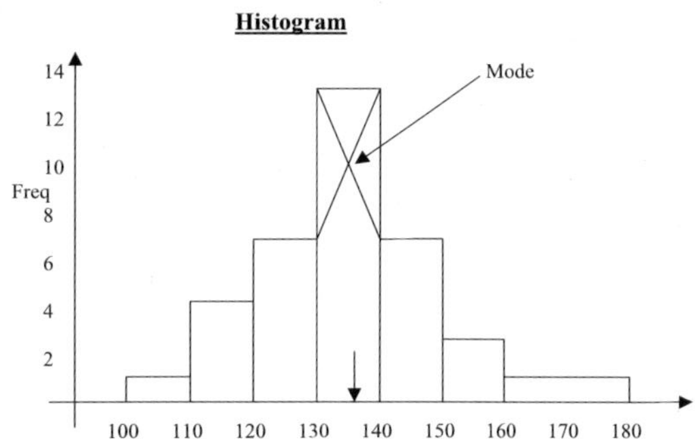

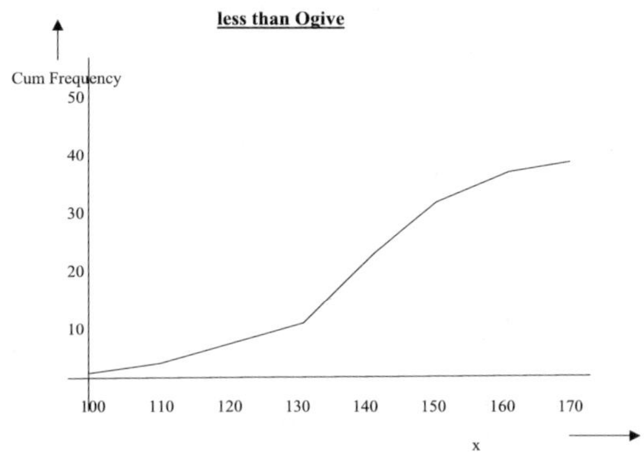

Scattergram

A common method to describe the relationship between two quantitative variables (a bivariate relationship) is to plot the data on a scattergram. This is a simple and powerful tool but no measure of reliability can be attached to inferences made about bivariate populations based on scattergrams of sample data. When an increase or decrease in one variable is associated with an increase or decrease in the second variable the two variables are said to be positively or negatively correlated. Both a relationship, and the strength of that relationship, can be determined between the variables by linear regression form of analysis. This can be visually and quantitatively presented and is an effective display.

The above graphical techniques are used frequently for summarising and describing quantitative data but these are often, also, associated with numerical methods for accomplishing this objective. A large number of numerical methods are available to describe quantitative data sets. Most of these methods measure one of two data characteristics 1) the central tendency of the set, that is, the tendency of the data to cluster and 2) the variability of the set, that is, the spread of the data.

Arithmetic Mean

The most popular measure of central tendency is the arithmetic mean. This is the sum of the measurements divided by the number of measurements contained in the data set. In many business cases the sample mean, x, is used to estimate or make an inference about a population since we may not have access to measurements for the entire population. However, in this case the accuracy of the estimate depends on the size of the sample (the larger the sample, the more accurate the estimate will tend to be) and the variability of the data (the more variable the data the less accurate the estimate).

Median

Another important measure of central tendency is the median. This is the middle number when the quantitative data set is arranged in ascending or descending order. This is of most value in describing large data sets and is the point where 50% of the data lies above the mid point and 50% below it. In certain situations the median may be a better measure of central tendency than the mean. It is less sensitive to extremely large or small values. In general, extreme values (large or small) affect the mean more than the median since these values are used explicitly to calculate the mean. The median is not affected directly by extreme values since only the middle value is explicitly used to calculate the median. Consequently if measurements are pulled towards one end of the distribution the mean will shift toward that tail more than the median.

Mode

The mode is particularly useful for describing qualitative data. The modal category is the class that occurs most frequently. Because it emphasises data concentrations, the mode is also used with quantitative data sets to locate the region in which much of the data is concentrated. However, for some quantitative data sets, the mode may not be very meaningful since there may be more than one mode in the sample. A more meaningful measure is the modal class. This can be obtained from a relative frequency histogram. However, for most data, the mean and median provide more descriptive data than the mode.

Positively Skewed Distribution

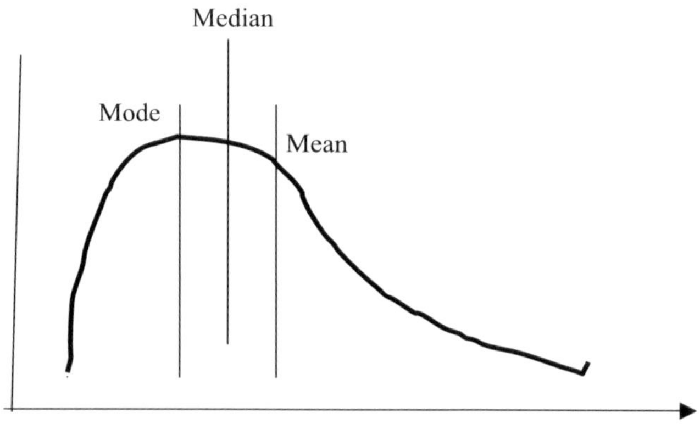

Standard Deviation

These measures of central tendency provide only a partial description of a quantitative data set. The description is incomplete without a measure of the variability of the data set. Knowledge of the data's variability along with its centre can help us visualise the shape of the data as well as its extreme values. The simplest measure of the variability of a quantitative set is its range. This is equal to the largest less the smallest measurement. The range is easy to compute and to understand but it is an insensitive measure of data variation when the data sets are large – two data sets can have the same range but be vastly different with respect to data variation. The variation of such data can be obtained by measuring the distance between each measurement and the mean. To cater for the + and – signs of the deviations, the deviations are squared to provide the sample variance, $s^2 = \sum(x_i - x)^2/(n - 1)$. This is the preliminary step in calculating the standard deviation of the data set, $\sqrt{s^2}$. Sample statistics like s^2 are primarily used to estimate population parameters like σ^2 ; (n -1) is preferred to n when defining the sample variance. To understand how the standard variation provides a measure of variability of a data set, it is necessary to determine how many measurements fall with I, 2 or 3 standard deviations of the mean. The empirical rule for interpreting the standard deviation of data that is bell shaped and symmetrical (where the mean, median and mode are approximately the same) is that approximately 68% of deviations fall within 1 standard deviation of the mean ($\mu \pm \sigma$), 95% fall within 2 standard deviations ($\mu \pm 2\sigma$) and 99.7% fall within 3 standard deviations ($\mu \pm 2\sigma$), for populations. In addition to the above it may be of interest to describe the relative quantitative location of a particular measurement within a data set. One such method is the percentile ranking. These are of practical value only for large data sets. The measurements are ranked in order and a rule is selected to define the location of each percentile. For example, if your company reports that its annual sales are in the 75th percentile of all companies in the industry, the implication is that 75% of all companies have annual sales less than your company and 25% have annual sales exceeding your company.

Time Series Plot

Most of the above methods have been concerned with describing the information contained in a sample or population of data. Often these data are viewed as having been produced at a similar point in time. Therefore, time has not been a factor. However, data of interest to managers are often produced over a time period. When data is produced over time it is important to record both the measurements and the time period associated with each measurement. With this information a time series plot can be constructed to describe the time series data and to learn about the process that generated the data and to monitor the movement (trend) and changes (variations) in the variable being examined. This type of information would not be revealed by most other graphical displays.

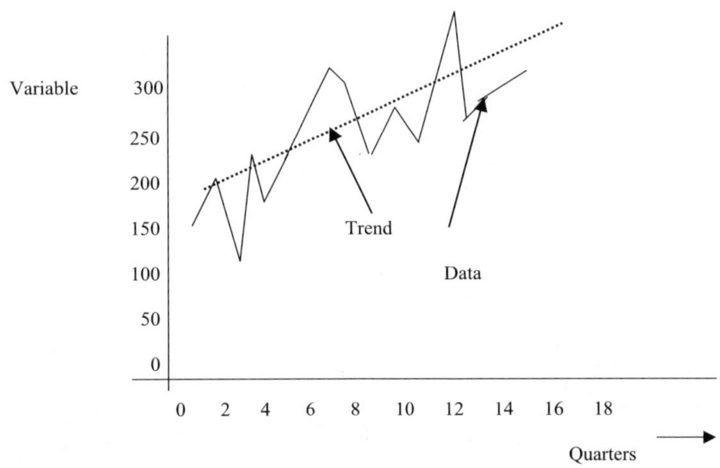

Time Series Plot: Original data v Trend.

Lies, Damned lies and Statistics. Distorting the Truth

Many of the presentations outlined can misrepresent or distort, or allow the target audience to misinterpret, the data presented. One common way to change the impression created by a pictorial or graphical presentation is to change the scale on either one or both axes. By stretching the vertical axis or by increasing the distance between vertical units can give a misleading visual impression of the data. In one case a histogram may appear to be vertically elongated and horizontally compressed or vice versa and may lead to incorrect conclusions. A visual distortion can be achieved with bar graphs by making the width of the bars proportional to the height. A similar effect can be achieved by using a scale break for the vertical axis. Further distortions can also occur with numerical descriptive measures. If a measure of central tendency only is reported in a sample, this can lead to a distortion of the information. Both a measure of central tendency and a measure of variability are needed to obtain an accurate mental image of a data set. The conclusion! Look at graphical descriptions with a critical eye, ignore the visual changes and concentrate on the actual numerical changes associated with the graph or chart.

Measures of Dispersion

Measures of central tendency, Mean, Median, Mode, etc., indicate the central position of a series. They indicate the general magnitude of the data but fail to reveal all the peculiarities and characteristics of the series. In other words, they fail to reveal the degree of the spread out or the extent of the variability in individual items of the distribution. This can be explained by certain other measures, known as 'Measures of Dispersion' or Variation. We can understand variation with the help of the following example:

Series 1	Series 11	Series III
10	2	10
10	8	12
10	20	8
$\Sigma X = 30$	**30**	**30**

In all three series, the value of arithmetic mean is 10. On the basis of this average, we can say that the series are alike. If we carefully examine the composition of three series, we find the following differences:

(i) In case of 1st series, three items are equal; but in 2nd and 3rd series, the items are unequal and do not follow any specific order.

(ii) The magnitude of deviation, item-wise, is different for the 1st, 2nd and 3rd series. But all these deviations cannot be ascertained if the value of simple mean is taken into consideration.

(iii) In these three series, it is quite possible that the value of arithmetic mean is 10; but the value of median may differ from each other. This can be understood as follows.

I	II	III
10	2	8
10 Median	8 Median	10 Median
10	20	12

The value of Median' in 1st series is 10, in 2nd series = 8 and in 3rd series = 10. Therefore, the value of the Mean and Median are not identical.

(iv) Even though the average remains the same, the nature and extent of the distribution of the size of the items may vary. In other words, the structure of the frequency distributions may differ even (though their means are identical.

Dispersion

Simplest meaning that can be attached to the word 'dispersion' is a lack of uniformity in the sizes or quantities of the items of a group or series. According to Reiglemen, "Dispersion is the extent to which the magnitudes or quantities of the items differ, the degree of diversity." The word dispersion may also be used to indicate the spread of the data.

In all these definitions, we can find the basic property of dispersion as a value that indicates the extent to which all other values are dispersed about the central value in a particular distribution.

Properties of a Good Measure of Dispersion

There are certain pre-requisites for a good measure of dispersion:

1. It should be simple to understand.
2. It should be easy to compute.
3. It should be rigidly defined.
4. It should be based on each individual item of the distribution.
5. It should be capable of further algebraic treatment.
6. It should have sampling stability.
7. It should not be unduly affected by the extreme items.

Types of Dispersion

The measures of dispersion can be either 'absolute' or "relative". Absolute measures of dispersion are expressed in the same units in which the original data are expressed. For example, if the series is expressed as Marks of the students in a particular subject; the absolute dispersion will provide the value in Marks. The only difficulty is that if two or more series are expressed in different units, the series cannot be compared on the basis of dispersion.

'Relative' or 'Coefficient' of dispersion is the ratio or the percentage of a measure of absolute dispersion to an appropriate average. The basic advantage of this measure is that two or more series can be compared with each other despite the fact they are expressed in different units. Theoretically, 'Absolute measure' of dispersion is better. But from a practical point of view, relative or coefficient of dispersion is considered better as it is used to make comparison between series.

Methods of Dispersion

Methods of studying dispersion are divided into two types:

(i) Mathematical Methods: We can study the 'degree' and 'extent' of variation with the use of these methods. The measures of dispersion included in this category are:

(a) Range

(b) Quartile Deviation

(c) Average Deviation

(d) Standard deviation and coefficient of variation.

(ii) Graphic Methods: If only the extent of variation is studied, whether it is higher or lower, a Lorenz-curve is put to use.

Mathematical Methods

- Range

  Two sections of 10 students each in class XII in a school were given a common test in Economics (40 maximum marks). The scores of the students are given below:

  Section A: 6 9 11 13 15 21 23 28 29 35

  Section B: 15 16 16 17 18 19 20 21 23 25

  The average score in section A is 19. The average score in section B is 19.

  In the above cited example, we observe that:

- The scores of all the students in section A are ranging from 6 to 35.

- The scores of the students in section B are ranging from 15 to 25.

  The difference between the largest and the smallest scores in section A is 29 (35-6).

  The difference between the largest and smallest scores in section B is 10 (25-15).

  Thus, the difference between the largest and the smallest value of a data, is termed as the range of the distribution. Range does not consider all the values of a series, i.e. it takes only the extreme items and middle items are not considered significant. Therefore, Range is not sufficient to explain about the character of the distribution. The concept of range is useful in the field of quality control and to study the variations in the prices of the shares etc.

- Quartile Deviation

  The quartile deviation is a slightly better measure of absolute dispersion than the range, although it ignores the observations on the ends (tails). It helps in knowing the range within which certain proportion of the items fall lay. It only considers the values of the 'Upper quartile' (Q3) and the 'Lower quartile' (Q1).

Inter Quartile Range = Q3 – Q1.

The Inter-Quartile Range is based upon the 50% of the values in a distribution which lay in the middle; and hence is unaffected by extreme values. Half of the Inter-Quartile Range is called Quartile Deviation (Q.D.).

Thus: Q .D . = (Q3 – Q1)/2

Q.D. is therefore also called Semi Inter Quartile Range.

In individual and discrete series, Q1 is the size of $[(n+1)/4]^{th}$ value, but in a continuous distribution, it is the size of $n/4^{th}$ value. Similarly, for Q3 and median also, n is used in place of n+1.

A relative measure of dispersion based on the quartile deviation is called the coefficient of quartile deviation. It is just a number without any units of measurement. It can be used for comparing the dispersion of two or more sets of data.

Coefficient of Quartile Deviation $\dfrac{\frac{Q_3 - Q_1}{2}}{\frac{Q_3 + Q_1}{2}} = \dfrac{Q_3 - Q_1}{Q_3 + Q_1}$

- Average Deviation

  Average deviation can be defined as the arithmetic mean of the absolute deviations (ignoring the negative signs) of various items from Mean, Mode or Median.

  Calculation of mean deviation:

  Individual Series

  $$\text{M.D.} = \frac{\sum \text{IDI}}{\text{N}}$$

  Discrete Series

  $$\text{M.D.} = \frac{\sum \text{f IDI}}{\text{N}}$$

  Continuous Series

  $$\frac{\sum fIDI}{N}$$

Where,

MD = Mean deviation

| D | = Deviations from mean or median ignoring + Signs

N = Number of item (Individual Series)

N = Total number of Frequencies (Discrete and continuous series)

F = Number of frequencies.

- Standard Deviation

  Standard deviation is one of the best and popularly used measures of dispersion. Standard deviation is the square root of the arithmetic mean of the squares of deviation of its items from their arithmetic mean. The concept of standard deviation, which was introduced by Karl Pearson is useful in assessing the representativeness of the mean. It has a practical significance because it does not come with the problems associated with a range, quartile deviation or average deviation.

  Calculations for the same, are as under:

Individual Series

1. Actual Mean Method

$$\sigma = \sqrt{\frac{\sum x^2}{N}}$$

$$x = X - \bar{X}_I$$

2. Assumed Mean Method

$$\sigma = \sqrt{\frac{\sum d^2}{N} - \left(\frac{\sum d}{N}\right)^2}$$

Discrete/Continuous Series

1. Actual Mean Method

$$\sigma = \sqrt{\frac{\sum fx^2}{\sum f}}$$

$$x = x - \bar{x}$$

2. Assumed Mean Method

$$\sigma = \sqrt{\frac{\sum fd^2}{\sum f} - \left(\frac{\sum fd}{\sum f}\right)^2}$$

3. Step Deviation Method

$$\sigma = \sqrt{\frac{\sum fd^{12}}{\sum f} - \left(\frac{\sum fd^{1}}{\sum f}\right)^{2}} \times C$$

Coefficient of Variation

This Is the most apt measure when two or more groups of similar data are to be compared with respect to stability (or uniformly or consistency or homogeneity). It is the ratio of the standard deviation to the mean.

$$CV = \frac{\sigma}{\overline{X}} \times 100$$

Where C.V. = Coefficient of variation

σ= Standard deviation

X = Arithmetic mean

Graphical Methods

Lorenz Curve: A Lorenz Curve can be defined as a graph on which the cumulative percentage of total national income (or some other variable) is plotted against the cumulative percentage of the corresponding population (ranked in increasing size of share). The extent to which the curve sags below a straight diagonal line indicates the degree of inequality of distribution.

Data Distribution

Data Distribution describes the systems and processes a company has for gathering key performance metrics and getting them to the right people at the right time in order to support the company's growth. How your company builds your specific data distribution philosophy centers around how you want to tell your company's story and who you want to tell that story to.

In short, Data Distribution is how well your company turns this:

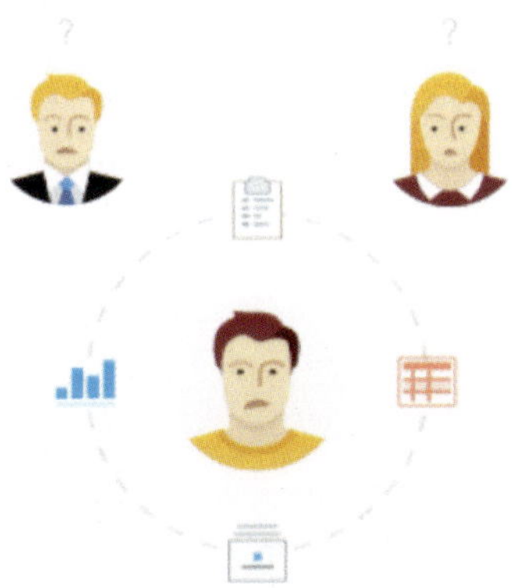

Into this:

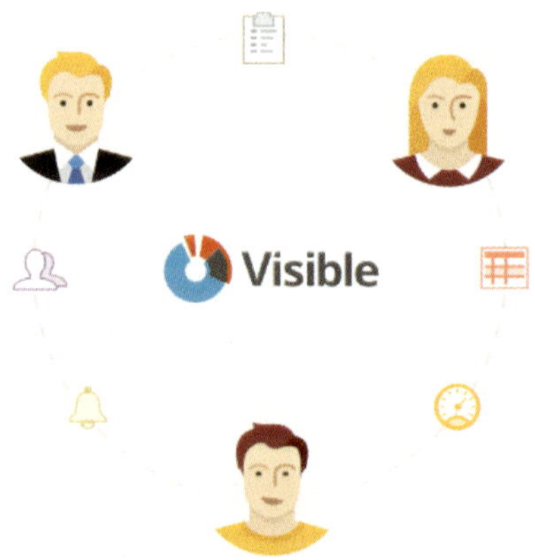

Importance of Data Distribution

Taking a company from its first round of funding to ultimate success (define that how you will) is no easy task. Companies fail for a number of different reasons and one of the more inexcusable is a breakdown in communication between founding teams, CEOs and investors, or leaders of different teams within in organization.

Building a solid process for your company's Data Distribution means professionalizing the way that you approach communication to your stakeholders. There is a responsibility that comes with deploying capital for others (often millions of dollars) and employing people (often dozens) to help build your vision.

Implementing Data Distribution

The way that a company tracks and analyzes the key performance indicators around its product development and distribution as well as its customers and employees is key in determining whether its data distribution system will be effective and yield long term positive results.

Blake Koriath, CFO at SaaS-focused seed fund High Alpha, likes to start wide when working with companies, focusing first on business model and company stage, then digging into exactly who will be viewing specific metrics and when.

Once you understand this and are committed to the idea of building out a data gathering system, your next step is to actually select the full set of metrics that make sense for your company. This is where things can get complicated, as there are hundreds of metrics to choose from as well as different time frames to consider and different ways of calculating certain metrics. Additionally, the amount of data produced in a growing technology company can be overwhelming for teams and founders.

Luckily, many thorough frameworks – crafted through years of experience by top investors and founders – already exist and can give you a great baseline to work from, no matter your business model or stage.

Remember, as Pablo Picasso whose paintings even most VCs can't afford is credited with saying, "great artists steal."

Data Analysis

Data analysis is a primary component of data mining and Business Intelligence (BI) and is key to gaining the insight that drives business decisions. Organizations and enterprises analyze data from a multitude of sources using Big Data management solutions and customer experience management solutions that utilize data analysis to transform data into actionable insights.

Data analysis is "all the ways you can break down the data, assess trends over time, and compare one sector or measurement to another. It can also include the various ways the data is visualized to make the trends and relationships intuitive at a glance." Data analysis involves asking questions about what happened, what is happening, and what will happen (predictive analytics). "Analytics is generally the data crunching, question-answering phase leading up to the decision-making phase in the overall Business Intelligence process."

Data Analysis Model

While each company has its own data requirements and goals, there are seven steps that remain consistent across organizations and their data analysis processes:

- Decide on the objectives – Determine objectives for data science teams to develop a quantifiable way to determine whether the business is progressing toward its goals; identify metrics or performance indicators early.
- Identify business levers – Identify goals, metrics, and levers early in data analysis projects to give scope and focus to data analysis; this means the business should be willing to make changes to improve its key metrics and reach its goals as well.
- Data collection – Gather as much data from diverse sources as possible in order to build better models and gain more actionable insights.
- Data cleaning – Improve data quality to generate the right results and avoid making

incorrect conclusions; automate the process but involve employees to oversee the data cleaning and ensure accuracy.

- Grow a data science team – Include on your science team individuals with advanced degrees in statistics who will focus on data modeling and predictions, as well as infrastructure engineers, software developers, and ETL experts; then, give the team the large-scale data analysis platforms they need to automate data collection and analysis.
- Optimize and repeat – Perfect your data analysis model so you can repeat the process to generate accurate predictions, reach goals, and monitor and report consistently.

Data Analysis Process

There are several phases that can be distinguished, described below. The phases are iterative, in that feedback from later phases may result in additional work in earlier phases.

Data Requirements

The data is necessary as inputs to the analysis, which is specified based upon the requirements of those directing the analysis or customers (who will use the finished product of the analysis). The general type of entity upon which the data will be collected is referred to as an experimental unit (e.g., a person or population of people). Specific variables regarding a population (e.g., age and income) may be specified and obtained. Data may be numerical or categorical (i.e., a text label for numbers).

Data Collection

Data is collected from a variety of sources. The requirements may be communicated by analysts to custodians of the data, such as information technology personnel within an organization. The data may also be collected from sensors in the environment, such as traffic cameras, satellites, recording devices, etc. It may also be obtained through interviews, downloads from online sources, or reading documentation.

Data Processing

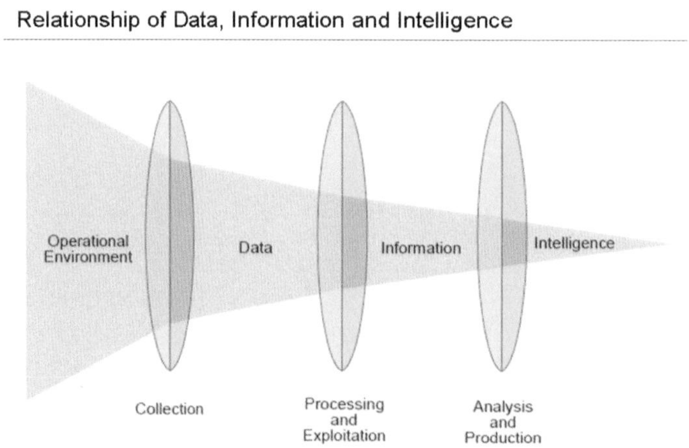

The phases of the intelligence cycle used to convert raw information into actionable intelligence or knowledge are conceptually similar to the phases in data analysis.

Data initially obtained must be processed or organised for analysis. For instance, these may involve placing data into rows and columns in a table format (i.e., structured data) for further analysis, such as within a spreadsheet or statistical software.

Data Cleaning

Once processed and organised, the data may be incomplete, contain duplicates, or contain errors. The need for data cleaning will arise from problems in the way that data is entered and stored. Data cleaning is the process of preventing and correcting these errors. Common tasks include record matching, identifying inaccuracy of data, overall quality of existing data, deduplication, and column segmentation. Such data problems can also be identified through a variety of analytical techniques. For example, with financial information, the totals for particular variables may be compared against separately published numbers believed to be reliable. Unusual amounts above or below pre-determined thresholds may also be reviewed. There are several types of data cleaning that depend on the type of data such as phone numbers, email addresses, employers etc. Quantitative data methods for outlier detection can be used to get rid of likely incorrectly entered data. Textual data spell checkers can be used to lessen the amount of mistyped words, but it is harder to tell if the words themselves are correct.

Exploratory Data Analysis

Once the data is cleaned, it can be analyzed. Analysts may apply a variety of techniques referred to as exploratory data analysis to begin understanding the messages contained in the data. The process of exploration may result in additional data cleaning or additional requests for data, so these activities may be iterative in nature. Descriptive statistics, such as the average or median, may be generated to help understand the data. Data visualization may also be used to examine the data in graphical format, to obtain additional insight regarding the messages within the data.

Modeling and Algorithms

Mathematical formulas or models called algorithms may be applied to the data to identify relationships among the variables, such as correlation or causation. In general terms, models may be developed to evaluate a particular variable in the data based on other variable(s) in the data, with some residual error depending on model accuracy (i.e., Data = Model + Error).

Inferential statistics includes techniques to measure relationships between particular variables. For example, regression analysis may be used to model whether a change in advertising (independent variable X) explains the variation in sales (dependent variable Y). In mathematical terms, Y (sales) is a function of X (advertising). It may be described as $Y = aX + b + \text{error}$, where the model is designed such that a and b minimize the error when the model predicts Y for a given range of values of X. Analysts may attempt to build models that are descriptive of the data to simplify analysis and communicate results.

Data Product

A data product is a computer application that takes data inputs and generates outputs, feeding them back into the environment. It may be based on a model or algorithm. An example is an application that analyzes data about customer purchasing history and recommends other purchases the customer might enjoy.

Communication

Data visualization to understand the results of a data analysis.

Once the data is analyzed, it may be reported in many formats to the users of the analysis to support their requirements. The users may have feedback, which results in additional analysis. As such, much of the analytical cycle is iterative.

When determining how to communicate the results, the analyst may consider data visualization techniques to help clearly and efficiently communicate the message to the audience. Data visualization uses information displays (such as tables and charts) to help communicate key messages contained in the data. Tables are helpful to a user who might lookup specific numbers, while charts (e.g., bar charts or line charts) may help explain the quantitative messages contained in the data.

Quantitative Messages

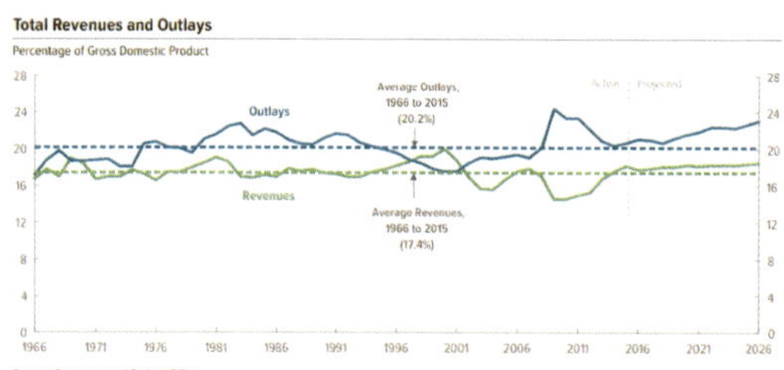

A time series illustrated with a line chart demonstrating trends in U.S. federal spending and revenue over time.

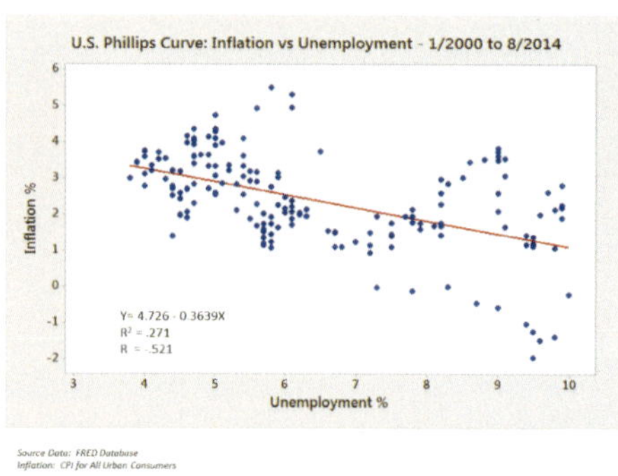

A scatterplot illustrating correlation between two variables (inflation and unemployment) measured at points in time.

Stephen Few described eight types of quantitative messages that users may attempt to understand or communicate from a set of data and the associated graphs used to help communicate the message. Customers specifying requirements and analysts performing the data analysis may consider these messages during the course of the process.

1. Time-series: A single variable is captured over a period of time, such as the unemployment rate over a 10-year period. A line chart may be used to demonstrate the trend.
2. Ranking: Categorical subdivisions are ranked in ascending or descending order, such as a ranking of sales performance (the *measure*) by sales persons (the *category*, with each sales person a *categorical subdivision*) during a single period. A bar chart may be used to show the comparison across the sales persons.
3. Part-to-whole: Categorical subdivisions are measured as a ratio to the whole (i.e., a percentage out of 100%). A pie chart or bar chart can show the comparison of ratios, such as the market share represented by competitors in a market.
4. Deviation: Categorical subdivisions are compared against a reference, such as a comparison of actual vs. budget expenses for several departments of a business for a given time period. A bar chart can show comparison of the actual versus the reference amount.
5. Frequency distribution: Shows the number of observations of a particular variable for given interval, such as the number of years in which the stock market return is between intervals such as 0–10%, 11–20%, etc. A histogram, a type of bar chart, may be used for this analysis.
6. Correlation: Comparison between observations represented by two variables (X,Y) to determine if they tend to move in the same or opposite directions. For example, plotting unemployment (X) and inflation (Y) for a sample of months. A scatter plot is typically used for this message.
7. Nominal comparison: Comparing categorical subdivisions in no particular order, such as the sales volume by product code. A bar chart may be used for this comparison.
8. Geographic or geospatial: Comparison of a variable across a map or layout, such as the unemployment rate by state or the number of persons on the various floors of a building. A cartogram is a typical graphic used.

Techniques for Analyzing Quantitative Data

Author Jonathan Koomey has recommended a series of best practices for understanding quantitative data. These include:

- Check raw data for anomalies prior to performing your analysis.
- Re-perform important calculations, such as verifying columns of data that are formula driven.
- Confirm main totals are the sum of subtotals.
- Check relationships between numbers that should be related in a predictable way, such as ratios over time.

- Normalize numbers to make comparisons easier, such as analyzing amounts per person or relative to GDP or as an index value relative to a base year.
- Break problems into component parts by analyzing factors that led to the results, such as DuPont analysis of return on equity.

For the variables under examination, analysts typically obtain descriptive statistics for them, such as the mean (average), median, and standard deviation. They may also analyze the distribution of the key variables to see how the individual values cluster around the mean.

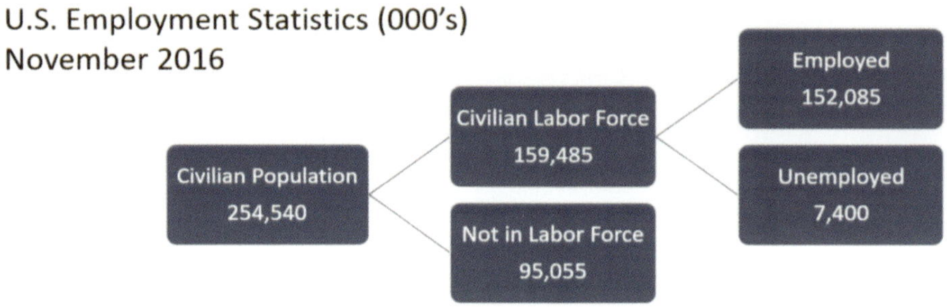

Unemployment rate	= $\frac{\text{Unemployed}}{\text{Civilian Labor Force}}$	= $\frac{7{,}400}{159{,}485}$	=	4.6%
Labor Force Participation Rate	= $\frac{\text{Civilian Labor Force}}{\text{Civilian Population}}$	= $\frac{159{,}485}{254{,}540}$	=	62.7%
Employment to Population Ratio	= $\frac{\text{Employed}}{\text{Civilian Population}}$	$\frac{152{,}085}{254{,}540}$	=	59.7%

An illustration of the MECE principle used for data analysis.

The consultants at McKinsey and Company named a technique for breaking a quantitative problem down into its component parts called the MECE principle. Each layer can be broken down into its components; each of the sub-components must be mutually exclusive of each other and collectively add up to the layer above them. The relationship is referred to as "Mutually Exclusive and Collectively Exhaustive" or MECE. For example, profit by definition can be broken down into total revenue and total cost. In turn, total revenue can be analyzed by its components, such as revenue of divisions A, B, and C (which are mutually exclusive of each other) and should add to the total revenue (collectively exhaustive).

Analysts may use robust statistical measurements to solve certain analytical problems. Hypothesis testing is used when a particular hypothesis about the true state of affairs is made by the analyst and data is gathered to determine whether that state of affairs is true or false. For example, the hypothesis might be that "Unemployment has no effect on inflation", which relates to an economics concept called the Phillips Curve. Hypothesis testing involves considering the likelihood of Type I and type II errors, which relate to whether the data supports accepting or rejecting the hypothesis.

Regression analysis may be used when the analyst is trying to determine the extent to which independent variable X affects dependent variable Y (e.g., "To what extent do changes in the unemployment rate (X) affect the inflation rate (Y)?"). This is an attempt to model or fit an equation line or curve to the data, such that Y is a function of X.

Necessary condition analysis (NCA) may be used when the analyst is trying to determine the extent to which independent variable X allows variable Y (e.g., "To what extent is a certain unemployment rate (X) necessary for a certain inflation rate (Y)?"). Whereas (multiple) regression analysis uses additive logic where each X-variable can produce the outcome and the X's can compensate for each other (they are sufficient but not necessary), necessary condition analysis (NCA) uses necessity logic, where one or more X-variables allow the outcome to exist, but may not produce it (they are necessary but not sufficient). Each single necessary condition must be present and compensation is not possible.

Barriers to Effective Analysis

Barriers to effective analysis may exist among the analysts performing the data analysis or among the audience. Distinguishing fact from opinion, cognitive biases, and innumeracy are all challenges to sound data analysis.

Confusing Fact and Opinion

> "You are entitled to your own opinion, but you are not entitled to your own facts."
>
> *Daniel Patrick Moynihan*

Effective analysis requires obtaining relevant facts to answer questions, support a conclusion or formal opinion, or test hypotheses. Facts by definition are irrefutable, meaning that any person involved in the analysis should be able to agree upon them. For example, in August 2010, the Congressional Budget Office (CBO) estimated that extending the Bush tax cuts of 2001 and 2003 for the 2011–2020 time period would add approximately $3.3 trillion to the national debt. Everyone should be able to agree that indeed this is what CBO reported; they can all examine the report. This makes it a fact. Whether persons agree or disagree with the CBO is their own opinion.

As another example, the auditor of a public company must arrive at a formal opinion on whether financial statements of publicly traded corporations are "fairly stated, in all material respects." This requires extensive analysis of factual data and evidence to support their opinion. When making the leap from facts to opinions, there is always the possibility that the opinion is erroneous.

Cognitive Biases

There are a variety of cognitive biases that can adversely affect analysis. For example, confirmation bias is the tendency to search for or interpret information in a way that confirms one's preconceptions. In addition, individuals may discredit information that does not support their views.

Analysts may be trained specifically to be aware of these biases and how to overcome them. In his book *Psychology of Intelligence Analysis*, retired CIA analyst Richards Heuer wrote that analysts should clearly delineate their assumptions and chains of inference and specify the degree and source of the uncertainty involved in the conclusions. He emphasized procedures to help surface and debate alternative points of view.

Innumeracy

Effective analysts are generally adept with a variety of numerical techniques. However, audiences may not have such literacy with numbers or numeracy; they are said to be innumerate. Persons communicating the data may also be attempting to mislead or misinform, deliberately using bad numerical techniques.

For example, whether a number is rising or falling may not be the key factor. More important may be the number relative to another number, such as the size of government revenue or spending relative to the size of the economy (GDP) or the amount of cost relative to revenue in corporate financial statements. This numerical technique is referred to as normalization or common-sizing. There are many such techniques employed by analysts, whether adjusting for inflation (i.e., comparing real vs. nominal data) or considering population increases, demographics, etc.

Analysts may also analyze data under different assumptions or scenarios. For example, when analysts perform financial statement analysis, they will often recast the financial statements under different assumptions to help arrive at an estimate of future cash flow, which they then discount to present value based on some interest rate, to determine the valuation of the company or its stock. Similarly, the CBO analyzes the effects of various policy options on the government's revenue, outlays and deficits, creating alternative future scenarios for key measures.

Practitioner Notes

Initial Data Analysis

The most important distinction between the initial data analysis phase and the main analysis phase, is that during initial data analysis one refrains from any analysis that is aimed at answering the original research question. The initial data analysis phase is guided by the following four questions:

1. Quality of Data

The quality of the data should be checked as early as possible. Data quality can be assessed in several ways, using different types of analysis: frequency counts, descriptive statistics (mean, standard deviation, median), normality (skewness, kurtosis, frequency histograms, n: variables are compared with coding schemes of variables external to the data set, and possibly corrected if coding schemes are not comparable.

- Test for common-method variance.

The choice of analyses to assess the data quality during the initial data analysis phase depends on the analyses that will be conducted in the main analysis phase.

2. Quality of Measurements

The quality of the measurement instruments should only be checked during the initial data analysis phase when this is not the focus or research question of the study. One should check whether structure of measurement instruments corresponds to structure reported in the literature.

There are two ways to assess measurement:

Analysis of homogeneity (internal consistency), which gives an indication of the reliability of a measurement instrument. During this analysis, one inspects the variances of the items and the scales, the Cronbach's α of the scales, and the change in the Cronbach's alpha when an item would be deleted from a scale

3. Initial Transformations

After assessing the quality of the data and of the measurements, one might decide to impute missing data, or to perform initial transformations of one or more variables, although this can also be done during the main analysis phase.

Possible transformations of variables are:

- Square root transformation (if the distribution differs moderately from normal)
- Log-transformation (if the distribution differs substantially from normal)
- Inverse transformation (if the distribution differs severely from normal)
- Make categorical (ordinal / dichotomous) (if the distribution differs severely from normal, and no transformations help)

4. Did the Implementation of the Study Fulfill the Intentions of the Research Design

One should check the success of the randomization procedure, for instance by checking whether background and substantive variables are equally distributed within and across groups.

If the study did not need or use a randomization procedure, one should check the success of the non-random sampling, for instance by checking whether all subgroups of the population of interest are represented in sample.

Other possible data distortions that should be checked are:

- dropout (this should be identified during the initial data analysis phase)
- Item nonresponse (whether this is random or not should be assessed during the initial data analysis phase)
- Treatment quality (using manipulation checks).

Characteristics of Data Sample

In any report or article, the structure of the sample must be accurately described. It is especially important to exactly determine the structure of the sample (and specifically the size of the subgroups) when subgroup analyses will be performed during the main analysis phase. The characteristics of the data sample can be assessed by looking at:

- Basic statistics of important variables
- Scatter plots
- Correlations and associations
- Cross-tabulations

Final Stage of the Initial Data Analysis

During the final stage, the findings of the initial data analysis are documented, and necessary, preferable, and possible corrective actions are taken.

Also, the original plan for the main data analyses can and should be specified in more detail or rewritten.

In order to do this, several decisions about the main data analyses can and should be made:

- In the case of non-normals: should one transform variables; make variables categorical (ordinal/dichotomous); adapt the analysis method?
- In the case of missing data: should one neglect or impute the missing data; which imputation technique should be used?
- In the case of outliers: should one use robust analysis techniques?
- In case items do not fit the scale: should one adapt the measurement instrument by omitting items, or rather ensure comparability with other (uses of the) measurement instrument(s)?
- In the case of (too) small subgroups: should one drop the hypothesis about inter-group differences, or use small sample techniques, like exact tests or bootstrapping?
- In case the randomization procedure seems to be defective: can and should one calculate propensity scores and include them as covariates in the main analyses?

Analysis

Several analyses can be used during the initial data analysis phase:

- Univariate statistics (single variable)
- Bivariate associations (correlations)
- Graphical techniques (scatter plots)

It is important to take the measurement levels of the variables into account for the analyses, as special statistical techniques are available for each level:

- Nominal and ordinal variables
    - Frequency counts (numbers and percentages)
    - Associations
        - circumambulations (crosstabulations)
        - hierarchical loglinear analysis (restricted to a maximum of 8 variables)
        - loglinear analysis (to identify relevant/important variables and possible confounders)
    - Exact tests or bootstrapping (in case subgroups are small)
    - Computation of new variables
- Continuous variables

- Distribution
  - Statistics (M, SD, variance, skewness, kurtosis)
  - Stem-and-leaf displays
  - Box plots

Nonlinear Analysis

Nonlinear analysis will be necessary when the data is recorded from a nonlinear system. Nonlinear systems can exhibit complex dynamic effects including bifurcations, chaos, harmonics and subharmonics that cannot be analyzed using simple linear methods. Nonlinear data analysis is closely related to nonlinear system identification.

Main Data Analysis

In the main analysis phase analyses aimed at answering the research question are performed as well as any other relevant analysis needed to write the first draft of the research report.

Exploratory and Confirmatory Approaches

In the main analysis phase either an exploratory or confirmatory approach can be adopted. Usually the approach is decided before data is collected. In an exploratory analysis no clear hypothesis is stated before analysing the data, and the data is searched for models that describe the data well. In a confirmatory analysis clear hypotheses about the data are tested.

Exploratory data analysis should be interpreted carefully. When testing multiple models at once there is a high chance on finding at least one of them to be significant, but this can be due to a type 1 error. It is important to always adjust the significance level when testing multiple models with, for example, a Bonferroni correction. Also, one should not follow up an exploratory analysis with a confirmatory analysis in the same dataset. An exploratory analysis is used to find ideas for a theory, but not to test that theory as well. When a model is found exploratory in a dataset, then following up that analysis with a confirmatory analysis in the same dataset could simply mean that the results of the confirmatory analysis are due to the same type 1 error that resulted in the exploratory model in the first place. The confirmatory analysis therefore will not be more informative than the original exploratory analysis.

Stability of Results

It is important to obtain some indication about how generalizable the results are. While this is hard to check, one can look at the stability of the results. Are the results reliable and reproducible? There are two main ways of doing this:

- Cross-validation: By splitting the data in multiple parts we can check if an analysis (like a fitted model) based on one part of the data generalizes to another part of the data as well.
- Sensitivity analysis: A procedure to study the behavior of a system or model when global parameters are (systematically) varied. One way to do this is with bootstrapping.

Statistical Methods

Many statistical methods have been used for statistical analyses. A very brief list of four of the more popular methods is:

- General linear model: A widely used model on which various methods are based (e.g. t test, ANOVA, ANCOVA, MANOVA). Usable for assessing the effect of several predictors on one or more continuous dependent variables.
- Generalized linear model: An extension of the general linear model for discrete dependent variables.
- Structural equation modelling: Usable for assessing latent structures from measured manifest variables.
- Item response theory: Models for (mostly) assessing one latent variable from several binary measured variables (e.g. an exam).

Benefits and Challenges of Data Analysis

Data analysis is a proven way for organizations and enterprises to gain the information they need to make better decisions, serve their customers, and increase productivity and revenue. The benefits of data analysis are almost too numerous to count, and some of the most rewarding benefits include getting the right information for your business, getting more value out of IT departments, creating more effective marketing campaigns, gaining a better understanding of customers, and so on.

But, there is so much data available today that data analysis is a challenge. Namely, handling and presenting all of the data are two of the most challenging aspects of data analysis. Traditional architectures and infrastructures are not able to handle the sheer amount of data that is being generated today, and decision makers find it takes longer than anticipated to get actionable insight from the data.

Fortunately, data management solutions and customer experience management solutions give enterprises the ability to listen to customer interactions, learn from behavior and contextual information, create more effective actionable insights, and execute more intelligently on insights in order to optimize and engage targets and improve business practices.

Data Mining

Data mining is a process used by companies to turn raw data into useful information. By using software to look for patterns in large batches of data, businesses can learn more about their customers and develop more effective marketing strategies as well as increase sales and decrease costs. Data mining depends on effective data collection and warehousing as well as computer processing.

Grocery stores are well-known users of data mining techniques. Many supermarkets offer free loyalty cards to customers that give them access to reduced prices not available to non-members. The cards make it easy for stores to track who is buying what, when they are buying it and at what price. The stores can then use this data, after analyzing it, for multiple purposes, such as offering customers coupons targeted to their buying habits and deciding when to put items on sale or when to sell them at full price. Data mining can be a cause for concern when only selected information, which is not representative of the overall sample group, is used to prove a certain hypothesis.

For businesses, data mining is used to discover patterns and relationships in the data in order to help make better business decisions. Data mining can help spot sales trends, develop smarter marketing campaigns, and accurately predict customer loyalty. Specific uses of data mining include:

- *Market segmentation* - Identify the common characteristics of customers who buy the same products from your company.
- *Customer churn* - Predict which customers are likely to leave your company and go to a competitor.
- *Fraud detection* - Identify which transactions are most likely to be fraudulent.
- *Direct marketing* - Identify which prospects should be included in a mailing list to obtain the highest response rate.
- *Interactive marketing* - Predict what each individual accessing a Web site is most likely interested in seeing.
- *Market basket analysis* - Understand what products or services are commonly purchased together; e.g., beer and diapers.
- *Trend analysis* - Reveal the difference between a typical customer this month and last.

Data mining technology can generate new business opportunities by:

- *Automated prediction of trends and behaviors*: Data mining automates the process of finding predictive information in a large database. Questions that traditionally required extensive hands-on analysis can now be directly answered from the data. A typical example of a predictive problem is targeted marketing. Data mining uses data on past promotional mailings to identify the targets most likely to maximize return on investment in future mailings. Other predictive problems include forecasting bankruptcy and other forms of default, and identifying segments of a population likely to respond similarly to given events.
- *Automated discovery of previously unknown patterns*: Data mining tools sweep through databases and identify previously hidden patterns. An example of pattern discovery is the

analysis of retail sales data to identify seemingly unrelated products that are often purchased together. Other pattern discovery problems include detecting fraudulent credit card transactions and identifying anomalous data that could represent data entry keying errors.

Using massively parallel computers, companies dig through volumes of data to discover patterns about their customers and products. For example, grocery chains have found that when men go to a supermarket to buy diapers, they sometimes walk out with a six-pack of beer as well. Using that information, it's possible to lay out a store so that these items are closer.

Working of Data Mining

How is data mining able to tell you important things that you didn't know or what is going to happen next? That technique that is used to perform these feats is called modeling. Modeling is simply the act of building a model (a set of examples or a mathematical relationship) based on data from situations where the answer is known and then applying the model to other situations where the answers aren't known. Modeling techniques have been around for centuries, of course, but it is only recently that data storage and communication capabilities required to collect and store huge amounts of data, and the computational power to automate modeling techniques to work directly on the data, have been available.

As a simple example of building a model, consider the director of marketing for a telecommunications company. He would like to focus his marketing and sales efforts on segments of the population most likely to become big users of long distance services. He knows a lot about his customers, but it is impossible to discern the common characteristics of his best customers because there are so many variables. From his existing database of customers, which contains information such as age, sex, credit history, income, zip code, occupation, etc., he can use data mining tools, such as neural networks, to identify the characteristics of those customers who make lots of long distance calls. For instance, he might learn that his best customers are unmarried females between the age of 34 and 42 who make in excess of $60,000 per year. This, then, is his model for high value customers, and he would budget his marketing efforts to accordingly.

Data Mining Tools and Techniques

Data mining techniques are used in many research areas, including mathematics, cybernetics, genetics and marketing. While data mining techniques are a means to drive efficiencies and predict customer behavior, if used correctly, a business can set itself apart from its competition through the use of predictive analysis.

Web mining, a type of data mining used in customer relationship management, integrates information gathered by traditional data mining methods and techniques over the web. Web mining aims to understand customer behavior and to evaluate how effective a particular website is.

Other data mining techniques include network approaches based on multitask learning for classifying patterns, ensuring parallel and scalable execution of data mining algorithms, the mining of large databases, the handling of relational and complex data types, and machine learning. Machine learning is a type of data mining tool that designs specific algorithms from which to learn and predict.

Applications of Data Mining

Future Healthcare

Data mining holds great potential to improve health systems. It uses data and analytics to identify best practices that improve care and reduce costs. Researchers use data mining approaches like multi-dimensional databases, machine learning, soft computing, data visualization and statistics. Mining can be used to predict the volume of patients in every category. Processes are developed that make sure that the patients receive appropriate care at the right place and at the right time. Data mining can also help healthcare insurers to detect fraud and abuse.

Market Basket Analysis

Market basket analysis is a modelling technique based upon a theory that if you buy a certain group of items you are more likely to buy another group of items. This technique may allow the retailer to understand the purchase behaviour of a buyer. This information may help the retailer to know the buyer's needs and change the store's layout accordingly. Using differential analysis comparison of results between different stores, between customers in different demographic groups can be done.

Education

There is a new emerging field, called Educational Data Mining, concerns with developing methods that discover knowledge from data originating from educational Environments. The goals of EDM are identified as predicting students' future learning behaviour, studying the effects of educational support, and advancing scientific knowledge about learning. Data mining can be used by an institution to take accurate decisions and also to predict the results of the student. With the results the institution can focus on what to teach and how to teach. Learning pattern of the students can be captured and used to develop techniques to teach them.

Manufacturing Engineering

Knowledge is the best asset a manufacturing enterprise would possess. Data mining tools can be very useful to discover patterns in complex manufacturing process. Data mining can be used in system-level designing to extract the relationships between product architecture, product portfolio, and customer needs data. It can also be used to predict the product development span time, cost, and dependencies among other tasks.

CRM

Customer Relationship Management is all about acquiring and retaining customers, also improving customers' loyalty and implementing customer focused strategies. To maintain a proper relationship with a customer a business need to collect data and analyse the information. This is where data mining plays its part. With data mining technologies the collected data can be used for analysis. Instead of being confused where to focus to retain customer, the seekers for the solution get filtered results.

Fraud Detection

Billions of dollars have been lost to the action of frauds. Traditional methods of fraud detection are time consuming and complex. Data mining aids in providing meaningful patterns and turning data into information. Any information that is valid and useful is knowledge. A perfect fraud detection system should protect information of all the users. A supervised method includes collection of sample records. These records are classified fraudulent or non-fraudulent. A model is built using this data and the algorithm is made to identify whether the record is fraudulent or not.

Intrusion Detection

Any action that will compromise the integrity and confidentiality of a resource is an intrusion. The defensive measures to avoid an intrusion includes user authentication, avoid programming errors, and information protection. Data mining can help improve intrusion detection by adding a level of focus to anomaly detection. It helps an analyst to distinguish an activity from common everyday network activity. Data mining also helps extract data which is more relevant to the problem.

Lie Detection

Apprehending a criminal is easy whereas bringing out the truth from him is difficult. Law enforcement can use mining techniques to investigate crimes, monitor communication of suspected terrorists. This filed includes text mining also. This process seeks to find meaningful patterns in data which is usually unstructured text. The data sample collected from previous investigations are compared and a model for lie detection is created. With this model processes can be created according to the necessity.

Customer Segmentation

Traditional market research may help us to segment customers but data mining goes in deep and increases market effectiveness. Data mining aids in aligning the customers into a distinct segment and can tailor the needs according to the customers. Market is always about retaining the customers. Data mining allows to find a segment of customers based on vulnerability and the business could offer them with special offers and enhance satisfaction.

Financial Banking

With computerised banking everywhere huge amount of data is supposed to be generated with new transactions. Data mining can contribute to solving business problems in banking and finance by finding patterns, causalities, and correlations in business information and market prices that are not immediately apparent to managers because the volume data is too large or is generated too quickly to screen by experts. The managers may find these information for better segmenting,targeting, acquiring, retaining and maintaining a profitable customer.

Corporate Surveillance

Corporate surveillance is the monitoring of a person or group's behaviour by a corporation. The data collected is most often used for marketing purposes or sold to other corporations, but is also regularly shared with government agencies. It can be used by the business to tailor their products desirable by their customers. The data can be used for direct marketing purposes, such as the targeted advertisements on Google and Yahoo, where ads are targeted to the user of the search engine by analyzing their search history and emails.

Research Analysis

History shows that we have witnessed revolutionary changes in research. Data mining is helpful in data cleaning, data pre-processing and integration of databases. The researchers can find any similar data from the database that might bring any change in the research. Identification of any co-occurring sequences and the correlation between any activities can be known. Data visualisation and visual data mining provide us with a clear view of the data.

Criminal Investigation

Criminology is a process that aims to identify crime characteristics. Actually crime analysis includes exploring and detecting crimes and their relationships with criminals. The high volume of crime datasets and also the complexity of relationships between these kinds of data have made criminology an appropriate field for applying data mining techniques. Text based crime reports can be converted into word processing files. These information can be used to perform crime matching process.

Bio Informatics

Data Mining approaches seem ideally suited for Bioinformatics, since it is data-rich. Mining biological data helps to extract useful knowledge from massive datasets gathered in biology, and in other related life sciences areas such as medicine and neuroscience. Applications of data mining to bioinformatics include gene finding, protein function inference, disease diagnosis, disease prognosis, disease treatment optimization, protein and gene interaction network reconstruction, data cleansing, and protein sub-cellular location prediction.

Benefits of Data Mining

In general, the benefits of data mining come from the ability to uncover hidden patterns and relationships in data that can be used to make predictions that impact businesses.

Specific data mining benefits vary depending on the goal and the industry. Sales and marketing departments can mine customer data to improve lead conversion rates or to create one-to-one marketing campaigns. Data mining information on historical sales patterns and customer behaviors can be used to build prediction models for future sales, new products and services.

Companies in the financial industry use data mining tools to build risk models and detect fraud. The manufacturing industry uses data mining tools to improve product safety, identify quality issues, manage the supply chain and improve operations.

Data Visualization

Data visualization is a general term that describes any effort to help people understand the significance of data by placing it in a visual context. Patterns, trends and correlations that might go undetected in text-based data can be exposed and recognized easier with data visualization software.

Today's data visualization tools go beyond the standard charts and graphs used in Microsoft Excel spreadsheets, displaying data in more sophisticated ways such as infographics, dials and gauges, geographic maps, sparklines, heat maps, and detailed bar, pie and fever charts. The images may include interactive capabilities, enabling users to manipulate them or drill into the data for querying and analysis. Indicators designed to alert users when data has been updated or predefined conditions occur can also be included.

Importance of Data Visualization

Data visualization has become the de facto standard for modern business intelligence (BI). The success of the two leading vendors in the BI space, Tableau and Qlik -- both of which heavily emphasize visualization -- has moved other vendors toward a more visual approach in their software. Virtually all BI software has strong data visualization functionality.

Data visualization tools have been important in democratizing data and analytics and making data-driven insights available to workers throughout an organization. They are typically easier to operate than traditional statistical analysis software or earlier versions of BI software. This has led to a rise in lines of business implementing data visualization tools on their own, without support from IT.

Data visualization software also plays an important role in big data and advanced analyticsprojects. As businesses accumulated massive troves of data during the early years of the big data trend, they needed a way to quickly and easily get an overview of their data. Visualization tools were a natural fit.

Visualization is central to advanced analytics for similar reasons. When a data scientist is writing advanced predictive analytics or machine learning algorithms, it becomes important to visualize the outputs to monitor results and ensure that models are performing as intended. This is because visualizations of complex algorithms are generally easier to interpret than numerical outputs.

Characteristics of Effective Graphical Displays

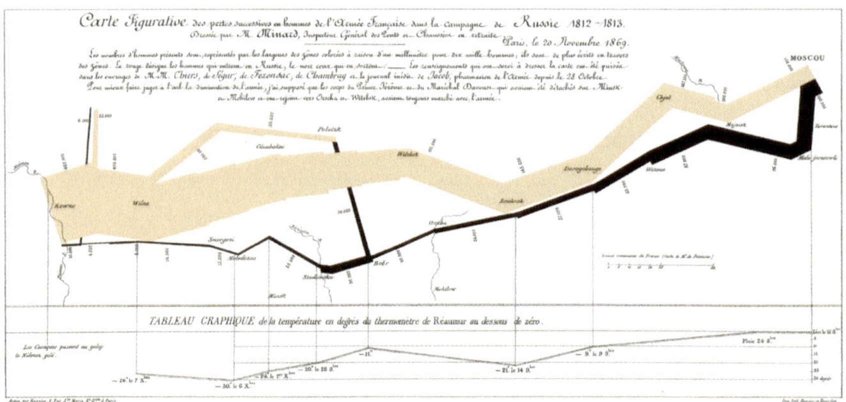

Charles Joseph Minard's 1869 diagram of Napoleonic France's invasion of Russia, an early example of an information graphic

> "The greatest value of a picture is when it forces us to notice what we never expected to see."
>
> *John Tukey*

Professor Edward Tufte explained that users of information displays are executing particular *analytical tasks* such as making comparisons or determining causality. The *design principle* of the information graphic should support the analytical task, showing the comparison or causality.

In his 1983 book *The Visual Display of Quantitative Information*, Edward Tufte defines 'graphical displays' and principles for effective graphical display in the following passage: "Excellence in statistical graphics consists of complex ideas communicated with clarity, precision and efficiency. Graphical displays should:

- Show the data.
- Induce the viewer to think about the substance rather than about methodology, graphic design, the technology of graphic production or something else.
- Avoid distorting what the data has to say.
- Present many numbers in a small space.
- Make large data sets coherent.
- Encourage the eye to compare different pieces of data.
- Reveal the data at several levels of detail, from a broad overview to the fine structure.
- Serve a reasonably clear purpose: description, exploration, tabulation or decoration.
- Be closely integrated with the statistical and verbal descriptions of a data set.

Graphics *reveal* data. Indeed graphics can be more precise and revealing than conventional statistical computations."

For example, the Minard diagram shows the losses suffered by Napoleon's army in the 1812–1813 period. Six variables are plotted: the size of the army, its location on a two-dimensional surface (x and y), time, direction of movement, and temperature. The line width illustrates a comparison (size of the army at points in time) while the temperature axis suggests a cause of the change in army size. This multivariate display on a two dimensional surface tells a story that can be grasped immediately while identifying the source data to build credibility. Tufte wrote in 1983 that: "It may well be the best statistical graphic ever drawn."

Not applying these principles may result in misleading graphs, which distort the message or support an erroneous conclusion. According to Tufte, chartjunk refers to extraneous interior decoration of the graphic that does not enhance the message, or gratuitous three dimensional or perspective effects. Needlessly separating the explanatory key from the image itself, requiring the eye to travel back and forth from the image to the key, is a form of "administrative debris." The ratio of "data to ink" should be maximized, erasing non-data ink where feasible.

The Congressional Budget Office summarized several best practices for graphical displays in a

June 2014 presentation. These included: a) Knowing your audience; b) Designing graphics that can stand alone outside the context of the report; and c) Designing graphics that communicate the key messages in the report.

Bar Chart

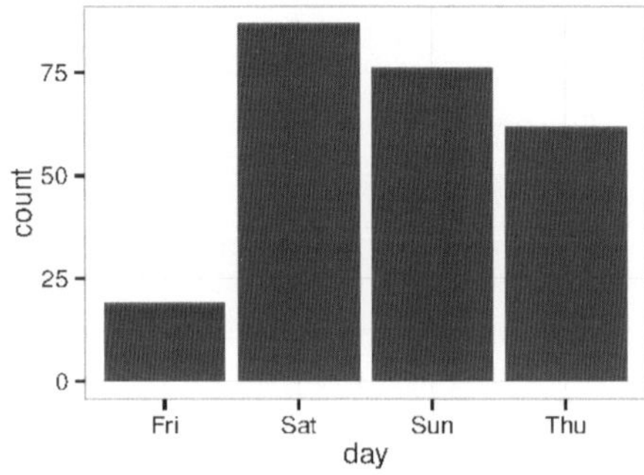

Bar chart of tips by day of week

Visual Dimensions

- Length/count
- Category
- Color

Example Usages : Comparison of values, such as sales performance for several persons or businesses in a single time period. For a single variable measured over time (trend) a line chart is preferable.

Histogram

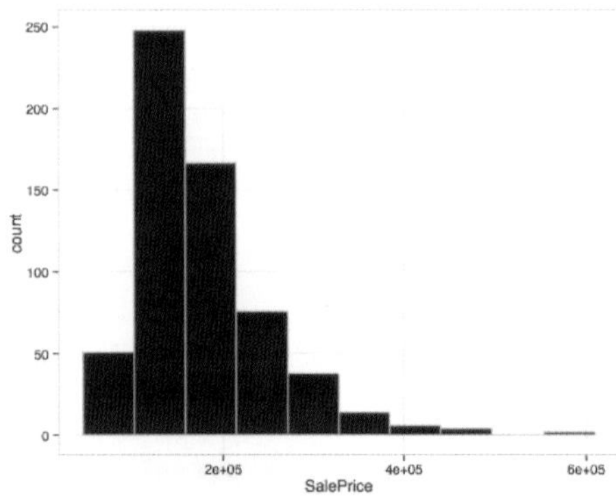

Histogram of housing prices

Visual Dimensions

- Bin limits
- Count/length
- Color

Example Usages : Determining frequency of annual stock market percentage returns within particular ranges (bins) such as 0-10%, 11-20%, etc. The height of the bar represents the number of observations (years) with a return % in the range represented by the bin.

Scatter Plot

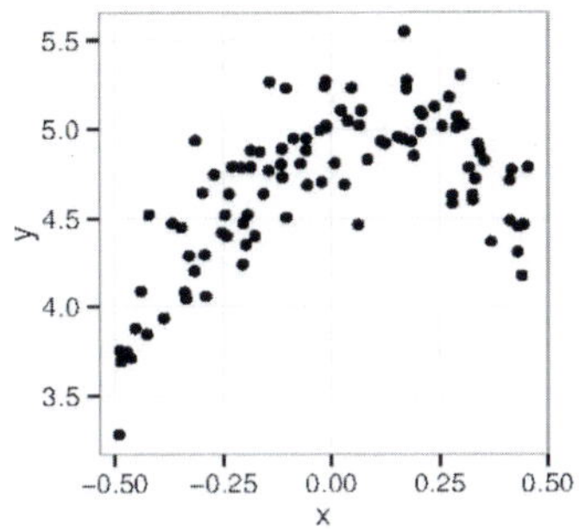

Basic scatterplot of two variables

Visual Dimensions

- x position
- y position
- (symbol/glyph)
- (color)
- (size)

Example Usages : Determining the relationship (e.g., correlation) between unemployment (x) and inflation (y) for multiple time periods.

Scatter Plot (3D)

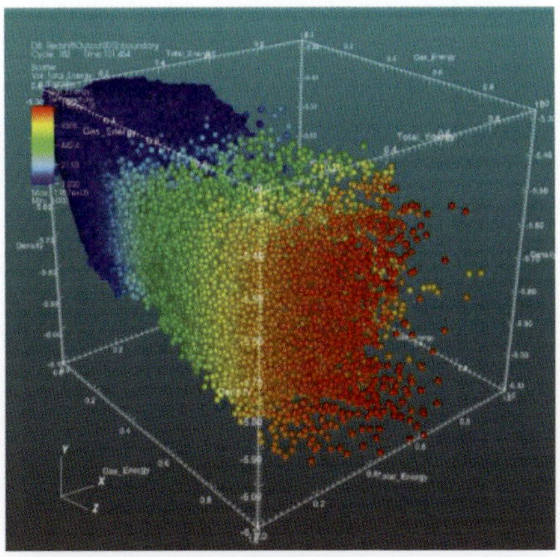

Scatter Plot

- Position x
- Position y

- Position z
- Color

Network

Network Analysis

- Nodes size
- Nodes color
- Ties thickness
- Ties color
- Spatialization

Example Usages:

- Finding clusters in the network (e.g. grouping Facebook friends into different clusters).
- Discovering bridges (information brokers or boundary spanners) between clusters in the network.
- Determining the most influential nodes in the network (e.g. A company wants to target a small group of people on Twitter for a marketing campaign).
- Finding outlier actors who do not fit into any cluster or are in the periphery of a network.

Streamgraph

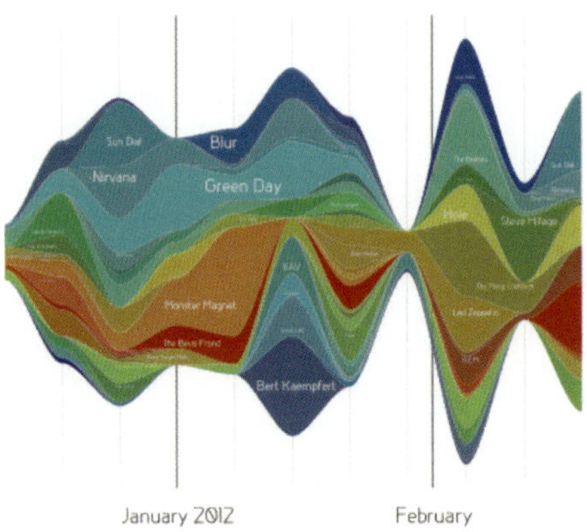

Streamgraph

- Width
- Color
- Time (flow)

Treemap

Treemap

- Size
- Color

Example Usages : disk space by location/file type.

Gantt Chart

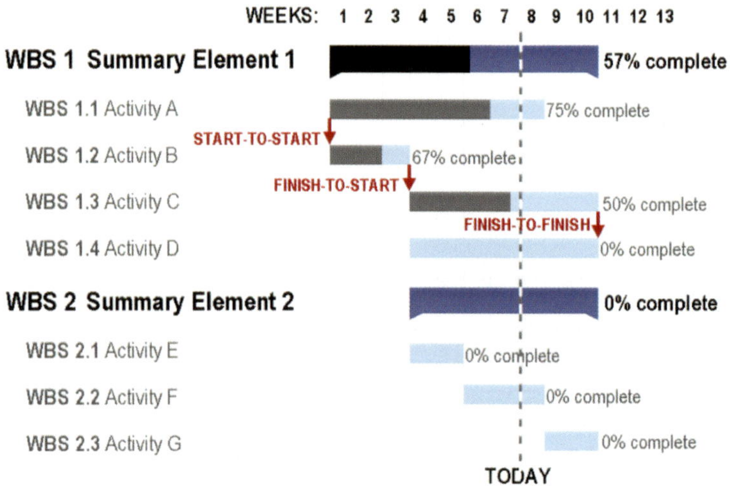

Gantt Chart

- Color
- Time (flow)

Example Usages : schedule / progress, e.g. in project planning.

Heat Map

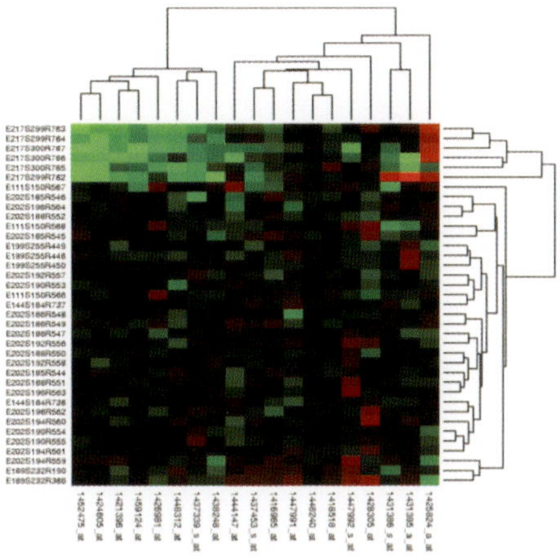

Heat map

- Row
- Column
- Cluster
- Color

Example Usages : Analyzing risk, with green, yellow and red representing low, medium, and high risk, respectively.

PhenoPlot

Glyph-based

- Ellipses dimensions
- Color
- Proportional filling
- Jagged versus straight lines

Example Usages :

- High dimensional data.
- Representing shape measurements of cells.
- Visualizing markers' abundance in various cellular compartments.
- Visualizing tumor data such as size, grade and cellularity.

Role of Visualization in Data Impact Business Cleansing

The simplest way to explain the importance of visualization is to look at visualization as the means to making sense of data. Even the most basic, widely-used data visualization tools that combine simple pie charts and bar graphs help people comprehend large amounts of information fast and easily, compared to paper reports and spreadsheets.

This powerful advantage of visualization and, obviously, visual cortex and pattern recognition capabilities of the human brain allow data scientists and decision makers to quickly grasp the meaning, identify trends and even notice inconsistencies and errors.

In other words, visualization is the initial filter for the quality of data streams. Combining data from various sources, visualization tools perform preliminary standardization, shape data in a unified way and create easy-to-verify visual objects. As a result, these tools become indispensable for data cleansing and vetting and help companies prepare quality assets to derive valuable insights.

Predictive Analytics

Predictive analytics is a form of advanced analytics that uses both new and historical data to forecast activity, behavior and trends. It involves applying statistical analysis techniques, analytical queries and automated machine learning algorithms to data sets to create predictive models that place a numerical value -- or *score* -- on the likelihood of a particular event happening.

Predictive analytics software applications use variables that can be measured and analyzed to predict the likely behavior of individuals, machinery or other entities. For example, an insurance company is likely to take into account potential driving safety variables, such as age, gender, location, type of vehicle and driving record, when pricing and issuing auto insurance policies.

Multiple variables are combined into a predictive model capable of assessing future probabilities with an acceptable level of reliability. The software relies heavily on advanced algorithms and methodologies, such as logistic regressionmodels, time series analysis and decision trees.

Predictive analytics has grown in prominence alongside the emergence of big data systems. As enterprises have amassed larger and broader pools of data in Hadoop clusters and other big data platforms, they have created increased data mining opportunities to gain predictive insights. Heightened development and commercialization of machine learning tools by IT vendors has also helped expand predictive analytics capabilities.

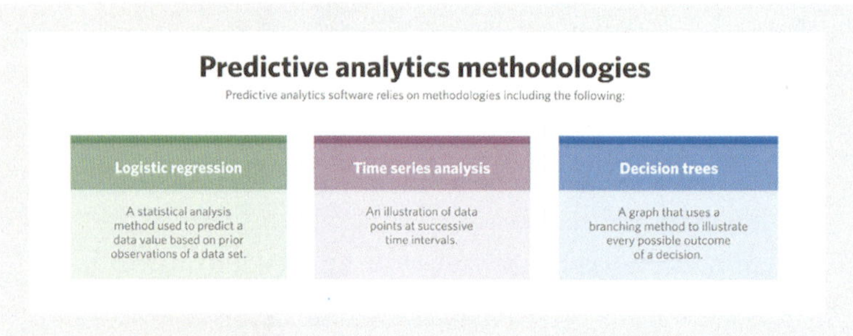

Marketing, financial services and insurance companies have been notable adopters of predictive analytics, as have large search engine and online services providers. Predictive analytics is also commonly used in industries such as healthcare, retail and manufacturing.

Business applications for predictive analytics include targeting online advertisements, analyzing customer behavior to determine buying patterns, flagging potentially fraudulent financial transactions, identifying patients at risk of developing particular medical conditions and detecting impending parts failures in industrial equipment before they occur.

Predictive Analytics Process

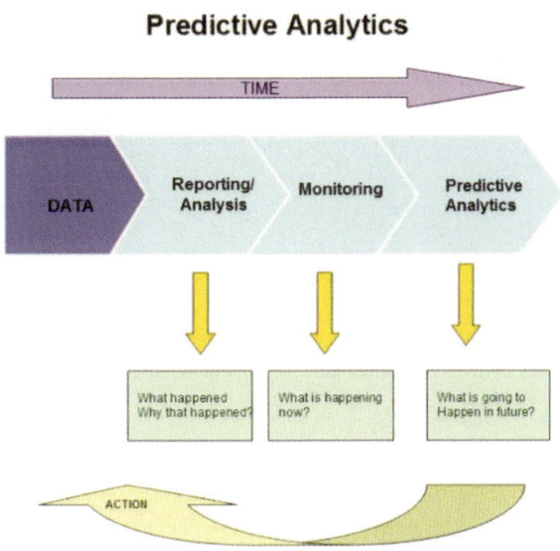

Step 1 Define Project:

Define the project outcomes, deliverables, scoping of the effort, business objectives, identify the data sets which are going to be used.

Step 2 Data Collection:

Data Mining for predictive analytics prepares data from multiple sources for analysis. This provides a complete view of the customer interactions.

Step 3. Data Analysis:

Data Analysis is the process of inspecting, cleaning, transforming, and modeling data with the objective of discovering useful information, arriving at conclusions.

Step 4. Statistics:

Statistical Analysis enables to validate the assumptions, hypotheses and test them with using standard statistical models.

Step 5. Modeling:

Predictive Modeling provides the ability to automatically create accurate predictive models about future. There are also options to choose the best solution with multi model evaluation.

Step 6. Deployment:

Predictive Model Deployment provides the option to deploy the analytical results in to the every day decision making process to get results, reports and output by automating the decisions based on the modeling.

Step 7. Model Monitoring:

Models are managed and monitored to review the model performance to ensure that it is providing the results expected.

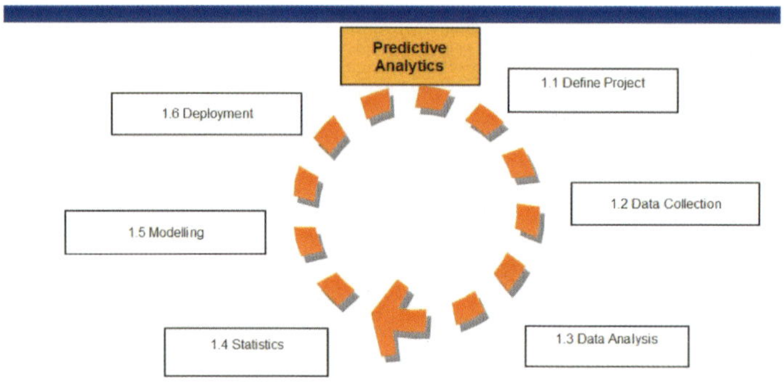

Applications of Predictive Analytics

- Customer relationship management (CRM): Predictive analysis applications are used to achieve CRM objectives such as marketing campaigns, sales, and customer services. Analytical customer relationship management can be applied throughout the customers life cycle, right from acquisition, relationship growth, retention, and win back.
- Health Care: Predictive analysis applications in health care can determine the patients who are at the risk of developing certain conditions such as diabetes, asthma and other lifetime illnesses. The clinical decision support systems incorporate predictive analytics to support medical decision making at the point of care.
- Collection Analytics: Predictive analytics applications optimize the allocation of collection resources by identifying the effective collection agencies, contact strategies, legal actions to increase the recovery and also reducing the collection costs.
- Cross Sell: Predictive analytics applications analyze customers spending, usage and other behavior, leading to efficient cross sales, or selling additional products to current customers for an organization that offers multiple products.
- Fraud detection: Predictive analytics applications can find inaccurate credit applications, fraudulent transactions both done offline and online, identity thefts and false insurance claims.
- Risk management: Predictive analytics applications predicts the best portfolio to maximize return in capital asset pricing model and probabilistic risk assessment to yield accurate forecasts.
- Direct Marketing: Predictive analytics can also help to identify the most effective combination of product versions, marketing material, communication channels and timing that should be used to target a given consumer.

- Underwriting: Predictive analytics can help underwrite the quantities by predicting the chances of illness, default, bankruptcy. Predictive analytics can streamline the process of customer acquisition by predicting the future risk behavior of a customer using application level data.

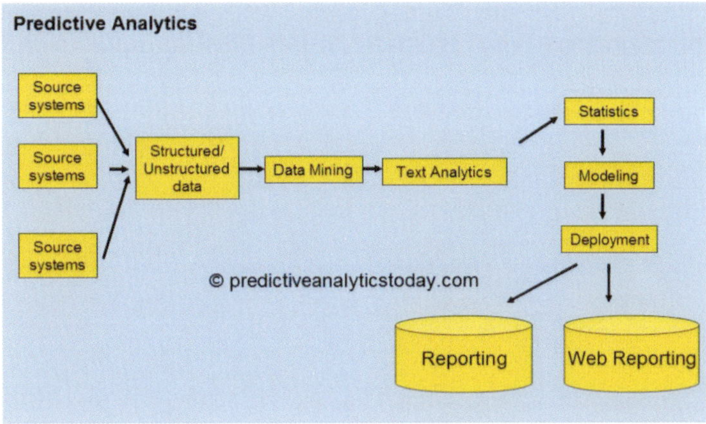

Analytics Tools

A wide range of tools is used in predictive modeling and analytics. IBM, Microsoft, SAS Institute and many other software vendors offer predictive analytics tools and related technologies supporting machine learning and deep learning applications.

In addition, open source software plays a big role in the predictive analytics market. The open source R analytics language is commonly used in predictive analytics applications, as are the P ython and Scala programming languages. Several open source predictive analytics and machine learning platforms are also available, including a library of algorithms built into the Spark processing engine.

Five leading customer analytics tools

PLATFORM	FEATURES
Adobe Analytics	▪ Platform for standardized video and ad engagement ▪ Predictive workbench through machine learning ▪ Live stream with real-time events ▪ Data workbench ▪ Mobile app campaign tool
Google Analytics 360	▪ Data studio ▪ Surveys ▪ Value of marketing channels through attribution ▪ Audience center to match customers with the right message ▪ Analytics ▪ Tag Manager allowing tag updates without editing code
IBM Watson Customer Experience Analytics	▪ Role-based dashboards ▪ Journey analytics ▪ Mindset analysis ▪ Event alerts ▪ Site optimization
SAP Hybris Marketing Cloud	▪ Gains customer insights ▪ Categorizes customers based on score values ▪ Builds customer target groups ▪ Triggers successful campaigns
SAS Customer Intelligence 360	▪ Utilizes customer-centric data model ▪ Records activities of all visitors ▪ Contextualizes captured data ▪ Better business goal creation ▪ Digital asset management

Analytics teams can use the base open source editions of R and other analytics languages or pay for the commercial versions offered by vendors such as Microsoft. The commercial tools can be expensive, but they come with technical support from the vendor, while users of pure open source releases must troubleshoot on their own or seek help through open source community support sites.

References

- Funkhouser, Howard Gray (Jan 1936). "A Note on a Tenth Century Graph". Osiris. 1: 260–262. doi:10.1086/368425. JSTOR 301609
- Measures-of-dispersion: toppr.com, Retrieved 14 June 2018
- Dragicevic, Pierre; Jansen, Yvonne (2012). "List of Physical Visualizations and Related Artefacts". Retrieved 2018-01-12
- What-is-data-analysis: ngdata.com, Retrieved 30 April 2018
- Tufte, Edward (1983). The Visual Display of Quantitative Information. Cheshire, Connecticut: Graphics Press. ISBN 0-9613921-4-2
- 14-useful-applications-of-data-mining: bigdata-madesimple.com, Retrieved 18 June 2018
- What-is-predictive-analytics: predictiveanalyticstoday.com, Retrieved 25 May 2018
- Manuela Aparicio and Carlos J. Costa (November 2014). "Data visualization". Communication Design Quarterly Review. 3 (1): 7–11. doi:10.1145/2721882.2721883
- Data-mining: searchsqlserver.techtarget.com, Retrieved 08 April 2018
- Friendly, Michael (2001). "Milestones in the history of thematic cartography, statistical graphics, and data visualization". Retrieved 2017-11-19
- Data-visualization-strategy-for-business: iotforall.com, Retrieved 26 April 2018

3

Probability, Sampling and Statistical Distributions

Probability refers to the measurement of the likelihood of occurrence of an event. The estimation of characteristics of a population is based on an analysis of a selection of a statistical sample. The aim of this chapter is to explore the concepts of probability, sampling and statistical distributions for business. It includes topics such as set theory, probability distribution, interval estimation, inference, sampling, large sample theory, sampling distribution, point estimation, etc.

Probability

Probability is a branch of mathematics that deals with calculating the likelihood of a given event's occurrence, which is expressed as a number between 1 and 0. An event with a probability of 1 can be considered a certainty: for example, the probability of a coin toss resulting in either "heads" or "tails" is 1, because there are no other options, assuming the coin lands flat. An event with a probability of .5 can be considered to have equal odds of occurring or not occurring: for example, the probability of a coin toss resulting in "heads" is .5, because the toss is equally as likely to result in "tails." An event with a probability of 0 can be considered an impossibility: for example, the probability that the coin will land (flat) without either side facing up is 0, because either "heads" or "tails" must be facing up. A little paradoxical, probability theory applies precise calculations to quantify uncertain measures of random events.

In its simplest form, probability can be expressed mathematically as: the number of occurrences of a targeted event divided by the number of occurrences plus the number of failures of occurrences (this adds up to the total of possible outcomes):

$$p(a) = p(a)/\left[p(a) + p(b)\right]$$

Calculating probabilities in a situation like a coin toss is straightforward, because the outcomes are mutually exclusive: either one event or the other must occur. Each coin toss is an independent event; the outcome of one trial has no effect on subsequent ones. No matter how many consecutive times one side lands facing up, the probability that it will do so at the next toss is always .5 (50-50). The mistaken idea that a number of consecutive results (six "heads" for example) makes it more likely that the next toss will result in a "tails" is known as the gambler's fallacy , one that has led to the downfall of many a bettor.

Probability theory had its start in the 17th century, when two French mathematicians, Blaise Pascal and Pierre de Fermat carried on a correspondence discussing mathematical problems dealing with games of chance. Contemporary applications of probability theory run the gamut of human inquiry, and include aspects of computer programming, astrophysics, music, weather prediction, and medicine.

Importance of Probability in a Business

As a small-business owner, you may act on hunches, guesses and instincts. After such actions, you might even say you thought a certain outcome was "probable." However, the mathematics of probability has rules that you can use in a much more disciplined way than guesswork to predict possible outcomes for your business plans.

Classical Approach

The classical approach to using probability depends on several future events that are equally likely to happen. In rolling a die, for example, the odds are equally likely for rolling a 1, 2, 3, 4, 5 or 6. If you roll the die once, you have a 1 in 6 chance of getting the number you want. The formula is the number of favorable outcomes divided by the total number of possible outcomes. Note that if you roll the die twice, the odds are 2 in 12 that you will get the number you want (this is the same value as 1/6). This is because the possible outcomes double if you throw the die twice.

Using the Classical Approach in Business

You can use the classical approach to probability when making business decisions where you don't know the likelihood of several possible outcomes. You assume they are all equally likely, then look at how many attempts you will be able to make. However, in your business, if 6 possible outcomes are equally likely, but they are not affected by how many times you try, you can cut your odds in half with repeated effort. For example, if you make 2 tries, your effort will have a 2 in 6 chance. Notice that 2/6 = 1/3. You have moved from a 1 in 6 chance of success to a 1 in 3 chance.

Relative Frequency Approach

The relative frequency approach uses the past to make predictions about the future. You look at how many times an event has happened and then look at how many opportunities exist for the event to occur. The formula is the number of times an event occurred divided by the total number of opportunities for the event to occur.

Using Relative Frequency Approach in Business

You can use relative frequency to improve your business decisions. For example if your research shows there are 75 failures for every 100 business startups attempted, you would say that 75 out of 100 startups fail. This reduces to 3/4. That would mean 3 out of 4 startups fail. If you don't do something to change your odds, you can expect that failure probability. This mathematical reality can give you a sense of urgency in your efforts to be the 1 out of 4 that succeeds. In fact, you could study the successes to see how they changed the odds in their favor.

Mutual Exclusivity

The concept of mutually exclusivity applies if the occurrence of one event prohibits the occurrence of another event. For example, assume you have two tasks on your to-do list. Both tasks are due today and both will take the entire day to complete. Whichever task you choose to complete means

the other will remain incomplete. These two tasks can't have the same outcome. Thus, these tasks are mutually exclusive.

Dependent Events

A second concept refers to the impact two separate events have on each other. Dependent events are those in which the occurrence of one event affects -- but doesn't prevent -- the probability of the other occurring. For example, assume a five-year goal is to purchase a new building and pay the full purchase price in cash. The expected funding source is investment returns from excess sales revenue investments. The probability of the purchase happening within the five-year period depends on whether sales revenues meet projected expectations. This makes these dependent events.

Interdependent Events

Interdependent events are those in which the occurrence of one event has no effect of the probability of another event. For example, assume consumer demand for hairbrushes is falling to an all-time low. The concept of interdependence says that declining demand for hairbrushes and the probability that demand for shampoo will also decline share no relationship. In the same way, if you intend to purchase a new building by investing personal funds instead of relying on investment returns from excess sales revenues, the purchase of a new building and sales revenues share no relationship. Thus, these are now interdependent events.

Set Theory

Set theory is a mathematical abstract concerned with the grouping of sets of numbers that have commonality. For example, all even numbers make up a set, and all odd numbers comprise a set. All numbers that end in zero make up a set of numbers that can be divided by 10. Using and comparing sets enables the creation of theories and rules that have practically unlimited scope, whether in mathematics or applied to areas such as business.

Applied to business operations, set theory can assist in planning and operations. Every element of business can be grouped into at least one set such as accounting, management, operations, production and sales. Within those sets are other sets. In operations, for example, there are sets of warehouse operations, sales operations and administrative operations. In some cases, sets intersect—as sales operations can intersect the operations set and the sales set.

Rough-Set Theory

Rough-set theory postulates that all things have something in common with at least one other thing. The difficulty in quantifying these sets gives rise to the name "rough sets." These sets provide a way of comparing and drawing conclusions regarding operational elements that may not be fully defined or quantified. An example of rough sets used in operations is a historical comparison of the Great Depression of the 1930s with the Credit Crisis of 2008. These sets are not the same, but they do intersect at certain points, and these intersections can reveal important clues to the effect of management operations before and during periods of financial crises.

Set Theory in Operations

Set theory is used in almost every discipline including engineering, business, medical and related health sciences, along with the natural sciences. In business operations, it can be applied at every level where intersecting and non-intersecting sets are identified. For example, the sets for warehouse operations and sales operations are both intersected by the inventory set. To improve the cost of goods sold, the solution might be found by examining where inventory intersects both sales and warehouse operations.

Probability Distribution

A probability distribution is a statistical function that describes all the possible values and likelihoods that a random variable can take within a given range. This range will be bounded between the minimum and maximum possible values, but precisely where the possible value is likely to be plotted on the probability distribution depends on a number of factors. These factors include the distribution's mean (average), standard deviation, skewness and kurtosis. Perhaps the most common probability distribution is the normal distribution, or "bell curve," although several distributions exist that are commonly used. Typically, the data generating process of some phenomenon will dictate its probability distribution.This process is called the probability density function.

Probability distributions can also be used to create cumulative distribution functions (CDFs), which adds up the probability of occurrences cumulatively and will always start at zero and end at 100 percent.

Academics, financial analysts and fund managers alike may determine a particular stock's probability distribution to evaluate the possible expected returns that the stock may yield in the future. The stock's history of returns, which can be measured from any time interval, will likely be composed of only a fraction of the stock's returns, which will subject the analysis to sampling error. By increasing the sample size, this error can be dramatically reduced.

Types of Probability Distributions

Bernoulli Distribution

At the beginning of any cricket match, how do you decide who is going to bat or ball? A toss! It all depends on whether you win or lose the toss, right? Let's say if the toss results in a head, you win. Else, you lose. There's no midway.

A Bernoulli distribution has only two possible outcomes, namely 1 (success) and 0 (failure), and a single trial. So the random variable X which has a Bernoulli distribution can take value 1 with the probability of success, say p, and the value 0 with the probability of failure, say q or 1-p.

Here, the occurrence of a head denotes success, and the occurrence of a tail denotes failure. Probability of getting a head = 0.5 = Probability of getting a tail since there are only two possible outcomes.

The probability mass function is given by: $p^x (1-p)^{1-x}$ where x € (0, 1).

It can also be written as:

$$P(x) = \begin{cases} 1-p, x = 0 \\ p, x = 1 \end{cases}$$

Here, the probability of success(p) is not same as the probability of failure. So, the chart below shows the Bernoulli Distribution of our fight.

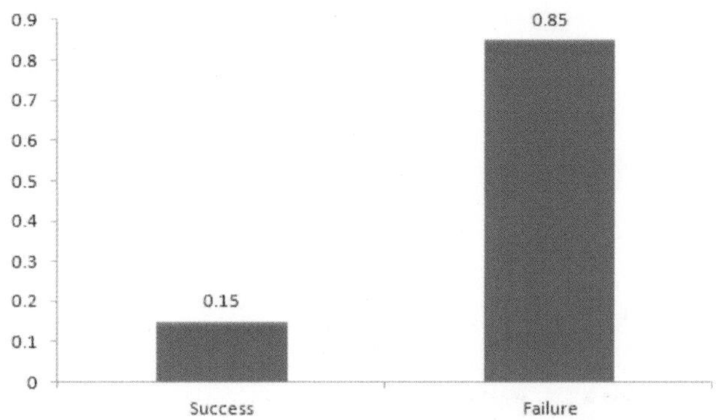

Here, the probability of success = 0.15 and probability of failure = 0.85. Basically expected value of any distribution is the mean of the distribution. The expected value of a random variable X from a Bernoulli distribution is found as follows:

$$E(X) = 1*p + 0*(1-p) = p$$

The variance of a random variable from a bernoulli distribution is:

$$V(X) = E(X^2) - [E(X)]^2 = p - p^2 = p(1-p)$$

There are many examples of Bernoulli distribution such as whether it's going to rain tomorrow or not where rain denotes success and no rain denotes failure and Winning (success) or losing (failure) the game.

Uniform Distribution

When you roll a fair die, the outcomes are 1 to 6. The probabilities of getting these outcomes are equally likely and that is the basis of a uniform distribution. Unlike Bernoulli Distribution, all the n number of possible outcomes of a uniform distribution are equally likely.

A variable X is said to be uniformly distributed if the density function is:

$$f(x) = \frac{1}{b-a} \quad \text{For} \quad -\infty < a \le x \le b < \infty$$

The graph of a uniform distribution curve looks like

You can see that the shape of the Uniform distribution curve is rectangular, the reason why Uniform distribution is called rectangular distribution.

For a Uniform Distribution, a and b are the parameters.

The number of bouquets sold daily at a flower shop is uniformly distributed with a maximum of 40 and a minimum of 10.

Let's try calculating the probability that the daily sales will fall between 15 and 30.

The probability that daily sales will fall between 15 and 30 is (30-15)*(1/(40-10)) = 0.5

Similarly, the probability that daily sales are greater than 20 is = 0.667

The mean and variance of X following a uniform distribution is:

$$\text{Mean} \quad -> E(X) = (a+b)/2$$

$$\text{Variance} \quad -> V(X) = (b-a)^2/12$$

The standard uniform density has parameters a = 0 and b = 1, so the PDF for standard uniform density is given by:

$$f(x) = \begin{cases} 1, & 0 \le x \le 1 \\ 0, & \text{otherwise} \end{cases}$$

Binomial Distribution

Suppose that you won the toss today and this indicates a successful event. You toss again but you lost this time. If you win a toss today, this does not necessitate that you will win the toss tomorrow. Let's assign a random variable, say X, to the number of times you won the toss. What can be the possible value of X? It can be any number depending on the number of times you tossed a coin.

There are only two possible outcomes. Head denoting success and tail denoting failure. Therefore, probability of getting a head = 0.5 and the probability of failure can be easily computed as: q = 1- p = 0.5.

A distribution where only two outcomes are possible, such as success or failure, gain or loss, win or lose and where the probability of success and failure is same for all the trials is called a Binomial Distribution.

Each trial is independent since the outcome of the previous toss doesn't determine or affect the outcome of the current toss. An experiment with only two possible outcomes repeated n number of times is called binomial. The parameters of a binomial distribution are n and p where n is the total number of trials and p is the probability of success in each trial.

On the basis of the above explanation, the properties of a Binomial Distribution are

1. Each trial is independent.
2. There are only two possible outcomes in a trial- either a success or a failure.
3. A total number of n identical trials are conducted.
4. The probability of success and failure is same for all trials. (Trials are identical.)

The mathematical representation of binomial distribution is given by:

$$P(x) = \frac{n!}{(n-x)!x!} p^x q^{n-x}$$

A binomial distribution graph where the probability of success does not equal the probability of failure looks like

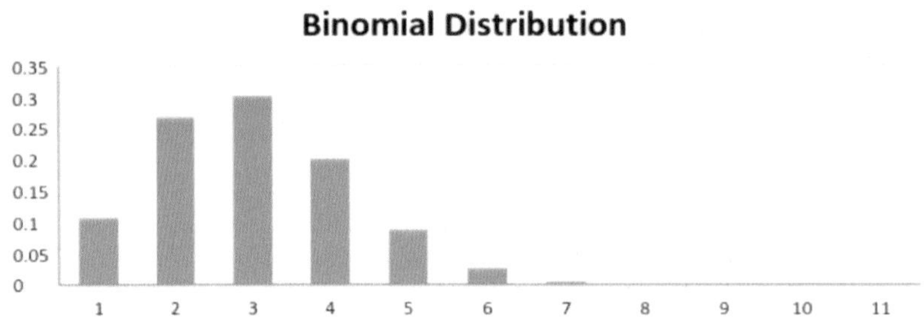

Now, when probability of success = probability of failure, in such a situation the graph of binomial distribution looks like

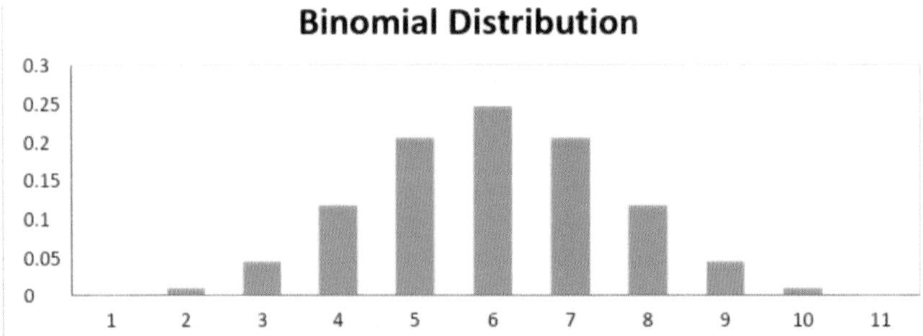

The mean and variance of a binomial distribution are given by:

$$\text{Mean} -> \mu = n * p$$

$$\text{Variance} -> \text{Var}(X) = n * p * q$$

Normal Distribution

Normal distribution represents the behavior of most of the situations in the universe. The large sum of (small) random variables often turns out to be normally distributed, contributing to its widespread application. Any distribution is known as Normal distribution if it has the following characteristics:

1. The mean, median and mode of the distribution coincide.
2. The curve of the distribution is bell-shaped and symmetrical about the line $x=\mu$.
3. The total area under the curve is 1.
4. Exactly half of the values are to the left of the center and the other half to the right.

A normal distribution is highly different from Binomial Distribution. However, if the number of trials approaches infinity then the shapes will be quite similar.

The PDF of a random variable X following a normal distribution is given by:

$$f(x)=\frac{1}{\sqrt{2\pi\sigma}}e^{\{-\frac{1}{2}(\frac{x-u}{\sigma})^2\}} \quad \text{For } -\infty < X < \infty$$

The mean and variance of a random variable X which is said to be normally distributed is given by:

Mean $-> E(X) = \mu$

Variance $-> Var(X) = \sigma\wedge 2$

Here, μ (mean) and σ (standard deviation) are the parameters.

The graph of a random variable X ~ N (μ, σ) is shown below:

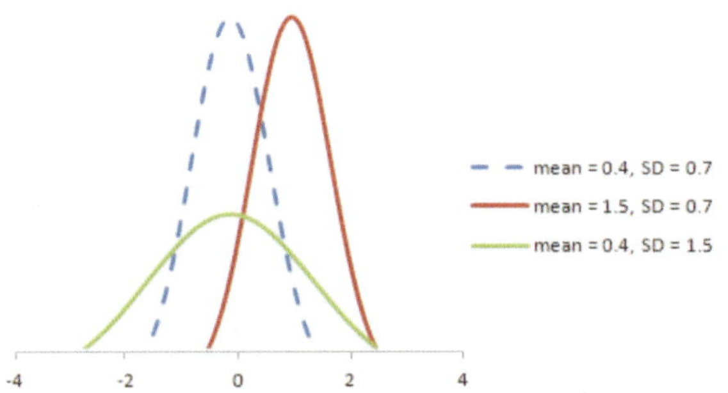

A standard normal distribution is defined as the distribution with mean 0 and standard deviation 1. For such a case, the PDF becomes:

$$f(x)=\frac{1}{\sqrt{2\pi}}e^{-x^2/2} \quad \text{For } -\infty < x < \infty$$

Standard Normal Distribution

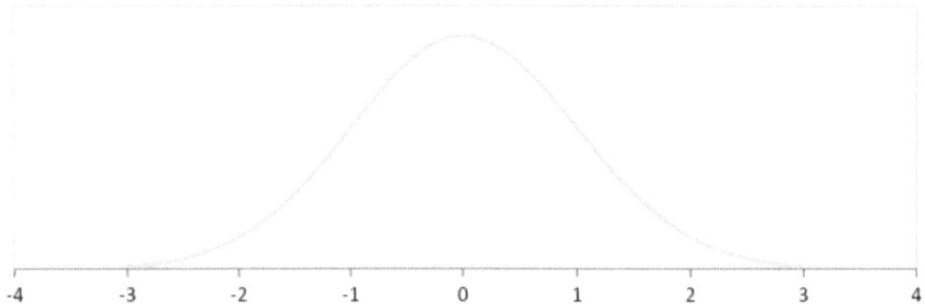

Poisson Distribution

Suppose you work at a call center, approximately how many calls do you get in a day? It can be any number. Now, the entire number of calls at a call center in a day is modeled by Poisson distribution. Some more examples are:

1. The number of emergency calls recorded at a hospital in a day.
2. The number of thefts reported in an area on a day.
3. The number of customers arriving at a salon in an hour.
4. The number of suicides reported in a particular city.
5. The number of printing errors at each page of the book.

You can now think of many examples following the same course. Poisson Distribution is applicable in situations where events occur at random points of time and space wherein our interest lies only in the number of occurrences of the event.

A distribution is called Poisson distribution when the following assumptions are valid:

1. Any successful event should not influence the outcome of another successful event.
2. The probability of success over a short interval must equal the probability of success over a longer interval.
3. The probability of success in an interval approaches zero as the interval becomes smaller.

Now, if any distribution validates the above assumptions then it is a Poisson distribution. Some notations used in Poisson distribution are:

- λ is the rate at which an event occurs,
- t is the length of a time interval,
- And X is the number of events in that time interval.

Here, X is called a Poisson Random Variable and the probability distribution of X is called Poisson distribution.

Let μ denote the mean number of events in an interval of length t. Then, $\mu = \lambda * t$.

The PMF of X following a Poisson distribution is given by:

$$P(X = x) = e^{-\mu} \frac{\mu^x}{x!} \qquad \text{For } x = 0, 1, 2, \ldots\ldots$$

The mean μ is the parameter of this distribution. μ is also defined as the λ times length of that interval. The graph of a Poisson distribution is shown below:

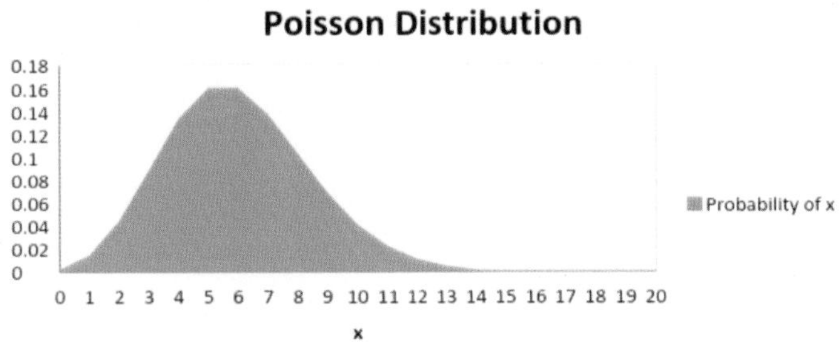

The graph shown below illustrates the shift in the curve due to increase in mean.

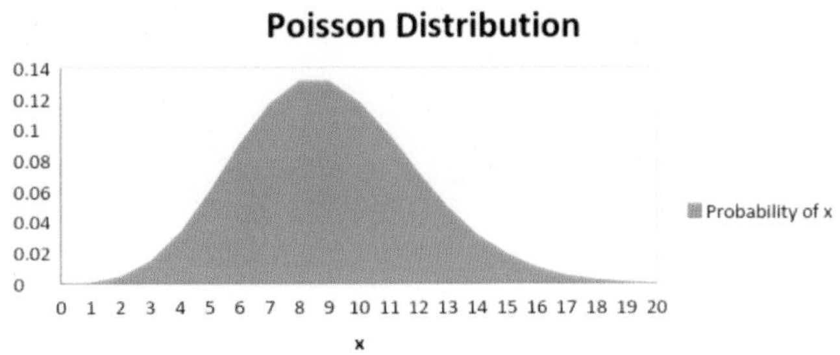

It is perceptible that as the mean increases, the curve shifts to the right.

The mean and variance of X following a Poisson distribution:

$$\text{Mean} \quad -> E(X) = \mu$$

$$\text{Variance} \quad -> Var(X) = \mu$$

Exponential Distribution

Let's consider the call center example one more time. What about the interval of time between the calls ? Here, exponential distribution comes to our rescue. Exponential distribution models the interval of time between the calls.

Other examples are:

1. Length of time beteeen metro arrivals,
2. Length of time between arrivals at a gas station
3. The life of an Air Conditioner

Exponential distribution is widely used for survival analysis. From the expected life of a machine to the expected life of a human, exponential distribution successfully delivers the result.

A random variable X is said to have an exponential distribution with PDF:

$$f(x) = \{ \lambda e^{-\lambda x}, x \geq 0$$

and parameter $\lambda > 0$ which is also called the rate.

For survival analysis, λ is called the failure rate of a device at any time t, given that it has survived up to t.

Mean and Variance of a random variable X following an exponential distribution:

$$\text{Mean} \quad -> E(X) = 1/\lambda$$

$$\text{Variance} \quad -> Var(X) = (1/\lambda)^2$$

Also, the greater the rate, the faster the curve drops and the lower the rate, flatter the curve. This is explained better with the graph shown below:

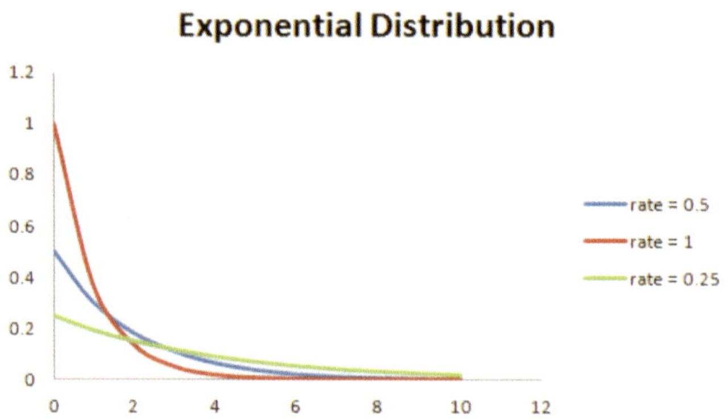

To ease the computation, there are some formulas given below:

$P\{X \leq x\} = 1 - e^{-\lambda x}$, corresponds to the area under the density curve to the left of x.

$P\{X > x\} = e^{-\lambda x}$, corresponds to the area under the density curve to the right of x.

$P\{x1 < X \leq x2\} = e^{-\lambda x1} - e^{-\lambda x2}$, corresponds to the area under the density curve between x1 and x2.

Relations between the Distributions

Relation between Bernoulli and Binomial Distribution:

1. Bernoulli Distribution is a special case of Binomial Distribution with a single trial.
2. There are only two possible outcomes of a Bernoulli and Binomial distribution, namely success and failure.
3. Both Bernoulli and Binomial Distributions have independent trails.

1. Relation between Poisson and Binomial Distribution

Poisson Distribution is a limiting case of binomial distribution under the following conditions:

1. The number of trials is indefinitely large or $n \to \infty$.
2. The probability of success for each trial is same and indefinitely small or $p \to 0$.
3. $np = \lambda$, is finite.

2. Relation between Normal and Binomial Distribution and Normal and Poisson Distribution

Normal distribution is another limiting form of binomial distribution under the following conditions:

1. The number of trials is indefinitely large, $n \to \infty$.
2. Both p and q are not indefinitely small.

The normal distribution is also a limiting case of Poisson distribution with the parameter $\lambda \to \infty$.

3. Relation between Exponential and Poisson Distribution

If the times between random events follow exponential distribution with rate λ, then the total number of events in a time period of length t follows the Poisson distribution with parameter λt.

Scenario Analysis

Probability distributions can be used to create scenario analyses. A scenario analysis uses probability distributions to create several, theoretically distinct possibilities for the outcome of a particular course of action or future event. For example, a business might create three scenarios: worst-case, likely and best-case. The worst-case scenario would contain some value from the lower end of the probability distribution; the likely scenario would contain a value towards the middle of the distribution; and the best-case scenario would contain a value in the upper end of the scenario.

Sales Forecasting

One practical use for probability distributions and scenario analysis in business is to predict future levels of sales. It is essentially impossible to predict the precise value of a future sales level; however, businesses still need to be able to plan for future events. Using a scenario analysis based on a probability distribution can help a company frame its possible future values in terms of a likely sales level and a worst-case and best-case scenario. By doing so, the company can base its business plans on the likely scenario but still be aware of the alternative possibilities.

Risk Evaluation

In addition to predicting future sales levels, probability distribution can be a useful tool for evaluating risk. Consider, for example, a company considering entering a new business line. If the company needs to generate $500,000 in revenue in order to break even and their probability distribution tells them that there is a 10 percent chance that revenues will be less than \$500,000, the company knows roughly what level of risk it is facing if it decides to pursue that new business line.

Random Variable

A *random variable*, usually written X, is a variable whose possible values are numerical outcomes of a random phenomenon. There are two types of random variables, *discrete* and *continuous*.

Discrete Random Variables

A *discrete random variable* is one which may take on only a countable number of distinct values such as 0,1,2,3,4,........ Discrete random variables are usually (but not necessarily) counts. If a random variable can take only a finite number of distinct values, then it must be discrete. Examples of discrete random variables include the number of children in a family, the Friday night attendance at a cinema, the number of patients in a doctor's surgery, the number of defective light bulbs in a box of ten.

The *probability distribution* of a discrete random variable is a list of probabilities associated with each of its possible values. It is also sometimes called the probability function or the probability mass function.

Suppose a random variable X may take k different values, with the probability that $X = x_i$ defined to be $P(X = x_i) = p_i$. The probabilities p_i must satisfy the following:

1: $0 < p_i < 1$ for each i

2: $p_1 + p_2 + \ldots + p_k = 1.$

Example

Suppose a variable X can take the values 1, 2, 3, or 4.
The probabilities associated with each outcome are described by the following table:

Outcome	1	2	3	4
Probability	0.1	0.3	0.4	0.2

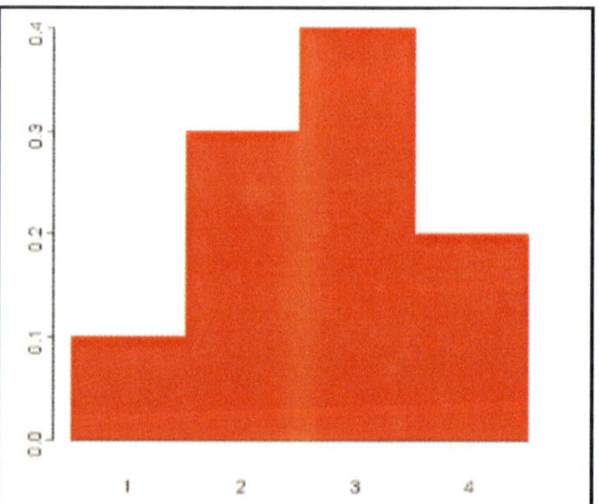

The probability that X is equal to 2 or 3 is the sum of the two probabilities:
$P(X = 2 \text{ or } X = 3) = P(X = 2) + P(X = 3) = 0.3 + 0.4 = 0.7$. Similarly, the probability that X is greater than 1 is equal to $1 - P(X = 1) = 1 - 0.1 = 0.9$, by the complement rule.
This distribution may also be described by the *probability histogram* in shown diagram.

All random variables (discrete and continuous) have a *cumulative distribution function*. It is a function giving the probability that the random variable X is less than or equal to x, for every value x. For a discrete random variable, the cumulative distribution function is found by summing up the probabilities.

Example The cumulative distribution function for the above probability distribution is calculated as follows: The probability that X is less than or equal to 1 is 0.1, the probability that X is less than or equal to 2 is 0.1+0.3 = 0.4, the probability that X is less than or equal to 3 is 0.1+0.3+0.4 = 0.8, and the probability that X is less than or equal to 4 is 0.1+0.3+0.4+0.2 = 1.	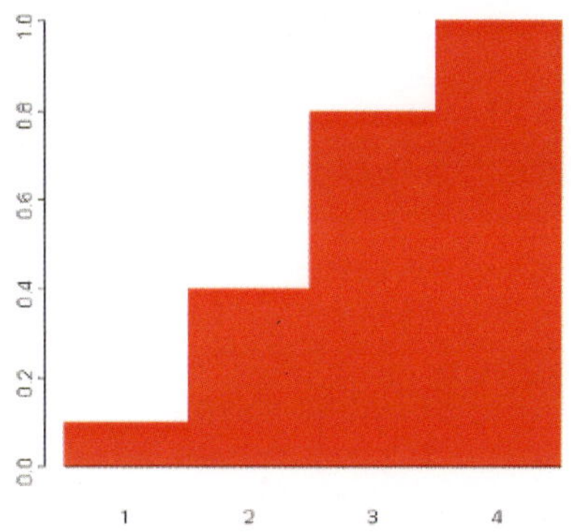

The probability histogram for the cumulative distribution of this random variable is shown in the diagram.

Continuous Random Variables

A *continuous random variable* is one which takes an infinite number of possible values. Continuous random variables are usually measurements. Examples include height, weight, the amount of sugar in an orange, the time required to run a mile.

A continuous random variable is not defined at specific values. Instead, it is defined over an *interval* of values, and is represented by the *area under a curve* (in advanced mathematics, this is known as an *integral*). The probability of observing any single value is equal to 0, since the number of values which may be assumed by the random variable is infinite.

Suppose a random variable *X* may take all values over an interval of real numbers. Then the probability that *X* is in the set of outcomes *A*, *P(A)*, is defined to be the area above *A* and under a curve. The curve, which represents a function *p(x)*, must satisfy the following:

1: The curve has no negative values (p(x) > 0 for all x).

2: The total area under the curve is equal to 1.

A curve meeting these requirements is known as a *density curve.*

Random Vectors and Joint Distributions

The concept of random vector is a multidimensional generalization of the concept of random variable.

Suppose that we conduct a probabilistic experiment and that the possible outcomes of the experiment are described by a sample space Ω.

A random vector is a vector whose value depends on the outcome of the experiment.

Let Ω be a sample space. A random vector X is a function from the sample space Ω to the set of K-dimensional real vectors $\mathbb{R}^K$:

$$X : \Omega \to \mathbb{R}^K$$

In rigorous probability theory, the function X is also required to be measurable (a concept found in measure theory.

The real vector $X(\infty)$ associated to a sample point $\infty \in \Omega$ is called a realization of the random vector.

The set of all possible realizations is called support and is denoted by R_x.

Notation

Denote by $P(E)$ the probability of an event $E \subseteq \Omega$. When dealing with random vectors, the following conventions are used:

- If $A \subseteq \mathbb{R}^k$, we often write $P(X \in A)$ with the meaning

  $P(X \in A) = P(\{\infty \in \Omega : X(\infty) \in A\})$

- If $A \subseteq \mathbb{R}^k$, we sometimes use the notation $P_x(A)$ with the meaning $P_x(A) = P(X \in A) = P(\{\infty \in \Omega : X(\infty) \in A\})$

  In applied work, it is very commonplace to build statistical models where a random vector X is defined by directly specifying P_X (in which case the specification of the sample space Ω is omitted altogether).

- We often write X instead of $X(\infty)$, that is, we omit the dependence on ∞.

The following example shows how a random vector can be defined on a sample space.

Example: Two coins are tossed. The possible outcomes of each toss can be either tail (T) or head (H). The sample space is

$$\Omega = \{TT, TH, HT, HH\}$$

The four possible outcomes are assigned equal probabilities:

$$P(\{TT\}) = P(\{TH\}) = P(\{HT\}) = P(\{HH\}) = \frac{1}{4}$$

If tail (T) is the outcome, we win one dollar, if head (H) is the outcome we lose one dollar. A 2-dimensional random vector X indicates the amount we win (or lose) on each toss:

$$X(\infty) = \begin{cases} [1\ 1] & \text{if } \infty = TT \\ [1\ -1] & \text{if } \infty = TH \\ [-1\ 1] & \text{if } \infty = HT \\ [-1 -1] & \text{if } \infty = HH \end{cases}$$

The probability of winning one dollar on both tosses is

$$P(X = [1\ \ 1]) = P(\{\infty \in \Omega : X(\infty) = [1\ 1]\}) = P(\{TT\}) = \frac{1}{4}$$

The probability of losing one dollar on the second toss is

$$P(X_2 = -1) = P(\{\infty \in \Omega : X_2(\infty) = -1\}) = P(\{TH, HH\}) = P(\{TH\}) + P(\{HH\}) = \frac{1}{2}$$

Discrete Random Vectors

This topic and the next one deal with discrete and continuous vectors, two kinds of random vectors that have special properties and are often found in applications.

Discrete vectors are defined as follows.

A random vector X is discrete if and only if:

1. its support R_X is a countable set;
2. there is a function $P_X : \mathbb{R}^K \to [0,1]$, called the joint probability mass function (or joint pmf, or joint probability function) of X, such that, for a $x \in R^K$:

$$px^{(x)} = \begin{cases} p(X = x) & \text{if } x \in R_x \\ 0 & \text{if } x \in R_x \end{cases}$$

The following notations are used interchangeably to indicate the joint probability mass function:

$$px(x) = px(x_1,..., x_k) = px_{1,...,}x_k(x_1,...., x_k)$$

In the second and third notation the K components of X are explicitly indicated.

Example: Suppose is a 2-dimensional random vector whose components (X_1 and X_2) can take only two values: 1or 0. Furthermore, the four possible combinations of 0 and 1 are all equally likely. X is an example of a discrete vector. Its support is $R_x = \left\{ \begin{bmatrix} 1 \\ 1 \end{bmatrix}, \begin{bmatrix} 1 \\ 0 \end{bmatrix}, \begin{bmatrix} 0 \\ 1 \end{bmatrix}, \begin{bmatrix} 0 \\ 0 \end{bmatrix} \right\}$

Its probability mass function is

$$px(x) = \begin{cases} \frac{1}{4} & \text{if } x = [1\ 1]^T \\ \frac{1}{4} & \text{if } x = [1\ 0]^T \\ \frac{1}{4} & \text{if } x = [0\ 1]^T \\ \frac{1}{4} & \text{if } x = [0\ 0]^T \\ 0 & \text{otherwise} \end{cases}$$

Continuous Random Vectors

Continuous vectors are defined as follows.

A random vector X is continuous (or absolutely continuous) if and only if:

1. Its support R_x is not countable;
2. There is a function $f_x : \mathbb{R}^K \rightarrow [0,\infty)$, called the joint probability density function (or joint pdf or joint density function) of X, such that, for any set $A \subseteq \mathbb{R}^K$ where

   $A = [a_1, b_1]x...x[a_K, b_K]$

   the probability that X belongs to A can be calculated as follows:

   $P(X \in A) = \int_{a_1}^{b_1} ... \int_{a_k}^{b_k} f_x(x_1,...,x_k)dx_k...dx_1$

   provided the above multiple integral is well defined.

The following notations are used interchangeably to indicate the joint probability density function:

$$fx(x) = fx(x_1,...,x_k) = fx_1,...,x_k(x_1,...,x_k)$$

In the second and third notation the K components of the random vector X are explicitly indicated.

Example: Suppose X is a 2-dimensional random vector whose components (X_1 and X_2) are independent uniform random variables (on the interval $[0,1]$). Then, X is an example of a continuous vector. Its support is

$$R_x = [0,1]x[0,1]$$

Its joint probability density function is

$$f_x(x) = \begin{cases} 1 \text{ if } x \in [0,1]x[0,1] \\ 0 \text{ otherwise} \end{cases}$$

The probability that the realization of X falls in the rectangle $\left[0,\frac{1}{2}\right]x\left[0,\frac{1}{2}\right]$ is

$$P\left(X \in \left[0,\frac{1}{2}\right]x\left[0,\frac{1}{2}\right]\right)$$

$$= \int_0^{1/2}\int_0^{1/2} fx(x_1,x_2)dx_2\, dx_1$$

$$= \int_0^{1/2}\int_0^{1/2} dx_2 dx_1$$

$$= \int_0^{1/2} [x_2]_0^{1/2} dx_1$$

$$= \int_0^{1/2} \frac{1}{2} dx_1$$

$$= \frac{1}{2}\int_0^{1/2} dx_1$$

$$= \frac{1}{2}[x_1]_0^{1/2}$$

$$= \frac{1}{2} \bullet \frac{1}{2} = \frac{1}{4}$$

Random Vectors in General

Random vectors, also those that are neither discrete nor continuous, are often described using their joint distribution function.

Let X be a random vector. The joint distribution function (or joint df, or joint cumulative distribution function, or joint cdf) of X is a function $f_x : \mathbb{R}^K \to [0,1]$ such that:

$$F_x(x) = P(X_1 \leq x_1, \ldots X_K \leq x_K), \forall x \in \mathbb{R}^K.$$

where the components of X and x are denoted by X_K and x_K respectively, for $k = 1, \ldots, K$.

The following notations are used interchangeably to indicate the joint distribution function:

$$F_x(x) = F_x(x_1, \ldots x_K) = Fx_1, \ldots, x_K(x_{1,\ldots,} x_K)$$

In the second and third notation the K components of the random vector X are explicitly indicated.

Joint Distribution

Sometimes, we talk about the joint distribution of a random vector, without specifying whether we are referring to:

- The joint distribution function;
- The joint pmf (in the case of discrete random vectors);
- The joint pdf (in the case of continuous random vectors).

This ambiguity is legitimate, since:

1. The joint pmf completely determines (and is completely determined by) the joint distribution function of a discrete vector;
2. The joint pdf completely determines (and is completely determined by) the joint distribution function of a continuous vector.

We use the term joint distribution when we are making statements that apply both to the distribution function and to the probability mass (or density) function of a random vector.

Marginal Distributions

If X and Y are discrete random variables and f (x,y) is the value of their joint probability distribution at (x,y), the functions given by: $g(x) = \Sigma_y f(x,y)$ and $h(y) = \Sigma_x f(x,y)$ are the marginal distributions of X and Y, respectively.

A marginal distribution gets it's name because it appears in the *margins* of a probability distribution table.

i/j	1	2	3	4	5	6	px(i)
1	1/36	1/36	1/36	1/36	1/36	1/36	1/6
2	1/36	1/36	1/36	1/36	1/36	1/36	1/6
3	1/36	1/36	1/36	1/36	1/36	1/36	1/6
4	1/36	1/36	1/36	1/36	1/36	1/36	1/6
5	1/36	1/36	1/36	1/36	1/36	1/36	1/6
6	1/36	1/36	1/36	1/36	1/36	1/36	1/6
py(j)	1/6	1/6	1/6	1/6	1/6	1/6	

Of course, it's not *quite* as simple as that. You can't just look at any old frequency distribution table and say that the last column (or row) is a "marginal distribution." Marginal distributions follow a couple of rules:

- The distribution must be from bivariate data. Bivariate is just another way of saying "two variables," like X and Y. In the table above, the random variables i and j are coming from the roll of two dice.
- A marginal distribution is where you are only interested in *one* of the random variables . In other words, either X or Y. If you look at the probability table above, the sum probabilities of one variable are listed in the bottom row and the other sum probabilities are listed in the right column. So this table has *two* marginal distributions.

Probability Density Function

Probability density function (PDF) is a statistical expression that defines a probability distribution for a continuous random variable as opposed to a discrete random variable. When the PDF is graphically portrayed, the area under the curve will indicate the interval in which the variable will fall. The total area in this interval of the graph equals the probability of a continuous random variable occurring.

Probability density function (PDF) is not to be confused with probability mass function (PMF), which is applicable for discrete random variables. The easiest way to think about the difference between discrete vs. continuous variables is that discrete ones can be counted (i.e., the number is finite and typically takes the form of an integer) and continuous ones cannot (i.e., infinite values are possible).

Example of PDF vs. PMF

To illustrate, the probability that today's temperature will be 80 degrees - and 80 degrees exactly - is measured by PMF; the probability that the temperature will be between 80 and 85 degrees is measured by PDF. PDF calculates the probability of a range of outcomes. In the latter case, the temperature could be 80.01, 80.001, 80.0001 degrees and so on (and never reach exactly 80), or 84.99, 84.999, 84.9999, etc. (and never hit exactly 85). On a PDF graph, the probability of a single outcome is always zero. This is because a single outcome is represented by a line, which has no area under a curve. However, for continuous random variables such as the temperature range in the foregoing example, PDF can be used to calculate the probability that today's temperature will fall between 80 and 85 degrees.

PDF most commonly follows a normal distribution (Gaussian). "Black swan" or extreme outlier events are possible, but an investor who would like to estimate the probability that the S&P 500 Index will rise between 8% to 10% in 12 months, for example, can use PDF. An economist who is interested in the probability that gross domestic product (GDP) growth will land between 1% and 1.5% this quarter would also find PDF helpful.

Probability density function is defined by following formula:

$$P(a \le X \le b) = \int_a^b f(x)\,d_x$$

Where,

- $[a, b]$ = Interval in which x lies.
- $P(a \le X \le b)$ = probability that some value x lies within this interval.
- $d_x = b - a$

Example

Problem statement

During the day, a clock at random stops once at any time. If x be the time when it stops and the PDF for x is given by:

$$f(x) = \begin{cases} 1/24, & \text{for } 0 \le x \le 240 \\ 0, & \text{otherwise} \end{cases}$$

Calculate the probability that clock stops between 2 pm and 2:45 pm.

Solution

We have found the value of the following:

$$P(14 \le X \le 14.45) = \int_{14}^{14.45} f(x)d_x$$

$$= \frac{1}{24}(14.45 - 14)$$

$$= \frac{1}{24}(0.45)$$

$$= 0.01875$$

Unlike a probability, a probability density function can take on values greater than one; for example, the uniform distribution on the interval [0, ½] has probability density $f(x) = 2$ for $0 \le x \le ½$ and $f(x) = 0$ elsewhere.

The standard normal distribution has probability density

$$f(x) = \frac{1}{\sqrt{2\pi}} e^{-x^2/2}.$$

If a random variable *X* is given and its distribution admits a probability density function *f*, then the expected value of *X* (if the expected value exists) can be calculated as

$$E[X] = \int_{-\infty}^{\infty} x\, f(x) dx.$$

Not every probability distribution has a density function: the distributions of discrete random variables do not; nor does the Cantor distribution, even though it has no discrete component, i.e., does not assign positive probability to any individual point.

A distribution has a density function if and only if its cumulative distribution function *F*(*x*) is absolutely continuous. In this case: *F* is almost everywhere differentiable, and its derivative can be used as probability density:

$$\frac{d}{dx} F(x) = f(x).$$

If a probability distribution admits a density, then the probability of every one-point set {*a*} is zero; the same holds for finite and countable sets.

Two probability densities *f* and *g* represent the same probability distribution precisely if they differ only on a set of Lebesgue measure zero.

In the field of statistical physics, a non-formal reformulation of the relation above between the derivative of the cumulative distribution function and the probability density function is generally used as the definition of the probability density function. This alternate definition is the following:

If *dt* is an infinitely small number, the probability that *X* is included within the interval (*t*, *t* + *dt*) is equal to *f*(*t*) *dt*, or:

$$\Pr(t < X < t + dt) = f(t)dt.$$

Link between Discrete and Continuous Distributions

It is possible to represent certain discrete random variables as well as random variables involving both a continuous and a discrete part with a generalized probability density function, by using the Dirac delta function. For example, let us consider a binary discrete random variable having the Rademacher distribution—that is, taking −1 or 1 for values, with probability ½ each. The density of probability associated with this variable is:

$$f(t) = \frac{1}{2}(\delta(t+1) + \delta(t-1)).$$

More generally, if a discrete variable can take n different values among real numbers, then the associated probability density function is:

$$f(t) = \sum_{i=1}^{n} p_i \delta(t - x_i),$$

where $x_1, \ldots, x_n$ are the discrete values accessible to the variable and $p_1, \ldots, p_n$ are the probabilities associated with these values.

This substantially unifies the treatment of discrete and continuous probability distributions. For instance, the above expression allows for determining statistical characteristics of such a discrete variable (such as its mean, its variance and its kurtosis), starting from the formulas given for a continuous distribution of the probability.

Families of Densities

It is common for probability density functions (and probability mass functions) to be parametrized—that is, to be characterized by unspecified parameters. For example, the normal distribution is parametrized in terms of the mean and the variance, denoted by ì and σ^2 respectively, giving the family of densities

$$f(x;\mu,\sigma^2) = \frac{1}{\sigma\sqrt{2\pi}} e^{\frac{1}{2}\left(\frac{x-\mu}{\sigma}\right)^2}.$$

It is important to keep in mind the difference between the domain of a family of densities and the parameters of the family. Different values of the parameters describe different distributions of different random variables on the same sample space (the same set of all possible values of the variable); this sample space is the domain of the family of random variables that this family of distributions describes. A given set of parameters describes a single distribution within the family sharing the functional form of the density. From the perspective of a given distribution, the parameters are constants, and terms in a density function that contain only parameters, but not variables, are part of the normalization factor of a distribution (the multiplicative factor that ensures that the area under the density—the probability of *something* in the domain occurring— equals 1). This normalization factor is outside the kernel of the distribution.

Since the parameters are constants, reparametrizing a density in terms of different parameters, to give a characterization of a different random variable in the family, means simply substituting the new parameter values into the formula in place of the old ones. Changing the domain of a probability density, however, is trickier and requires more work.

Densities Associated with Multiple Variables

For continuous random variables $X_1, \ldots, X_n$, it is also possible to define a probability density function associated to the set as a whole, often called joint probability density function. This density function is defined as a function of the n variables, such that, for any domain D in the n-dimensional space of the values of the variables $X_1, \ldots, X_n$, the probability that a realisation of the set variables falls inside the domain D is

$$\Pr(X_1,\ldots,X_n \in D) = \int_D f_{X_1,\ldots,X_n}(x_1,\ldots,x_n)dx_1\cdots dx_n.$$

If $F(x_1, \ldots, x_n) = \Pr(X_1 \le x_1, \ldots, X_n \le x_n)$ is the cumulative distribution function of the vector $(X_1, \ldots, X_n)$, then the joint probability density function can be computed as a partial derivative

$$f(x) = \frac{\partial^n F}{\partial x_1 \ldots \partial x_n}\Big|_x$$

Marginal Densities

For $i=1, 2, \ldots, n$, let $f_{Xi}(x_i)$ be the probability density function associated with variable X_i alone. This is called the marginal density function, and can be deduced from the probability density associated with the random variables $X_1, \ldots, X_n$ by integrating over all values of the other $n - 1$ variables:

$$f_{X_i}(x_i) = \int f(x_1,\ldots,x_n)dx_1\ldots dx_{i-1}\,dx_{i+1}\ldots dx_n.$$

Independence

Continuous random variables $X_1, \ldots, X_n$ admitting a joint density are all independent from each other if and only if

$$f_{X_1,\ldots,X_n}(x_1,\ldots,x_n) = f_{X_1}(x_1)\ldots f_{X_n}(x_n).$$

Corollary

If the joint probability density function of a vector of n random variables can be factored into a product of n functions of one variable

$$f_{X_1,\ldots,X_n}(x_1,\ldots,x_n) = f_1(x_1)\ldots f_n(x_n),$$

(where each f_i is not necessarily a density) then the n variables in the set are all independent from each other, and the marginal probability density function of each of them is given by

$$f_{X_i}(x_i) = \frac{f_i(x_i)}{\int f_i(x)dx}.$$

Example

This elementary example illustrates the above definition of multidimensional probability density functions in the simple case of a function of a set of two variables. Let us call $\vec{R}$ a 2-dimensional random vector of coordinates (X, Y): the probability to obtain $\vec{R}$ in the quarter plane of positive x and y is

$$\Pr(X > 0, Y > 0) = \int_0^\infty \int_0^\infty f_{X,Y}(x,y)dx\,dy.$$

Dependent Variables and Change of Variables

If the probability density function of a random variable X is given as $f_X(x)$, it is possible to calculate the probability density function of some variable $Y = g(X)$. This is also called a "change of variable" and is in practice used to generate a random variable of arbitrary shape $f_{g(X)} = f_Y$ using a known (for instance, uniform) random number generator.

If the function g is monotonic, then the resulting density function is

$$f_Y(y) = \left|\frac{d}{dy}\left(g^{-1}(y)\right)\right| \cdot f_X\left(g^{-1}(y)\right).$$

Here g^{-1} denotes the inverse function.

This follows from the fact that the probability contained in a differential area must be invariant under change of variables. That is,

$$|f_Y(y)dy| = |f_X(x)dx|,$$

or

$$f_Y(y) = \left|\frac{dx}{dy}\right| f_X(x) = \left|\frac{d}{dy}(x)\right| f_X(x) = \left|\frac{d}{dy}\left(g^{-1}(y)\right)\right| f_X\left(g^{-1}(y)\right) = \frac{f_X\left(g^{-1}(y)\right)}{\left|g'\left(g^{-1}(y)\right)\right|}.$$

For functions that are not monotonic, the probability density function for y is

$$\sum_{k=1}^{n(y)} \left|\frac{d}{dy} g_k^{-1}(y)\right| \cdot f_X\left(g_k^{-1}(y)\right),$$

where $n(y)$ is the number of solutions in x for the equation $g(x) = y$, and $g_k^{-1}(y)$ are these solutions.

It is tempting to think that in order to find the expected value $E(g(X))$, one must first find the probability density $f_{g(X)}$ of the new random variable $Y = g(X)$. However, rather than computing

$$E\left(g(X)\right) = \int_{-\infty}^{\infty} y f_{g(X)}(y)dy$$

one may find instead

$$E\left(g(X)\right) = \int_{-\infty}^{\infty} g(x) f_X(x)dx.$$

The values of the two integrals are the same in all cases in which both X and $g(X)$ actually have probability density functions. It is not necessary that g be a one-to-one function. In some cases the latter integral is computed much more easily than the former.

Multiple Variables

The above formulas can be generalized to variables (which we will again call y) depending on more than one other variable. $f(x_1, ..., x_n)$ shall denote the probability density function of the variables that y depends on, and the dependence shall be $y = g(x_1, ..., x_n)$. Then, the resulting density function is

$$\int_{y=g(x_1,\ldots,x_n)} \frac{f(x_1,\ldots,x_n)}{\sqrt{\sum_{j=1}^{n} \frac{\partial g}{\partial x_j}(x_1,\ldots,x_n)^2}} dV,$$

where the integral is over the entire $(n - 1)$-dimensional solution of the subscripted equation and the symbolic dV must be replaced by a parametrization of this solution for a particular calculation; the variables $x_1, ..., x_n$ are then of course functions of this parametrization.

This derives from the following, perhaps more intuitive representation: Suppose x is an n-dimensional random variable with joint density f. If $y = H(x)$, where H is a bijective, differentiable function, then y has density g:

$$g(y) = f(x)\left|\det\left(\frac{dx}{dy}\right)\right|$$

with the differential regarded as the Jacobian of the inverse of H, evaluated at y.

For example, in the 2-dimensional case $x = (x_1, x_2)$, suppose the transform H is given as $y_1 = H_1(x_1, x_2)$, $y_2 = H_2(x_1, x_2)$ with inverses $x_1 = H_1^{-1}(y_1, y_2)$, $x_2 = H_2^{-1}(y_1, y_2)$. The joint distribution for $y = (y_1, y_2)$ has density

$$g(y_1, y_2) = f_{X_1,X_2}\left(H_1^{-1}(y_1, y_2), H_2^{-1}(y_1, y_2)\right)\left|\frac{\partial H_1^{-1}}{\partial y_1}\frac{\partial H_2^{-1}}{\partial y_2} - \frac{\partial H_1^{-1}}{\partial y_2}\frac{\partial H_2^{-1}}{\partial y_1}\right|.$$

Using the delta-function (and assuming independence), the same result is formulated as follows.

If the probability density function of independent random variables X_i, $i = 1, 2, ..., n$ are given as $f_{Xi}(x_i)$, it is possible to calculate the probability density function of some variable $Y = G(X_1, X_2, ... X_n)$. The following formula establishes a connection between the probability density function of Y denoted by $f_Y(y)$ and $f_{Xi}(x_i)$ using the Dirac delta function:

$$f_Y(y) = \int_{-\infty}^{\infty}\int_{-\infty}^{\infty}\cdots\int_{-\infty}^{\infty} f_{X_1}(x_1)f_{X_2}(x_2)\ldots f_{X_n}(x_n)\delta\left(y - G(x_1, x_2, \ldots, x_n)\right)dx_1\,dx_2\ldots dx_n$$

Sums of Independent Random Variables

The probability density function of the sum of two independent random variables U and V, each of which has a probability density function, is the convolution of their separate density functions:

$$f_{U+V}(x) = \int_{-\infty}^{\infty} f_U(y)f_V(x - y)dy = (f_U * f_V)(x)$$

It is possible to generalize the previous relation to a sum of N independent random variables, with densities $U_1, \ldots, U_N$:

$$f_{U_1+\cdots+U_N}(x) = \left(f_{U_1} * \cdots * f_{U_N}\right)(x)$$

This can be derived from a two-way change of variables involving $Y=U+V$ and $Z=V$, similarly to the example below for the quotient of independent random variables.

Products and Quotients of Independent Random Variables

Given two independent random variables U and V, each of which has a probability density function, the density of the product $Y = UV$ and quotient $Y=U/V$ can be computed by a change of variables.

Example: Quotient Distribution

To compute the quotient $Y = U/V$ of two independent random variables U and V, define the following transformation:

$$Y = U / V$$

$$Z = V$$

Then, the joint density $p(y,z)$ can be computed by a change of variables from U,V to Y,Z, and Y can be derived by marginalizing out Z from the joint density.

The inverse transformation is

$$U = YZ$$

$$V = Z$$

The Jacobian matrix $J(U,V \mid Y,Z)$ of this transformation is

$$\begin{vmatrix} \frac{\partial u}{\partial y} & \frac{\partial u}{\partial z} \\ \frac{\partial v}{\partial y} & \frac{\partial v}{\partial z} \end{vmatrix} = \begin{vmatrix} z & y \\ 0 & 1 \end{vmatrix} = |z|.$$

Thus:

$$p(y,z) = p(u,v)J(u,v \mid y,z) = p(u)p(v)J(u,v \mid y,z) = p_U(yz)p_V(z)|z|.$$

And the distribution of Y can be computed by marginalizing out Z:

$$p(y) = \int_{-\infty}^{\infty} p_U(yz)p_V(z)|z|dz$$

Note that this method crucially requires that the transformation from U,V to Y,Z be bijective. The above transformation meets this because Z can be mapped directly back to V, and for a given V the quotient U/V is monotonic. This is similarly the case for the sum $U + V$, difference $U - V$ and product UV.

Exactly the same method can be used to compute the distribution of other functions of multiple independent random variables.

Example: Quotient of two standard normals

Given two standard normal variables U and V, the quotient can be computed as follows. First, the variables have the following density functions:

$$p(u) = \frac{1}{\sqrt{2\pi}} e^{-\frac{u^2}{2}}$$

$$p(v) = \frac{1}{\sqrt{2\pi}} e^{-\frac{v^2}{2}}$$

We transform as described above:

$$Y = U / V$$

$$Z \quad V$$

This leads to:

$$\begin{aligned}
p(y) &= \int_{-\infty}^{\infty} p_U(yz) p_V(z) |z| dz \\
&= \int_{-\infty}^{\infty} \frac{1}{\sqrt{2\pi}} e^{-\frac{1}{2}y^2z^2} \frac{1}{\sqrt{2\pi}} e^{-\frac{1}{2}z^2} |z| dz \\
&= \int_{-\infty}^{\infty} \frac{1}{\sqrt{2\pi}} e^{-\frac{1}{2}(y^2+1)z^2} |z| dz \\
&= 2\int_{-\infty}^{\infty} \frac{1}{2\pi} e^{-\frac{1}{2}(y^2+1)z^2} z dz \\
&= \int_{-\infty}^{\infty} \frac{1}{\pi} e^{-(y^2+1)u} du \qquad u = \tfrac{1}{2}z^2 \\
&= -\left. \frac{1}{\pi(y^2+1)} e^{-(y^2+1)u} \right]_{u=0}^{\infty} \\
&= \frac{1}{\pi(y^2+1)}
\end{aligned}$$

This is the density of a standard Cauchy distribution.

Inference

Inferential statistics use a random sample of data taken from a population to describe and make inferences about the population. Inferential statistics are valuable when examination of each member of an entire population is not convenient or possible. For example, to measure the diameter of each nail that is manufactured in a mill is impractical. You can measure the diameters of a representative random sample of nails. You can use the information from the sample to make generalizations about the diameters of all of the nails.

Inferential statistics relies upon gathering data on a sample of individuals within a much larger, often *impossible-to-measure* population.

In our example of estimating the mean adult weight of everyone in a country, an experimenter might select a random sample of adults from the population of interest, and then weigh everyone in that sample. The experimenter could then calculate the mean weight of his sample, and from that, draw an inference that the true mean weight of the entire population falls within a specified interval of values.

The reason the experimenter must use an interval of values—and not specify an exact value for the mean weight of the population—is because no sample is a perfect representation of the entire population, and thus every experiment will involve some sampling error. Thus, the results gained through inferential statistics will always contain some uncertainty.

In general, the larger your sample size, the more an experimenter can reduce the uncertainty in his results. As the sample size gets larger and approaches the size of the entire population, that uncertainty will approach zero—and inferential statistics will give way to descriptive statistics.

Suppose we want to estimate the characteristics of a population such as the average weight of all 30 year old women in Australia, or the percentage of voters in N.S.W. who think the Government is doing a good job to control inflation.

In practice we cannot obtain data from every member of the population. Instead, we obtain data from a sample and use the results to make inferences about the population.

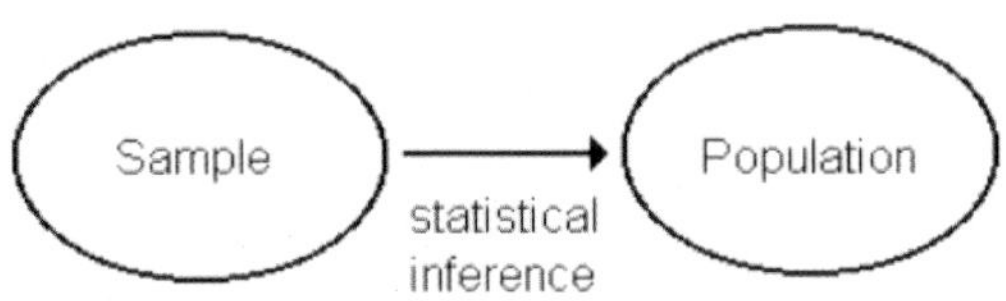

- Population - collection of all subjects or objects of interest (not necessarily people).
- Sample - subset of the population used to make inferences about the characteristics of the population.
- Population parameter - numerical characteristic of a population, a fixed and usually unknown quantity.

  e.g. average weight, μ, of all 30 year old women in Australia, e.g. % of voters, p, in N.S.W who think the Government is doing a good job to control inflation.

- Data - values measured or recorded on the sample.
- Sample statistic - numerical characteristic of the sample data such as the mean, proportion or variance. It can be used to provide estimates of the corresponding population parameters.

e.g. % of voters in an opinion poll in Sydney who think the Government is doing a good job to control inflation.

Different samples give different values for sample statistics. By taking many different samples and calculating a sample statistic for each sample (e.g. the sample mean), you could then draw a histogram of all the sample means. A statistic from a sample or randomised experiment can be regarded as a random variable and the histogram is an approximation to its probability distribution. The term sampling distribution is used to describe this distribution, i.e. how the statistic (regarded as a random variable) varies if random samples are repeatedly taken from the population.

Bias

If the sampling distribution is known then the ability of the sample statistic to estimate the corresponding population parameter can be determined.

In particular, the sampling distribution determines the expected value and variance of the sampling statistic. If the expected value of the statistic is equal to the population parameter, the estimator is unbiased. If the variance of the statistic is 'small' and it is also unbiased then an observed statistic is likely to be close to the population parameter.

Bias = distance between parameter and expected value of sample statistics

Subsequently, sample statistics can be classified as shown in the following diagrams.

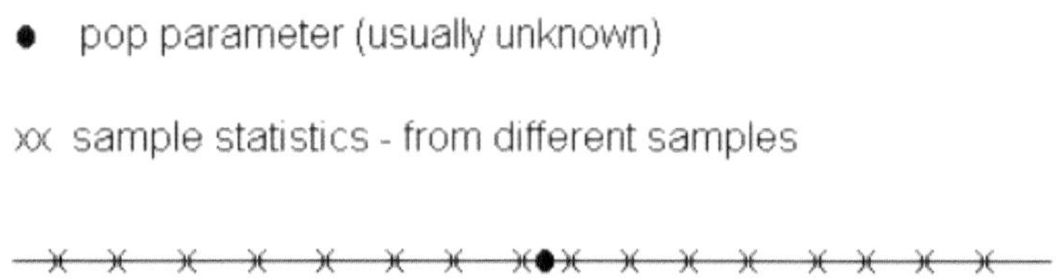

1.

Estimates have low bias because their average is near the population parameter, but have high variability because they are widely spread and a single sample value could be far from the parameter.

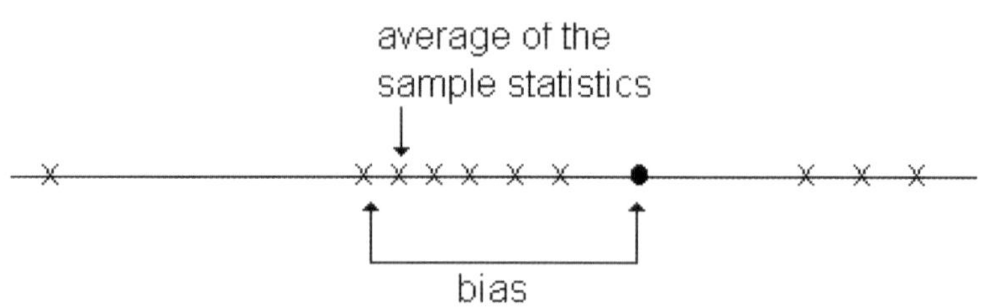

2.

Estimates have bias because the expected value is not equal to the parameter.

They also have high variability because they are widely spread out.

3.

In this case the estimates are biased because all of them are systematically higher than the population parameter

The sample statistics have, however, low variability because they are all close together.

4.

In this case the estimates have both low bias and low variability. Experimental design aims to simultaneously reduce bias and variability by producing a sampling distribution as shown in 4.

In general

Sample statistic = population parameter + bias + chance variation

Inferences about the characteristics of a population are based on data from a sample.

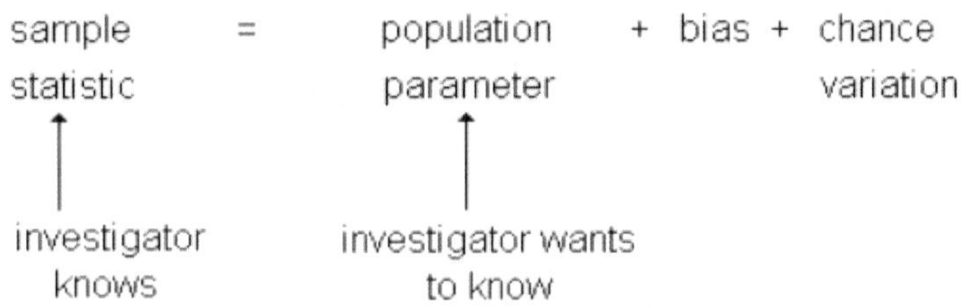

- If the sample is not representative of the population being studied, the sample statistic may be biased so you cannot use it to make valid inferences about the population parameter.
- To minimise bias the sample should be chosen by random sampling from a list of all individuals in the relevant population. This list is called the sampling frame. It is essential.
- For a simple random sample the individuals are chosen in such a way that each individual in the sampling frame has an equal chance of being selected. This may involve using computer generated random numbers to select the sample.

Models and Assumptions

Any statistical inference requires some assumptions. A statistical model is a set of assumptions concerning the generation of the observed data and similar data. Descriptions of statistical models usually emphasize the role of population quantities of interest, about which we wish to draw inference. Descriptive statistics are typically used as a preliminary step before more formal inferences are drawn.

Degree of Models/Assumptions

Statisticians distinguish between three levels of modeling assumptions:

- Fully parametric: The probability distributions describing the data-generation process are assumed to be fully described by a family of probability distributions involving only a finite number of unknown parameters. For example, one may assume that the distribution of population values is truly Normal, with unknown mean and variance, and that datasets are generated by 'simple' random sampling. The family of generalized linear models is a widely used and flexible class of parametric models.

- Non-parametric: The assumptions made about the process generating the data are much less than in parametric statistics and may be minimal. For example, every continuous probability distribution has a median, which may be estimated using the sample median or the Hodges–Lehmann–Sen estimator, which has good properties when the data arise from simple random sampling.

- Semi-parametric: This term typically implies assumptions 'in between' fully and non-parametric approaches. For example, one may assume that a population distribution has a finite mean. Furthermore, one may assume that the mean response level in the population depends in a truly linear manner on some covariate (a parametric assumption) but not make any parametric assumption describing the variance around that mean (i.e. about the presence or possible form of any heteroscedasticity). More generally, semi-parametric models can often be separated into 'structural' and 'random variation' components. One component is treated parametrically and the other non-parametrically. The well-known Cox model is a set of semi-parametric assumptions.

Importance of Valid Models/Assumptions

Whatever level of assumption is made, correctly calibrated inference in general requires these assumptions to be correct; i.e. that the data-generating mechanisms really have been correctly specified.

Incorrect assumptions of 'simple' random sampling can invalidate statistical inference. More complex semi- and fully parametric assumptions are also cause for concern. For example, incorrectly assuming the Cox model can in some cases lead to faulty conclusions. Incorrect assumptions of Normality in the population also invalidates some forms of regression-based inference. The use of any parametric model is viewed skeptically by most experts in sampling human populations: "most sampling statisticians, when they deal with confidence intervals at all, limit themselves to statements about [estimators] based on very large samples, where the central limit theorem ensures that these [estimators] will have distributions that are nearly normal." In particular, a normal distribution "would be a totally unrealistic and catastrophically unwise assumption to make if we were dealing with any kind of economic population." Here, the central limit theorem states that the distribution of the sample mean "for very large samples" is approximately normally distributed, if the distribution is not heavy tailed.

Approximate Distributions

Given the difficulty in specifying exact distributions of sample statistics, many methods have been developed for approximating these.

With finite samples, approximation results measure how close a limiting distribution approaches the statistic's sample distribution: For example, with 10,000 independent samples the normal distribution approximates (to two digits of accuracy) the distribution of the sample mean for many population distributions, by the Berry–Esseen theorem. Yet for many practical purposes, the normal approximation provides a good approximation to the sample-mean's distribution when there are 10 (or more) independent samples, according to simulation studies and statisticians' experience. Following Kolmogorov's work in the 1950s, advanced statistics uses approximation theory and functional analysis to quantify the error of approximation. In this approach, the metric geometry of probability distributions is studied; this approach quantifies approximation error with, for example, the Kullback–Leibler divergence, Bregman divergence, and the Hellinger distance.

With indefinitely large samples, limiting results like the central limit theorem describe the sample statistic's limiting distribution, if one exists. Limiting results are not statements about finite samples, and indeed are irrelevant to finite samples. However, the asymptotic theory of limiting distributions is often invoked for work with finite samples. For example, limiting results are often invoked to justify the generalized method of moments and the use of generalized estimating equations, which are popular in econometrics and biostatistics. The magnitude of the difference between the limiting distribution and the true distribution (formally, the 'error' of the approximation) can be assessed using simulation. The heuristic application of limiting results to finite samples is common practice in many applications, especially with low-dimensional models with log-concave likelihoods (such as with one-parameter exponential families).

Randomization-based Models

For a given dataset that was produced by a randomization design, the randomization distribution of a statistic (under the null-hypothesis) is defined by evaluating the test statistic for all of the plans that could have been generated by the randomization design. In frequentist inference, randomization allows inferences to be based on the randomization distribution rather than a subjective model, and this is important especially in survey sampling and design of experiments. Statistical inference from randomized studies is also more straightforward than many other situations. In Bayesian inference, randomization is also of importance: in survey sampling, use of sampling without replacement ensures the exchangeability of the sample with the population; in randomized experiments, randomization warrants a missing at random assumption for covariate information.

Objective randomization allows properly inductive procedures. Many statisticians prefer randomization-based analysis of data that was generated by well-defined randomization procedures. (However, it is true that in fields of science with developed theoretical knowledge and experimental control, randomized experiments may increase the costs of experimentation without improving the quality of inferences.) Similarly, results from randomized experiments are recommended by leading statistical authorities as allowing inferences with greater reliability than do observational studies of the same phenomena. However, a good observational study may be better than a bad randomized experiment.

The statistical analysis of a randomized experiment may be based on the randomization scheme stated in the experimental protocol and does not need a subjective model.

However, at any time, some hypotheses cannot be tested using objective statistical models, which accurately describe randomized experiments or random samples. In some cases, such randomized studies are uneconomical or unethical.

Model-based Analysis of Randomized Experiments

It is standard practice to refer to a statistical model, often a linear model, when analyzing data from randomized experiments. However, the randomization scheme guides the choice of a statistical model. It is not possible to choose an appropriate model without knowing the randomization scheme. Seriously misleading results can be obtained analyzing data from randomized experiments while ignoring the experimental protocol; common mistakes include forgetting the blocking used in an experiment and confusing repeated measurements on the same experimental unit with independent replicates of the treatment applied to different experimental units.

Paradigms for Inference

Different schools of statistical inference have become established. These schools—or "paradigms"—are not mutually exclusive, and methods that work well under one paradigm often have attractive interpretations under other paradigms.

Bandyopadhyay & Forster describe four paradigms: "(i) classical statistics or error statistics, (ii) Bayesian statistics, (iii) likelihood-based statistics, and (iv) the Akaikean-Information Criterion-based statistics". The classical (or frequentist) paradigm, the Bayesian paradigm, and the AIC-based paradigm are summarized below. The likelihood-based paradigm is essentially a sub-paradigm of the AIC-based paradigm.

Frequentist Inference

This paradigm calibrates the plausibility of propositions by considering (notional) repeated sampling of a population distribution to produce datasets similar to the one at hand. By considering the dataset's characteristics under repeated sampling, the frequentist properties of a statistical proposition can be quantified—although in practice this quantification may be challenging.

Examples of Frequentist Inference

- p-value
- Confidence interval

Frequentist Inference, Objectivity and Decision Theory

One interpretation of frequentist inference (or classical inference) is that it is applicable only in terms of frequency probability; that is, in terms of repeated sampling from a population. However, the approach of Neyman develops these procedures in terms of pre-experiment probabilities. That is, before undertaking an experiment, one decides on a rule for coming to a conclusion such that the probability of being correct is controlled in a suitable way: such a probability need not have a frequentist or repeated sampling interpretation. In contrast, Bayesian inference works in terms of conditional probabilities (i.e. probabilities conditional on the observed data), compared to the marginal (but conditioned on unknown parameters) probabilities used in the frequentist approach.

The frequentist procedures of significance testing and confidence intervals can be constructed without regard to utility functions. However, some elements of frequentist statistics, such as statistical decision theory, do incorporate utility functions. In particular, frequentist developments of optimal inference (such as minimum-variance unbiased estimators, or uniformly most powerful testing) make use of loss functions, which play the role of (negative) utility functions. Loss functions need not be explicitly stated for statistical theorists to prove that a statistical procedure has an optimality property. However, loss-functions are often useful for stating optimality properties: for example, median-unbiased estimators are optimal under absolute value loss functions, in that they minimize expected loss, and least squares estimators are optimal under squared error loss functions, in that they minimize expected loss.

While statisticians using frequentist inference must choose for themselves the parameters of interest, and the estimators/test statistic to be used, the absence of obviously explicit utilities and prior distributions has helped frequentist procedures to become widely viewed as 'objective'.

Bayesian Inference

The Bayesian calculus describes degrees of belief using the 'language' of probability; beliefs are positive, integrate to one, and obey probability axioms. Bayesian inference uses the available posterior beliefs as the basis for making statistical propositions. There are several different justifications for using the Bayesian approach.

Examples of Bayesian Inference

- Credible interval for interval estimation
- Bayes factors for model comparison

Bayesian Inference, Subjectivity and Decision Theory

Many informal Bayesian inferences are based on "intuitively reasonable" summaries of the posterior. For example, the posterior mean, median and mode, highest posterior density intervals, and Bayes Factors can all be motivated in this way. While a user's utility function need not be stated for this sort of inference, these summaries do all depend (to some extent) on stated prior beliefs, and are generally viewed as subjective conclusions. (Methods of prior construction which do not require external input have been proposed but not yet fully developed.)

Formally, Bayesian inference is calibrated with reference to an explicitly stated utility, or loss function; the 'Bayes rule' is the one which maximizes expected utility, averaged over the posterior uncertainty. Formal Bayesian inference therefore automatically provides optimal decisions in a decision theoretic sense. Given assumptions, data and utility, Bayesian inference can be made for essentially any problem, although not every statistical inference need have a Bayesian interpretation. Analyses which are not formally Bayesian can be (logically) incoherent; a feature of Bayesian procedures which use proper priors (i.e. those integrable to one) is that they are guaranteed to be coherent. Some advocates of Bayesian inference assert that inference *must* take place in this decision-theoretic framework, and that Bayesian inference should not conclude with the evaluation and summarization of posterior beliefs.

AIC-based Inference

The *Akaike information criterion* (AIC) is an estimator of the relative quality of statistical models for a given set of data. Given a collection of models for the data, AIC estimates the quality of each model, relative to each of the other models. Thus, AIC provides a means for model selection.

AIC is founded on information theory: it offers an estimate of the relative information lost when a given model is used to represent the process that generated the data. (In doing so, it deals with the trade-off between the goodness of fit of the model and the simplicity of the model.)

Minimum Description Length

The minimum description length (MDL) principle has been developed from ideas in information theory and the theory of Kolmogorov complexity. The (MDL) principle selects statistical models that maximally compress the data; inference proceeds without assuming counterfactual or non-falsifiable "data-generating mechanisms" or probability models for the data, as might be done in frequentist or Bayesian approaches.

However, if a "data generating mechanism" does exist in reality, then according to Shannon's source coding theorem it provides the MDL description of the data, on average and asymptotically. In minimizing description length (or descriptive complexity), MDL estimation is similar to maximum likelihood estimation and maximum a posteriori estimation (using maximum-entropy Bayesian priors). However, MDL avoids assuming that the underlying probability model is known; the MDL principle can also be applied without assumptions that e.g. the data arose from independent sampling.

The MDL principle has been applied in communication-coding theory in information theory, in linear regression, and in data mining.

The evaluation of MDL-based inferential procedures often uses techniques or criteria from computational complexity theory.

Fiducial Inference

Fiducial inference was an approach to statistical inference based on fiducial probability, also known as a "fiducial distribution". In subsequent work, this approach has been called ill-defined, extremely limited in applicability, and even fallacious. However this argument is the same as that which shows that a so-called confidence distribution is not a valid probability distribution and, since this has not invalidated the application of confidence intervals, it does not necessarily invalidate conclusions drawn from fiducial arguments. An attempt was made to reinterpret the early work of Fisher's fiducial argument as a special case of an inference theory using Upper and lower probabilities.

Structural Inference

Developing ideas of Fisher and of Pitman from 1938 to 1939, George A. Barnard developed "structural inference" or "pivotal inference", an approach using invariant probabilities on group families. Barnard reformulated the arguments behind fiducial inference on a restricted class of models on which "fiducial" procedures would be well-defined and useful.

Sampling

Sampling is a statistical methodology that uses a portion of a total population to represent the full population. As a subject, sampling considers the different methodologies one could use to survey a portion of the population and seeks to find a sample that is most indicative of the overall population. A sample's "representativeness" is also known as "generalizability," how a specific set of a population's members can be generalized to the whole population. To achieve a highly generalizable result, sampling can weigh certain factors or certain respondents differently to try and better represent the overall population. For instance, a highly generalized sample of an elementary school would not just include responses from students in the first grade, but from students in all grades, and from the appropriate proportion of the overall school. If there are 100 students in an elementary school, and are in first grade, then the sample should include no more 15% than responses from first graders.

A population to be sampled could be any number of things. It could be a literal population of people sampled for political opinion; a sample could be taken of a plant species to determine the prevalence of a pest; a population could be the entire clothing production of a factory to be checked for quality; or it could be checking the outputs of a given computer simulation to determine if the simulation is a fair approximation of reality. Studies that include the entire population are referred to as census studies, not samples. Such comprehensive studies are rarely carried out, as the cost (in time or money) might be too high, or the feasibility might be too low. For instance, collecting data on the detailed religious views of every citizen in the United States would be very expensive and maybe unfeasible, or determining the average age of bears in Siberia might be impossible to handle (as it would require determining where every bear is in a vast geography).

Sampling is a key tool in the scientific method, allowing researchers to provide evidence that generalizable theories are true simply from a sample of specific facts. Sampling also allows mathematicians to resolve complex paradoxes, for instance, the St. Petersburg paradox, and is used commonly in political polling to understand current social, philosophical, and moral trends.

Probability versus Non-probability Sampling

Sampling methods are either categorized as a probability or a non-probability sample. In probability samples, every member of a population has a known non-zero chance of being included in the sample. This allows researchers to calculate and report the sampling error, or the degree to which the sample might stray from the overall population. Whereas in non-probability samples, some members have a zero percent chance or an unknown percentage of being included.

Example

Imagine a polltaker visits a supermarket at 7 pm every Thursday to conduct a survey of the careers that the shoppers hold. By its very nature, this poll will exclude, at some unknown probability, those people who are working at that time. This could be bartenders, night time TV news anchors, nurses with evening shifts, etc. Or it might exclude people of a certain ethnic group who prefer to shop at their ethnic grocer. If the goal was to represent the population of people who buy groceries from that type of store at that time, it could have a low sample bias. But if its purpose was to represent the entire population in that geographic region, it would be a non-probability sample with an unknown (possibly high) sample bias.

Part of the reason for choosing one type of sampling methodology over another is cost. As a general rule, the larger the population to be sampled from, the larger the sample population must be (to ensure that it is representative) and the harder it can be to eliminate bias. If a researcher is trying to select people randomly from a classroom of people, there are many easy ways to do this that will ensure the sample is random and representative. If that same researcher is trying to select from a population of million, they're unlikely to select of the population, and any size sample would be considerably more expensive in time and money.

One thing that is rarely spoken to is that samples are usually not randomly accounting for time. That is, the sample is taken at whatever time the researchers gathered the data. Ten years earlier or ten years later, that population could change.

Probability Sampling

Random sampling is the most basic type of sampling, taking a truly $x\%$ random of the population a researcher wishes to study. The challenge is that true randomness is difficult to implement: to ensure that it's actually random, that is, every single member of the population has an equal probability of being selected. In theory, a random sample would look something like every member of the population is given a single raffle ticket, and then the sample is picked from the available raffle tickets. However, the larger the population gets, the harder it is to ensure that each member of the population is given the same chance of being selected as any other. That is, it can be hard to assign each member one raffle ticket and pick from all raffle tickets with equal probability.

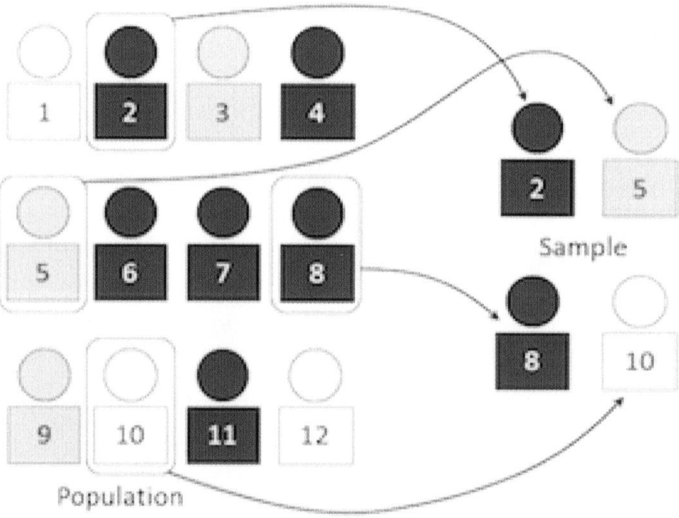

Random Sampling

It can be relatively easy to check if a sample is truly random by comparing the sample to known data about the tested population (provided such data is available). For example, a sample of the population of Australia should 50% be male and female 50% as the entire population is 50-50.

Systematic sampling is a method for implementing random sampling, essentially as a means to select every n^{th} member of the sample, where is some integer or some random integer, or some randomly generated number. For instance, a bakery could choose to select every 99th cake for testing and quality control, or it could pick every n^{th} cake where n is a randomly generated number between 50 and 200. Note: this only works if the population is itself in a random order, or where the count begins randomly at some number between 1 and n . If the population is somehow ordered, then selecting every 99th one will not be random.

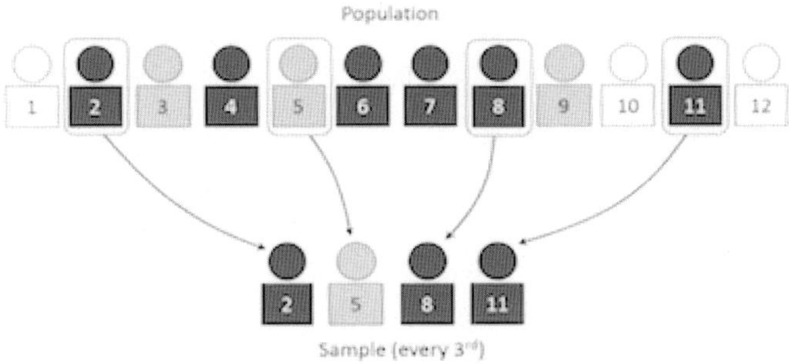

Systematic Sampling

Stratified sampling is a method to help ensure randomness in larger populations. The entire population is divided into strata, or different groups, based on some particular criteria. For instance, if a surveyor wanted to sample an entire city population, he might divide the city into geographic strata, or occupational ones, educational, wealth, etc. The number of members of the sample selected from the strata is proportional to the entire population. For instance, if District A represents 10% of the city's population, and a researcher wants a total sample of 1000 , then they will select 100 people from District A. Within the strata, sample members are selected randomly. For instance, it might be possible to randomly select a house and randomly select one member from the household to sample.

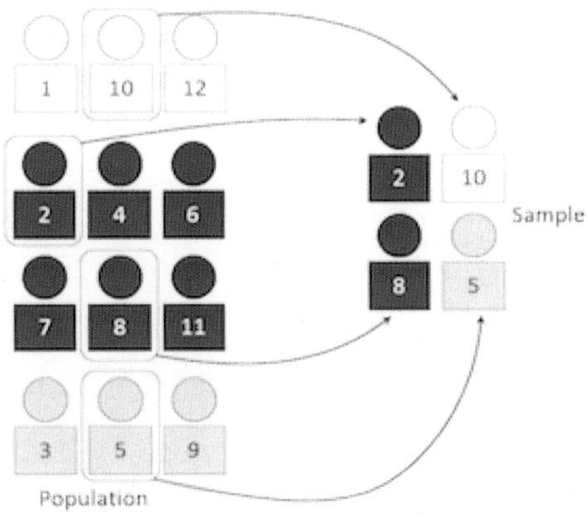

Stratified Sampling

Cluster sampling is a method whereby researchers pick random *clusters* for ease of sampling. For instance, a study of students in a school district might study every student in each of 20 schools. This is as opposed to random sampling which would likely end up with a few students from every school. Researchers may choose to study clusters for the ease of implementation (for instance it might be easier to get 20 principals of schools to agree to some minor school-day disruption than to get every principal to agree).

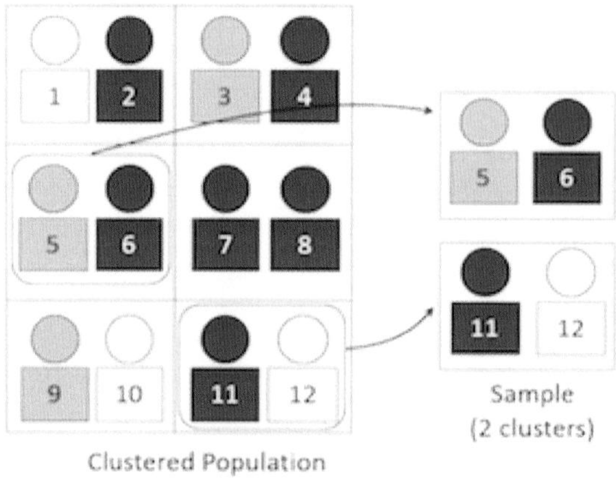

Cluster Sampling

Multistage sampling is a form of other sampling techniques whereby the researchers winnow down the final sample from larger and larger samples. For instance, in the above example of studying students in a school district, researchers used cluster sampling to select 20 schools. They could then conduct a second stage and use cluster sampling again to select 15 classrooms in each school, followed by a third stage where they use random sampling to choose 10 students in each class. Again, this helps to decrease costs but introduces opportunities at each stage for the researchers to deviate from a truly random or representative sample of the total population. For instance, if they were studying student performance and they happened to choose the two best performing or two worst performing schools in the population, then of 10% their sample are the biggest outliers in the total population.

Non-probability Sampling

Convenience sampling, also known as opportunity sampling, refers to a method where a researcher uses a non-random sample to approximate the truth. This is often used at the beginning of a study, or as a means of testing if a study is worthwhile, as a *convenient* sample; for instance, the first five people a researcher finds walking down the street may be much cheaper than conducting a truly random sample.

Judgement sampling is a form of convenience sampling where the researcher applies some judgment in selecting a convenient sample. For instance, a researcher studying coffee shop patrons could justifiably conclude that the population of people in their nearest coffee shop is representative of all the populations in all the coffee shops in the area they're studying, because that coffee shop is located in a centrally located, high-traffic commuter area, with wide swaths of education level, gender, occupation, wealth, ethnicity, and sexual orientation represented in this one coffee shop.

Snowball sampling is a type of non-probability sampling that occurs when members of the desired population are hard to find, such as patients with a rare disease, holders of an opinion that few like to publicly profess, or rare species. Researchers might ask members of the sample to recommend others to be surveyed or follow a rare species to find other kin. This methodology potentially introduces bias, as the sample may not represent a truly random section of the overall population, but it does so at the benefit of reducing costs significantly.

Sampling Errors

Errors in sampling usually manifest themselves as selection bias or random sampling bias. Such errors can occur

- when the researchers conducting the sampling have accidentally or deliberately constructed the study to be misrepresentative of the total population, or
- because the researchers used a truly random methodology and that random sample happened to not be representative of the overall population.

The key here is that there is an error because the sample does not represent the population.

Other sorts of errors are a product not of design, but of execution. These include things like non-responses by surveyed members of the population, data entry and processing errors, and measurement errors occurring when questions posed to respondents are misunderstood or tests conducted on sample members do not measure what they intended to measure. For instance, a question of "How much do you like this product?" seems like a good question, but may not actually collect the data the surveyor wanted. It may indicate how unwilling the respondent is to say anything negative or might inflate small issues they have with the product. A better question would be, "How likely are you to recommend this product to a friend or family member?" which is a commonly used question in surveying, known as the Net Promoter Score. The key with these errors is that even though the sample is random, the data processed may not accurately reflect the sample or the population.

In both cases, it can be difficult to determine if the sample is statistically valid. One solution is to reverse-engineer the results to see if they match the intended methodology (not necessarily if they match any particular result). For instance, one could see a sample with 75% women and think this is an error (that it should be closer to 50%). They could then test what the probability is that their sampling methodology produces that result.

Calculating Sampling Error

Sampling error can also refer to a calculation of error in a sample, also known as the margin of error. For instance, most published scientific studies that do experimentation include margin of error. They might say that with a 95% confidence interval the margin of error is 5%, meaning that they can say 95% with certainty that their results are $\pm 5\%$ accurate.

The basic formula for sample error is

$$z\sqrt{\frac{p(1-p)}{n}},$$

where is the z-score for the study's confidence interval, sometimes expressed as z^*, or the critical value. P is the portion of the sample who has the factor you're testing for, and n is the total sample population. Sometimes this formula is expressed $1.96\sqrt{\frac{p(1-p)}{n}}$ as which assumes a confidence interval of 95%.

Example

Suppose you are a researcher who has conducted a survey in a sample of 1,000 respondents. You're evaluating them to determine whether they are pro-their congressman or not. You have a confidence interval of 95%, and 700 respondents say they do not approve of their congressman. What is your margin of error?

We have

$$z\sqrt{\frac{p(1-p)}{n}} = 1.96\sqrt{\frac{(0.700)(0.300)}{1000}} = 2.84\%$$

which means that you can say, with 95% confidence, that 700 out of 1,000 Americans do not approve of their congressman, plus or minus 2.84%.

A -score table for other confidence intervals is below:

Confidence Interval	z -score
80%	1.28
90%	1.645
95%	2.33
99%	2.58
99.9%	3.29

The margin of error increases significantly as you decrease the sample size and attempt to increase the confidence interval.

Market Research

Expanding the customer base may mean finding new market niches. A market niche is a group of individuals that have similar demographics such as age, gender, income, geographic location, marital status and education levels. Sampling the population of that niche lets the business know whether this is a lucrative prospect and should be pursued or is lukewarm at best and can be put on the back burner.

New Product Development

One product development philosophy is to invent a new product and then find a market for it. The other philosophy is to listen to the market and develop a product that solves its problems or fills its needs. Both philosophies benefit from sampling the market -- the potential customers. For example, if you manufacture fruit drinks, you may find out that most of the market doesn't care one way or the other about using high-fructose corn syrup as an ingredient, but a smaller market segment does. That smaller segment is where to market your sugar-sweetened fruit drink.

Customer Satisfaction

A very small business most likely could ask all its customers about their level of satisfaction. However, that's not possible with a business that has several hundred customers a day, such as a retail website or restaurant. In that case, sampling the customers is the way to go. Sample at several different times and days to get the entire picture. Service businesses can use customer sampling as well. It may make sense to hire an outside firm to conduct the sampling and administer the survey, so the customers feel comfortable telling how they really feel, not what they think you want to hear.

Challenges of Sampling

Sampling has challenges. The population of the sample has to reflect the makeup of the general population it's being pulled from, otherwise the results aren't meaningful. The survey -- if one is being used -- shouldn't lead the participants to the answers the small-business person expects. The sampling should be completed within a short window, not over a long period of time, since the sample might change or an event may occur that changes their answers.

Sampling Frame

A sampling frame is a list of all the items in your population. It's a complete list of everyone or everything you want to study. The difference between a population and a sampling frame is that the population is general and the frame is specific. For example, the population could be "People who live in Jacksonville, Florida." The frame would name ALL of those people, from Adrian Abba to Felicity Zappa. A couple more examples:

Population: People in STAT101.

Sampling Frame: Adrian, Anna, Bob, Billy, Howie, Jess, Jin, Kate, Kaley, Lin, Manuel, Norah, Paul, Roger, Stu, Tim, Vanessa, Yasmin.

Population: Birds that are pink.

Sampling Frame:

- Brown-capped Rosy-Finch.
- White-winged Crossbill.
- American Flamingo.
- Roseate Spoonbill.
- Black Rosy-Finch.
- Cassin's Finch.

When you draw a sample in statistics, you need a list of items to draw the sample from. Take a very simple population: bingo balls numbered 1 to 99. You frame would be a list of all those balls: 1 , 2, 3...99. Once you have your list, you can go ahead and draw your sample.

Qualities of a Good Sampling Frame

You can't just use any list you come across. Care must be taken to make sure your sampling frame is adequate for your needs. For example, according to Alaska University, a good sample frame for a project on living conditions would:

1. Include all individuals in the target population.
2. Exclude all individuals not in the target population.
3. Includes accurate information that can be used to contact selected individuals.

Other general factors that you would want to make sure you have:

- An unique identifier for each member. This could be a simple numerical identifier (i.e. from 1 to 1000). Check to make sure there are no duplicates in the frame.
- A logical organization to the list. For example, put them in alphabetical order.
- Up to date information. This may need to be periodically checked (i.e. for address changes).

In some cases, it might be impossible, or very difficult, to get a sampling frame. For example, getting a list of prostitutes in your city isn't likely (mostly because of the fact that most prostitutes won't want to be found). Sometimes, techniques like snowball sampling must be used to make up for the lack of sampling frame. Snowball sampling is where you find one person (or a few people) for your survey or experiment. You then ask them to find someone else who would be willing to participate. Then that person finds someone else, and so on, until you have enough people for your needs.

Large Sample Theory

Large Sample Theory is a name given to the search for approximations to the behaviour of statistical procedures which are derived by computing limits as the sample size, n, tends to infinity. Suppose we have a data set with a fairly large sample size, say n = 100. We imagine our data set is one in a sequence of possible data sets - one for each possible value of n. If we have a sequence of statistics which converges to something as n tends to in nity we approximate the value of a probability, for instance, when n = 100 by the corresponding value when $n = \infty$.

Most large sample theory uses three main technical tools: the Law of Large Numbers (LLN), the Central Limit Theorem (CLT) and Taylor ex-pansion.

Theorem 1 (LLN) If $Y_1, Y_2, \ldots$ are *ii* d with mean μ then

$$\frac{\sum Y_i}{n} \to \mu$$

This is called the law of large numbers but it comes in two forms: Strong and Weak.

Theorem 2 (SLLN) If $Y_1, Y_2, \ldots$ are *ii* d with mean μ then

$$P\left(\lim_{n\to\infty} \frac{\sum Y_i}{n} = \mu \right) = 1.$$

The strong law is harder to prove than the weak law of large numbers:

Theorem 3 (WLLN) If Y_1, Y_2,... are iid with mean μ then for each positive $\in$

$$\lim P\left(\left|\frac{\sum Y_i}{n} - \mu\right| > \in\right) = 0$$

For *ii* d Y_i the stronger conclusion (the SLLN) holds but for our heuristics we will ignore the differences between these notions.

Now suppose that θ_0 is the true value of θ. Then

$$U(\theta) / n \to \mu(\theta)$$

where

$$\mu(\theta) = E_{\theta_0}\left[\frac{\partial \log f}{\partial \theta}(X_i, \theta)\right]$$
$$= \int \frac{\partial \log f}{\partial \theta}(x, \theta) f(x, \theta_0) dx$$

Estimating Equations

The same ideas arise in almost any model where estimates are derived by solving some equation. As an example I sketch large sample theory for Generalized Linear Models.

Generalized Linear Models

Suppose that for $i = 1, \ldots, n$ we have observations of the numbers of cancer cases Y_i in some group of people characterized by values x_i of some covariates. You are supposed to think of x_i as containing variables like age, or a dummy for sex or average income or . . .A parametric regression model for the Y_i might postulate that Y_i has a Poisson distribution with mean μ_i where the mean μ_i depends somehow on the covariate values. Typically we might assume that $g(\mu_i) = \beta o + x_i\, \beta$ where g is a so-called link function, often for this case $g(\mu) = \log(\mu)$ and $x_i\, \beta$ is a matrix product with x_i written as a row vector and μ a column vector. This is supposed to function as a \linear regression model with Poisson errors". We will do as a special case $\log(\mu_i) = \beta\, x_{i\,i}$ where $x_{i\,i}$ is a scalar.

The log likelihood is simply

$$\ell(\beta) = \sum Y_i \, log(\mu_i) - \mu_i)$$

ignoring irrelevant factorials. The score function is, since log $(\mu_i) = \beta x_i$

$$U(\beta) = \sum Y_i x_i - x_i \mu_i) = \sum x_i (Y_i - \mu_i)$$

(Notice again that the score has mean 0 when you plug in the true parameter value.) The key observation, however, is that it is not necessary to believe that Y_i has a Poisson distribution to make solving the equation U = 0 sensible.

Suppose only that $\log(E(Y_i)) = x_i\,\beta$. Then we have assumed that

$$E_\beta(U(\beta)) = 0$$

This was the key condition in proving that there was a root of the likelihood equations which was consistent and here it is what is needed, roughly, to prove that the equation $U(\beta) = 0$ has a consistent root $\hat{\beta}$. Ignoring higher order terms in a Taylor expansion will give

$$V(\beta)(\hat{\beta} - \beta) \approx U(\beta)$$

where $V = -U'$. In the MLE case we had identities relating the expectation of V to the variance of U. In general here we have

$$Var(U) = \sum x_i^2 Var(Y_i)$$

If Y_i is Poisson with mean μ_i (and so $Var(Y_i) = \mu_i$) this is

$$Var(U) = \sum x_i^2 \mu_i$$

Moreover we have

$$V_i = x_i^2 \quad _i$$

and so

$$V(\beta) = \sum x_i^2 \mu_i$$

The central limit theorem (the Lyapunov kind) will show that $U(\beta)$ has an approximate normal distribution with variance $\sigma_U^2 = \sum x_i^2 \mathrm{Var}(Y_i)$ and so

$$\hat{\beta} - \beta \approx N(0, \sigma_U^2 / (\sum x_i^2 \mu_i)^2$$

If $Var(Y_i) = \mu_i$, as it is for the Poisson case, the asymptotic variance simplifies to $1/\sum x_i^2 \mu_i$.

Notice that other estimating equations are possible. People suggest alternatives very often. If w_i is any set of deterministic weights (even possibly depending on μ_i then we could define

$$U(\beta) = \sum w_i (Y_i - \mu_i)$$

and still conclude that U = 0 probably has a consistent root which has an asymptotic normal distribution. This idea is being used all over the place these days: see, for example Zeger and Liang's Generalized estimating equations (GEE) which the econometricians call Generalized Method of Moments.

Problems with Maximum Likelihood

1. In problems with many parameters the approximations don't work very well and maximum likelihood estimators can be far from the right answer. See your homework for the Neyman Scott example where the MLE is not consistent.

2. When there are multiple roots of the likelihood equation you must choose the right root. To do so you might start with a different consistent estimator and then apply some iterative scheme like Newton Raphson to the likelihood equations to find the MLE. It turns out not many steps of NR are generally required if the starting point is a reasonable estimate.

Finding (Good) Preliminary Point Estimates

Method of Moments

Basic strategy: set sample moments equal to population moments and solve for the parameters.

The rth sample moment (about the origin) is

$$\frac{1}{n}\sum_{i=1}^{n} X_i^r$$

The rth population moment is

$$E(X^r)$$

Central moments are

$$\frac{1}{n}\sum_{i=1}^{n}(X_i - \bar{X})^r$$

And

$$E[(X-\mu)^r]$$

If we have p parameters we can estimate the parameters $\theta_1,\ldots,\theta_p$ by solving the system of p equations:

$$\mu_1 = \bar{X}$$

$$\mu_2' = \bar{X}^2$$

and so on to

$$\mu_p' = \bar{X}^p$$

You need to remember that the population moments μ_K' will be formulas involving the parameters.

Gamma Example

The Gamma(α,β) density is

$$f(x;\alpha,\beta) = \frac{1}{\beta\Gamma(\alpha)}\left(\frac{x}{\beta}\right)^{\alpha-1} \exp\left[-\frac{x}{\beta}\right] 1(x>0)$$

and has

$$\mu_1 = \alpha\hat{a}$$

And

$$\mu_2' = \alpha\hat{a}^2$$

This gives the equations

$$\alpha\hat{a} = \overline{X}$$

$$\alpha\hat{a}^2 = \overline{X^2}$$

Divide the second by the first to find the method of moments estimate of $\hat{a}$ is

$$\tilde{\beta} = \overline{X^2} / \overline{X}$$

Then from the first equation get

$$\tilde{\alpha} = \overline{X} / \tilde{\beta} = (\overline{X})^2 / \overline{X^2}$$

The equations are much easier to solve than the likelihood equations which involve the function

$$\psi(\alpha) = \frac{d}{d\alpha}\log(\Gamma(\alpha))$$

called the digamma function.

Sampling Distribution

A sampling distribution is a probability distribution of a statistic obtained through a large number of samples drawn from a specific population. The sampling distribution of a given population is the distribution of frequencies of a range of different outcomes that could possibly occur for a statistic of a population.

A lot of data drawn and used by academicians, statisticians, researchers, marketers, analysts, etc. are actually samples, not population. A sample is a subset of a population. For example, a medical researcher that wanted to compare the average weight of all babies born in North America from 1995 to 2005 to those born in South America within the same time period cannot within a reasonable amount of time draw the data for the entire population of over a million childbirths that occurred over the ten-year time frame. He will instead only use the weight of, say 100 babies, in each continent to make a conclusion. The weight of 200 babies used is the sample and the average weight calculated is the sample mean.

Now suppose that instead of taking just one sample of 100 newborn weights from each continent, the medical researcher takes repeated random samples from the general population, and computes the sample mean for each sample group. So, for North America, he pulls up data for 100 newborn weights recorded in the US, Canada, and Mexico as follows: four 100 samples from select hospitals in the US, five 70 samples from Canada, and three 150 records from Mexico, for a total of 1200 weights of newborn babies grouped in 12 sets. He also collects a sample data of 100 birth weights from each of the 12 countries in South America. Each sample has its own sample mean and the distribution of the sample means is known as the sample distribution.

The average weight computed for each of the 2400 sample set is the sampling distribution of the mean. Not just the mean can be calculated from a sample. Other statistics, such as the standard deviation, variance, proportion, and range can be calculated from a sample data. The standard deviation and variance measure the variability of the sampling distribution. The number of observations in a population, number of observations in a sample, and the procedure used to draw the sample sets determine the variability of a sampling distribution. The standard deviation of a sampling distribution is called the standard error. While the mean of a sampling distribution is equal to the mean of the population, the standard error depends on the standard deviation of the population, the size of the population, and the size of the sample. Knowing how spread apart the mean of each of the sample sets are from each other and from the population mean will give an indication of how close the sample mean is to the population mean. The standard error of the sampling distribution decreases as the sample size increases.

Normal Distribution and Shape

A population or one sample set of numbers will have a normal distribution. However, because a sampling distribution includes multiple sets of observations, it will not necessarily have a bell-curved shape. Following our example, the population average weight of babies in North America and in South America has a normal distribution because some babies will be underweight (below the mean) or overweight (above the mean), with most babies falling in between (around the mean). If the average weight of newborns in North America is seven pounds, the sample mean weight in each of the 12 sets of sample observations recorded for North America will be close to seven pounds as well. But if you graph each of the averages calculated in each of the 1200 sample groups, the resulting shape may result in a uniform distribution, but it is difficult to predict with certainty what the actual shape will turn out to be. The more samples the researcher uses from the population of over a million weight figures, the more the graph will start forming a normal distribution.

Standard Error

The standard deviation of the sampling distribution of a statistic is referred to as the standard error of that quantity. For the case where the statistic is the sample mean, and samples are uncorrelated, the standard error is:

$$\sigma_{\bar{x}} = \frac{\sigma}{\sqrt{n}}$$

where σ is the standard deviation of the population distribution of that quantity and n is the sample size (number of items in the sample).

An important implication of this formula is that the sample size must be quadrupled (multiplied by 4) to achieve half (1/2) the measurement error. When designing statistical studies where cost is a factor, this may have a role in understanding cost–benefit tradeoffs.

Examples

Population	Statistic	Sampling distribution
Normal: $\mathcal{N}(\mu, \sigma^2)$	Sample mean $\bar{X}$ samples of size n	$\bar{X} \sim \mathcal{N}(\mu, \frac{\sigma^2}{n})$ or (In case sigma is not known): $\bar{X} \sim \mathcal{T}(\mu, \frac{S^2}{n})$ Where S is the standard deviation of the sample and T is the Student's t-distribution.
Bernoulli: Bernoulli(p)	Sample proportion of "successful trials" $\bar{X}$	$n\bar{X} \sim \text{Binomial}(n, p)$
Two independent normal populations: $\mathcal{N}(\mu_1, \sigma_1^2)$ and $\mathcal{N}(\mu_2, \sigma_2^2)$	Difference between sample means, $\bar{X}_1 - \bar{X}_2$	$\bar{X}_1 - \bar{X}_2 \sim \mathcal{N}\left(\mu_1 - \mu_2, \frac{\sigma_1^2}{n_1} + \frac{\sigma_2^2}{n_2}\right)$
Any absolutely continuous distribution F with density f	Median $X_{(k)}$ from a sample of size n = 2k – 1, where sample is ordered $X_{(1)}$ to $X_{(n)}$	$f_{X_{(k)}}(x) = \frac{(2k-1)!}{(k-1)!^2} f(x)\left(F(x)(1-F(x))\right)^{k-1}$
Any distribution with distribution function F	Maximum $M = \max X_k$ from a random sample of size n	$F_M(x) = P(M \le x) = \prod P(X_k \le x) = \left(F(x)\right)^n$

Statistical Inference

In the theory of statistical inference, the idea of a sufficient statistic provides the basis of choosing a statistic (as a function of the sample data points) in such a way that no information is lost by replacing the full probabilistic description of the sample with the sampling distribution of the selected statistic.

In frequentist inference, for example in the development of a statistical hypothesis test or a confidence interval, the availability of the sampling distribution of a statistic (or an approximation to this in the form of an asymptotic distribution) can allow the ready formulation of such procedures, whereas the development of procedures starting from the joint distribution of the sample would be less straightforward.

In Bayesian inference, when the sampling distribution of a statistic is available, one can consider replacing the final outcome of such procedures, specifically the conditional distributions of any unknown quantities given the sample data, by the conditional distributions of any unknown quantities given selected sample statistics. Such a procedure would involve the sampling distribution of the statistics. The results would be identical provided the statistics chosen are jointly sufficient statistics.

Point Estimation

Point estimation is the process of finding an approximate value of some parameter—such as the mean (average)—of a population from random samples of the population. The accuracy of any particular approximation is not known precisely, though probabilistic statements concerning the accuracy of such numbers as found over many experiments can be constructed.

In simple terms, any statistic can be a point estimate. A statistic is an estimator of some parameter in a population. For example:

- The sample standard deviation (s) is a point estimate of the population standard deviation (σ).
- The sample mean ($\bar{x}$) is a point estimate of the population mean,
- The sample variance (s^2 is a point estimate of the population variance (σ^2).

It is desirable for a point estimate to be: (1) Consistent. The larger the sample size, the more accurate the estimate. (2) Unbiased. The expectation of the observed values of many samples ("average observation value") equals the corresponding population parameter. For example, the sample mean is an unbiased estimator for the population mean. (3) Most efficient or best unbiased—of all consistent, unbiased estimates, the one possessing the smallest variance (a measure of the amount of dispersion away from the estimate). In other words, the estimator that varies least from sample to sample. This generally depends on the particular distribution of the population. For example, the mean is more efficient than the median (middle value) for the normal distribution but not for more "skewed" (asymmetrical) distributions.

Several methods are used to calculate the estimator. The most often used, the maximum likelihood method, uses differential calculus to determine the maximum of the probability function of a number of sample parameters. The moments method equates values of sample moments (functions describing the parameter) to population moments. The solution of the equation gives the desired estimate. The Bayesian method, named for the 18th-century English theologian and mathematician Thomas Bayes, differs from the traditional methods by introducing a frequency function for the parameter being estimated. The drawback to the Bayesian method is that sufficient information on the distribution of the parameter is usually not available. One advantage is that the estimation can be easily adjusted as additional information becomes available.

Bayesian Point Estimation

Bayesian inference is typically based on the posterior distribution. Many Bayesian point estimators are the posterior distribution's statistics of central tendency, e.g., its mean, median, or mode:

- Posterior mean, which minimizes the (posterior) *risk* (expected loss) for a squared-error loss function; in Bayesian estimation, the risk is defined in terms of the posterior distribution, as observed by Gauss.

- The alternative hypothesis is that your business idea will not succeed in the target market as a standalone sustainable business.
- There are different reasons for the alternative hypothesis. Your job is to find all most important reasons that can lead to failure of your business idea.
- Each reason that leads to failure you can avoid if you as an entrepreneur prepare concrete action steps for them.

This is the process that you must apply before you start your business. Test your ideas if you are a startup entrepreneur, or before you start implementing them into your current business. Always use an alternative hypothesis, something opposite if you want to test future success.

The last, but not the least important thing is that you must always see things as they really are.

Test Statistic

A test statistic is a random variable that is calculated from sample data and used in a hypothesis test. You can use test statistics to determine whether to reject the null hypothesis. The test statistic compares your data with what is expected under the null hypothesis. The test statistic is used to calculate the p-value.

A test statistic measures the degree of agreement between a sample of data and the null hypothesis. Its observed value changes randomly from one random sample to a different sample. A test statistic contains information about the data that is relevant for deciding whether to reject the null hypothesis. The sampling distribution of the test statistic under the null hypothesis is called the null distribution. When the data show strong evidence against the assumptions in the null hypothesis, the magnitude of the test statistic becomes too large or too small depending on the alternative hypothesis. This causes the test's p-value to become small enough to reject the null hypothesis.

For example, the test statistic for a Z-test is the Z-statistic, which has the standard normal distribution under the null hypothesis. Suppose you perform a two-tailed Z-test with an α of 0.05, and obtain a Z-statistic (also called a Z-value) based on your data of 2.5. This Z-value corresponds to a p-value of 0.0124. Because this p-value is less than α, you declare statistical significance and reject the null hypothesis.

Different hypothesis tests use different test statistics based on the probability model assumed in the null hypothesis. Common tests and their test statistics include:

Hypothesis test	**Test statistic**
Z-test	Z-statistic
t-tests	t-statistic
ANOVA	F-statistic
Chi-square tests	Chi-square statistic

Student's T-test and T-statistic

The idea behind parametric tests is to provide the researcher with a statistical inference about the population by conducting statistically significant tests (like t-test) on the sample drawn from the population. The parametric test called t-test or Student's t-test is based on a student's t statistic. This statistic assumes that variables are drawn from the normal population. The mean of the population in this statistic of t-test has been assumed to be known. The distribution, called t-distribution, has a similar shape to that of a normal distribution, i.e. a bell shaped appearance.

The parametric test called t-test is useful for testing those samples whose size is less than 30. The reason behind this is that if the size of the sample is more than 30, then the distribution of the t-test and the normal distribution will not be distinguishable.

The parametric test is used for conducting statistically significant tests in the testing of hypotheses. There are basically three types of t-tests: one sample t-test, two independent sample t-test and paired sample t-test.

In the case of a one sample t-test, if a researcher in the field of psychology is working on a study where he wants to make sure that at least 65% of students will pass the IQ test, he can use the t-test. So, one sample t-test will be used after the hypothesis has been formulated in this particular case. The parametric test is then calculated by selecting an appropriate formula of t-test. In this case, the appropriate formula will be a t-test for a single mean. A selection of the level of significance is conducted to check the t-test of the null hypothesis. Usually, the researcher takes 0.05 as the appropriate level of significance while conducting the t-test. The level of significance refers to the minimum probability that there will be a false rejection of the null hypothesis. Now, if the value calculated from the t-test is more than the tabulated value, then the null hypothesis gets rejected at a particular level of significance. Similarly, if the value calculated from the t-test is less than the tabulated value, then the null hypothesis gets accepted at a particular level of significance.

In two independent sample t-tests, two samples that are not at all related to each other are tested. The main idea behind two independent sample t-tests is to draw out a statistical inference about the comparison of two independent samples of data. For example, in the field of psychology, if the researcher wants to compare the IQ level of students living in region A and region B, then a two independent sample t-test is useful. The region A and the region B are not at all related to each other, i.e. they are independent of each other. The procedure for conducting this t-test is the same, except that now the sample number is double instead of single. Also, in the case of t-test for single mean and two independent sample t-tests, there are different formulas for the degree of freedom. The degree of freedom is referred to as the restriction that a researcher puts forward while conducting parametric tests, like t-test in this case.

The paired sample t-test refers to that type of sample in which the variables form paired categories. For example, if a researcher wants to compare male and female smokers, paired sample t-test comes into play if the variable is in following form: male chain smoker and female chain smoker, male occasional smoker and female occasional smoker, etc.

t Score

The t score is a ratio between the difference between two groups and the difference within the groups. The larger the t score, the more difference there is between groups. The smaller the t score, the more similarity there is between groups. A t score of 3 means that the groups are three times as different *from* each other as they are within each other. When you run a t test, the bigger the t-value, the more likely it is that the results are repeatable.

- A large t-score tells you that the groups are different.
- A small t-score tells you that the groups are similar.

Student's *t*-distribution

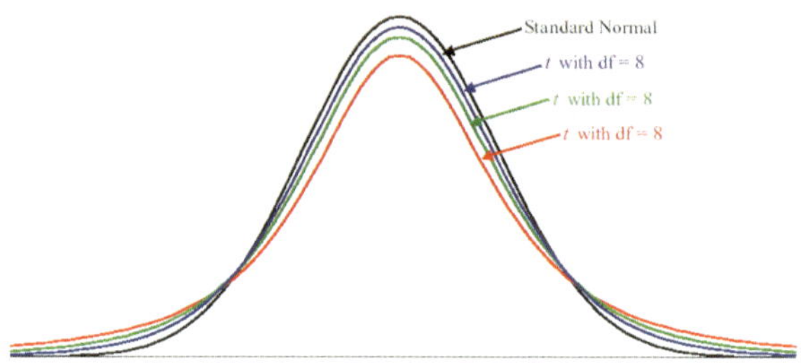

The t-distribution, used for the t-test.

T-Values and P-values

How big is "big enough"? Every t-value has a p-value to go with it. A p-value is the probability that the results from your sample data occurred by chance. P-values are from 0% to 100%. They are usually written as a decimal. For example, a p value of 5% is 0.05. Low p-values are good; They indicate your data did not occur by chance. For example, a p-value of .01 means there is only a 1% probability that the results from an experiment happened by chance. In most cases, a p-value of 0.05 (5%) is accepted to mean the data is valid.

The T Statistic is used in a T test when you are deciding if you should support or reject the null hypothesis. It's very similar to a Z-score and you use it in the same way: find a cut off point, find your t score, and compare the two. You use the t statistic when you have a small sample size, or if you don't know the population standard deviation.

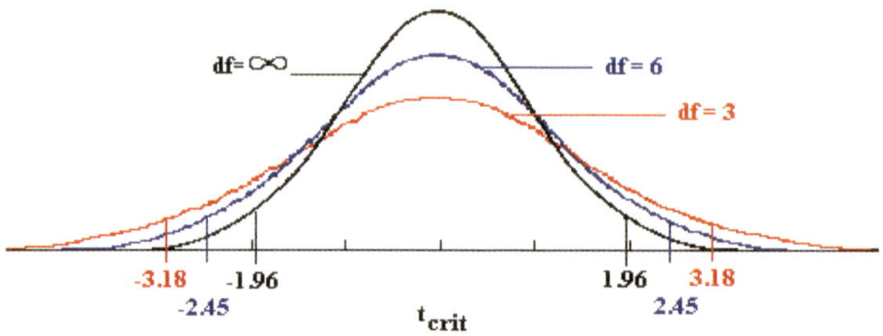

The T statistic doesn't really tell you much on its own. It's like the word "average" doesn't mean anything on it's own either, without some context. If I say "the average was 150," it means nothing. If I say "the average weight of dogs seen in a veterinary office was 50lbs," then the picture becomes clearer. In the same way, you need some more information along with your t statistic for it to make sense. You get this information by taking a sample and running a hypothesis test.

Use of t-Statistic

When you run a hypothesis test, you use the T statistic with a p value. The p-value tells you what the odds are that your results could have happened by chance. Let's say you and a group of friends score an average of 205 on a bowling game. You know the average bowler scores 79.7. Should you and your friends consider professional bowling? Or are those scores a fluke? Finding the t statistic and the probability value will give you a good idea. More technically, finding those values will give you evidence of a significant difference between your team's mean and the population mean (i.e. everyone).

The greater the T, the more evidence you have that your team's scores are significantly different from average. A smaller T value is evidence that your team's score is not significantly different from average. It's pretty obvious that your team's score (205) is significantly different from 79.7, so you'd want to take a look at the probability value. If the p-value is larger than 5%, the odds are your team getting those scores are due to chance. Very small (under 5%), you're onto something: think about going professional.

T Score vs. Z-Score

The Z-score allows you to decide if your sample is different from the population mean. In order to use z, you must know four things:

1. The population mean.
2. The population standard deviation.
3. The sample mean.
4. The sample size.

Usually in stats, you don't know anything about a population, so instead of a Z score you use a T Test with a T Statistic. The major difference between using a Z score and a T statistic is that you have to estimate the population standard deviation. The T test is also used if you have a small sample size (less than 30).

T Statistic Formula

The statistic can be found in so many different ways, there is no single formula for it. The formula depends on what type of test you are trying to do. For example:

- One sample t test. This is the most common type of t test you'll come across in elementary statistics. You can test the mean of a single group against a known mean. For example, the average IQ is 100. You can test a class of children with a mean score of 90 to see if that's significant, or if it just happened by chance.

- A paired t-test compares means from the same group at different times (say, one year apart). For example, you could try a new weight loss technique on a group of people and follow up a year later.

When to Choose a Paired T Test / Paired Samples T Test / Dependent Samples T Test

Choose the paired t-test if you have two measurements on the same item, person or thing. You should also choose this test if you have two items that are being measured with a unique condition. For example, you might be measuring car safety performance in Vehicle Research and Testing and subject the cars to a series of crash tests. Although the manufacturers are different, you might be subjecting them to the same conditions.

With a "regular" two sample t test, you're comparing the means for two different samples. For example, you might test two different groups of customer service associates on a business-related test or testing students from two universities on their English skills. If you take a random sample each group separately and they have different conditions, your samples are independent and you should run an independent samples t test (also called between-samples and unpaired-samples).

The null hypothesis for the for the independent samples t-test is $\mu_1 = \mu_2$. In other words, it assumes the means are equal. With the paired t test, the null hypothesis is that the *pairwise difference* between the two tests is equal (H_0: $\mu_d = 0$). The difference between the two tests is very subtle; which one you choose is based on your data collection method.

t-Distributions

When you perform a t-test for a single study, you obtain a single t-value. However, if we drew multiple random samples of the same size from the same population and performed the same t-test, we would obtain many t-values and we could plot a distribution of all of them. This type of distribution is known as a sampling distribution.

Fortunately, the properties of t-distributions are well understood in statistics, so we can plot them without having to collect many samples! A specific t-distribution is defined by its degrees of freedom (DF), a value closely related to sample size. Therefore, different t-distributions exist for every sample size. You can graph t-distributions using Minitab's probability distribution plots.

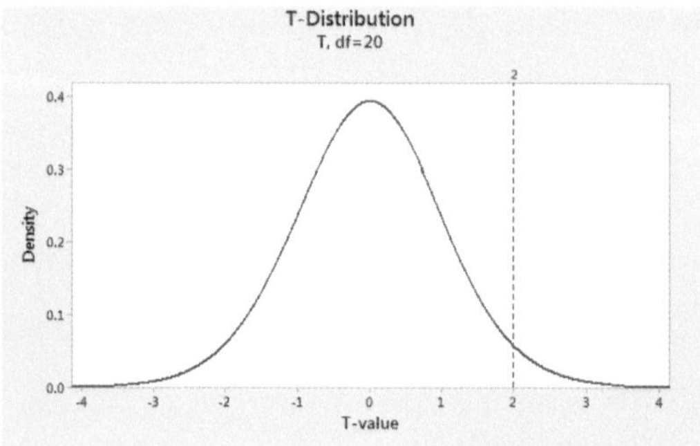

The graph above shows a t-distribution that has 20 degrees of freedom, which corresponds to a sample size of 21 in a one-sample t-test. It is a symmetric, bell-shaped distribution that is similar to the normal distribution, but with thicker tails. This graph plots the probability density function (PDF), which describes the likelihood of each t-value.

T-distributions assume that you draw repeated random samples from a population where the null hypothesis is true. You place the t-value from your study in the t-distribution to determine how consistent your results are with the null hypothesis.

The peak of the graph is right at zero, which indicates that obtaining a sample value close to the null hypothesis is the most likely. That makes sense because t-distributions assume that the null hypothesis is true. T-values become less likely as you get further away from zero in either direction. In other words, when the null hypothesis is true, you are less likely to obtain a sample that is very different from the null hypothesis.

Our t-value of 2 indicates a positive difference between our sample data and the null hypothesis. The graph shows that there is a reasonable probability of obtaining a t-value from -2 to +2 when the null hypothesis is true. Our t-value of 2 is an unusual value, but we don't know exactly *how* unusual. Our ultimate goal is to determine whether our t-value is unusual enough to warrant rejecting the null hypothesis. To do that, we'll need to calculate the probability.

Using t-Values and t-Distributions to Calculate Probabilities

The foundation behind any hypothesis test is being able to take the test statistic from a specific sample and place it within the context of a known probability distribution. For t-tests, if you take a t-value and place it in the context of the correct t-distribution, you can calculate the probabilities associated with that t-value.

A probability allows us to determine how common or rare our t-value is under the assumption that the null hypothesis is true. If the probability is low enough, we can conclude that the effect observed in our sample is inconsistent with the null hypothesis. The evidence in the sample data is strong enough to reject the null hypothesis for the entire population.

Before we calculate the probability associated with our t-value of 2, there are two important details to address.

First, we'll actually use the t-values of +2 and -2 because we'll perform a two-tailed test. A two-tailed test is one that can test for differences in both directions. For example, a two-tailed 2-sample t-test can determine whether the difference between group 1 and group 2 is statistically significant in either the positive or negative direction. A one-tailed test can only assess one of those directions.

Second, we can only calculate a non-zero probability for a range of t-values. As you'll see in the graph below, a range of t-values corresponds to a proportion of the total area under the distribution curve, which is the probability. The probability for any specific point value is zero because it does not produce an area under the curve.

With these points in mind, we'll shade the area of the curve that has t-values greater than 2 and t-values less than -2.

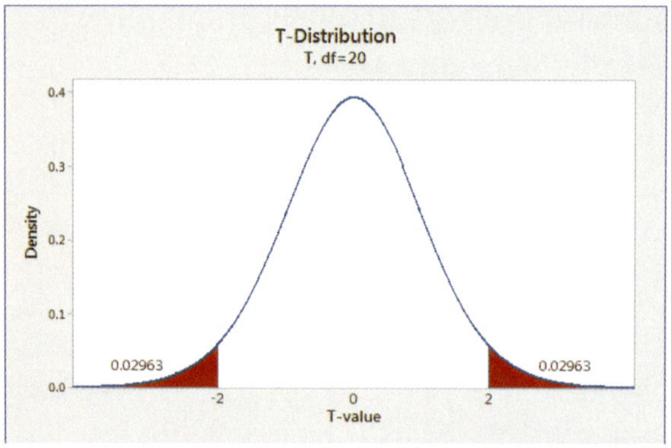

The graph displays the probability for observing a difference from the null hypothesis that is at least as extreme as the difference present in our sample data while assuming that the null hypothesis is actually true. Each of the shaded regions has a probability of 0.02963, which sums to a total probability of 0.05926. When the null hypothesis is true, the t-value falls within these regions nearly 6% of the time.

This probability has a name that you might have heard of—it's called the p-value! While the probability of our t-value falling within these regions is fairly low, it's not low enough to reject the null hypothesis using the common significance level of 0.05.

t-Distributions and Sample Size

As mentioned above, t-distributions are defined by the DF, which are closely associated with sample size. As the DF increases, the probability density in the tails decreases and the distribution becomes more tightly clustered around the central value. The graph below depicts t-distributions with 5 and 30 degrees of freedom

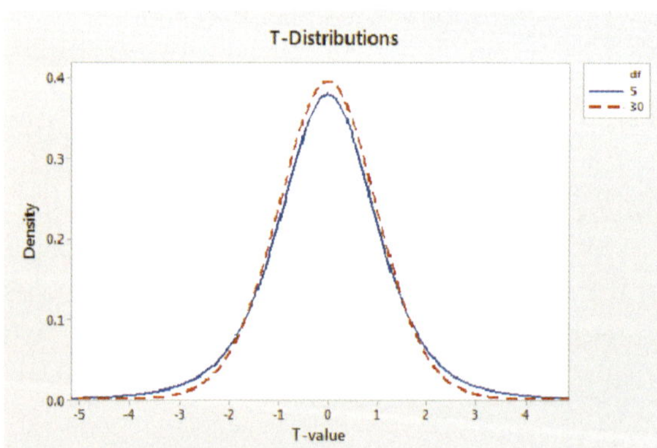

The t-distribution with fewer degrees of freedom has thicker tails. This occurs because the t-distribution is designed to reflect the added uncertainty associated with analyzing small samples. In other words, if you have a small sample, the probability that the sample statistic will be further away from the null hypothesis is greater even when the null hypothesis is true.

Small samples are more likely to be unusual. This affects the probability associated with any given t-value. For 5 and 30 degrees of freedom, a t-value of 2 in a two-tailed test has p-values of 10.2% and 5.4%, respectively.

Hotelling's T-squared Distribution

To motivate Hotelling's T^2, consider the square of the *t*-statistic for testing a hypothesis regarding a univariate mean. Recall that under the null hypothesis *t* has a distribution with *n*-1 degrees of freedom. Now consider squaring this test statistic as shown below:

$$t^2 = \frac{(x-\mu_0)^2}{s^2/n} = n(x-\mu_0)\left(\frac{1}{s^2}\right)(x-\mu_0) \sim F_{1,n-1}$$

When you square a *t*-distributed random variable with *n*-1 degrees of freedom, the result is an *F*-distributed random variable with 1 and *n*-1 degrees of freedom. We reject H_o at level α if t^2 is greater than the critical value from the *F*-table with 1 and *n*-1 degrees of freedom, evaluated at level α.

$$t^2 > F_{1,n-1,\alpha}$$

Consider the last term in the above expression for t^2. In the expression for Hotelling's T^2, the difference between the sample mean and μ_0 is replaced with the difference between the sample mean vector and the hypothesized mean vector μ_o. The inverse of the sample variance is replaced by the inverse of the sample variance-covariance matrix S, yielding the expression below:

$$T^2 = n(\bar{X}-\mu_0)'S^{-1}(\bar{X}-\mu_0)$$

For large *n*, T^2 is *approximately* chi-square distributed with *p* degrees of freedom. If we replace the sample variance-covariance matrix, S, by the population variance-covariance matrix, Σ

$$n(\bar{X}-\mu_0)'\Sigma^{-1}(\bar{X}-\mu_0),$$

then the resulting test is exactly chi-square distributed with *p* degrees of freedom when the data are normally distributed.

For small samples, the chi-square approximation for T^2 does not take into account variation due to estimating Σ with the sample variance-covariance matrix *S*.

Better results can be obtained from the transformation of the Hotelling T^2 statistic as below:

$$F = \frac{n-p}{P(n-1)}T^2 \sim F_{p,n-p}$$

Under null hypothesis, $H_o: \mu = \mu_o$, this will have a *F* distribution with *p* and *n-p* degrees of freedom. We reject the null hypothesis, $H_{o,}$ at level α if the test statistic *F* is greater than the critical value from the *F*-table with *p* and *n-p* degrees of freedom, evaluated at level α.

$$F > F_{p.n-p,\alpha}$$

Example: Women's Nutrition Data

The recommended intake and sample mean are given below:

Variable	Recommended Intake (μ_o)	Mean
Calcium	1000 mg	624.0 mg
Iron	15mg	11.1 mg
Protein	60g	65.8 g
Vitamin A	800 μg	839.6 μg
Vitamin C	75 mg	78.9 mg

as well as the sample variance-covariance matrix:

$$S = \begin{pmatrix} 157829.4 & 940.1 & 6075.8 & 102411.1 & 6701.6 \\ 940.1 & 35.8 & 114.1 & 2383.2 & 137.7 \\ 6075.8 & 114.1 & 934.9 & 7330.1 & 477.2 \\ 102411.1 & 2383.2 & 7330.1 & 2668452.4 & 22063.3 \\ 6701.6 & 137.7 & 477.2 & 22063.3 & 5416.3 \end{pmatrix}$$

Hotelling's T-square comes out to be:

$$T^2 = 1758.54$$

The *F*-statistic is:

$$F = 349.80 > 3.042 = F_{5,732,0.01}$$

For an 0.01 level test, the critical value is approximately 3.02. Because 349.80 is greater than this value, we can reject the null hypothesis that the average dietary intake meets recommendations.

$$(T^2 = 1758.54; F = 349.80; \text{d.f.} = 5,732; p < 0.0001)$$

The SAS program reports the *p*-value as 0.00. In this case, the *p*-values can never equal zero. It is preferable to state that the *p*-value is less than 0.0001.

For all women between 25 and 50 years old, the average dietary intake *does not* meet recommended standards. Returning to the table of sample means and recommended dietary intake, it appears that women fail to meet nutritional standards for calcium and iron, and perhaps exceed intakes for protein, vitamin A and vitamin C.

Welch's T-test

Mean comparison is the central theme of many classical statistical procedures. The well-known independent-sample t-test is often used to test the equality of two means from independent populations with equal variances, whereas Welch's t-test is generally preferred when the variances are not equal.

Let $Y_{11}, Y_{21}, \ldots, Yn_1 1$ and $Y_{12}, Y_{22}, \ldots, Y_{22}, \ldots, Yn_2 2$ be two independent random samples from two populations with means (or expected values) $\mu_j = E(y_{ij})$ and variances $\sigma_j^2 = Var(y_{ij})$ $j = 1, 2$. The sample counterparts of μ_j and σ_j^2 are $\bar{y}_j = \frac{1}{n_j}\sum_{i=1}^{n_j} Y_{ij}$ and $s_j^2 = \frac{1}{n_j - 1}\sum_{i=1}^{n_j}(y_{ij} - \bar{y}_j)^2$ respectively. Because $\bar{y}_j$ is an unbiased estimator of μ_j any difference between μ_1 and μ_2 should be reflected by $\bar{y}_1 - \bar{y}_2$. Of course, even when the null hypothesis

$$H_0 : \mu_1 = \mu_2$$

holds, $\bar{y}_1 = \bar{y}_2$ does not hold in general because of the sampling error, which is characterized by the variance

$$v^2 = Var(\bar{y}_1 - \bar{y}_2) = \frac{\sigma_1^2}{n_1} + \frac{\sigma_2^2}{n_2}$$

Notice that, when $\sigma_1^2 = \sigma_2^2 = \sigma^2$, v^2 will be simplified to $v_0^2 = \sigma^2(1/n_1 + 1/n_2)$ which is best estimated by

$$\hat{v}_0^2 = s_p^2(1/n_1 + 1/n_2),$$

where the pooled variance estimator is given by

$$\frac{(n-1)s_1^2 + (n_2 - 1)s_2^2}{n_1 + n_2 - 2}$$

The commonly used independent-sample t-statistic,

$$t_s = \frac{\bar{y}_1 - \bar{y}_2}{s_p\sqrt{1/n_1 + 1/n_2}}$$

is just the standardized mean difference using $\hat{v}_0$. As obtained by William S. Gosset in 1908, the t_s in Equation follows $t(n_1 + n_2 - 2)$ the Student's t-distribution with $(n_1 + n_2 - 2)$ degrees of freedom. It is commonly denoted by

$$t_s \sim t(n_1 + n_2 - 2),$$

where "~" stands for "following the distribution of ". When $\sigma_1^2 \neq \sigma_1^2$, $\hat{v}_0^2$ is no longer an unbiased estimator of v^2, but $\hat{v}^2 = s_1^2/n_1 + s_2^2/n_2$ n remains unbiased. A natural choice is to standardize $\bar{y}_1 - \bar{y}_2$ using $\hat{v}$, which leads to the so-called Welch's t-statistic

$$t_w = \frac{\bar{y}_1 - \bar{y}_2}{\sqrt{s_1^2/n_1 + s_2^2/n_2}}.$$

The exact distribution of t_w can be characterized by a series or an integral, and it is far more complicated than Student's t-distribution. Using complicated mathematics, Bernard L. Welch came up with

$$t_w \dot{\sim} t(df_w)$$,

where $\dot{\sim}$ stands for "approximately following the distribution of " and df_w is the degrees of freedom given by

$$df_w = \frac{\left(s_1^2/n_1 + s_2^2/n_2\right)^2}{\frac{(s_1^2/n_1)^2}{n_1-1} + \frac{(s_2^2/n_2)^2}{n_2-1}}.$$

In other words, it means approximating the distribution of t_w by the t-distribution with degrees of freedom df_w. The test that compares t_w against the distribution $t(df_w)$ for significance is called Welch's t-test. Notice that the df_w in Equation (8) is not necessarily an integer.

It's worth mentioning that the approximation in was also obtained by Franklin E. Satterthwaite in 1946 under a different context. Therefore, it is also called the Welch-Satterthwaite approximation.

Welch's t-test is not only simple to use but also provides accurate control of the Type I error. Let α_w be the actual Type I error rates of Welch's t-test. At nominal level $\alpha = .01, .05$, and .1, the maximum difference between α and α_w is approximately at .001 when both n_1 and n_2 are greater than 5; and α_w will be closer to α as n_1 and n_2 increase.

Welch's t-Test with Distribution Violations

Welch obtained the distribution $t(df_w)$ under the normality assumption. The approximation in it is affected by non-normal distributions, especially by the third central moments at smaller n_1 and n_2.

The actual Type I error rate α_w depends on $E(t_w)$, the expected value of the t_w in equation. When the two populations are normally distributed, $E(t_w) = 0$ under H_0 in equation. When the two populations are not normally distributed, under H_0, $E(t_w)$ can be approximated by

$$\lambda_w = \frac{1}{2v^3}\left(\frac{\mu_{32}}{n_2^2} - \frac{\mu_{31}}{n_1^2}\right)$$

Where v is given in Equation and $\mu_{3j} = E\left[(y_{ij} - \mu_j)^3\right]$ is the third central moment for the jth population, $j = 1, 2$. The fourth central moments have little effect on $E(t_w)$. The effect of $E(t_w)$ on the Type I error can be summarized as follows:

- When $\lambda_w = 0$, the expected value of t_w is closed to zero, and then α_w is very close to the nominal α. When two populations are normal, their third central moments are zero, and thus, $\alpha_w = 0$. Another case of $\lambda_w = 0$ is when two equal-sized samples are from distributions with the same third central moment.

- When $\lambda_w > 0$, Welch's t-test tends to reject more on the right and less on the left. Because the over-rejection on the right is greater than the under-rejection on the left, the Type I error of the two-tailed Welch's t-test α_w is typically greater than α.

- When $\lambda_w < 0$, the test tends to reject less on the right and more on the left, and $\alpha_w = \alpha$ for the two-tailed test.

Notice that the effect of non-normally distributed populations on α_w is most obvious when n_1 and n_2 are small, and it decreases as the two sample sizes increase. Actually, non-normal distributed populations only have minimal effect on Welch's t-test when both n_1 and n_2 are large, which can also be explained by Equation being close to zero.

Welch's t-Test versus Student's t-Test

Although it is unlikely for $\sigma_1^2 = \sigma_2^2$ with practical data, the Student's t-test is still most widely used probably because it has been taught in introductory textbooks. Under certain conditions, the Student's t-test can perform well even when $\sigma_1^2 \neq \sigma_2^2$. The conditions are closely related to whether there exists a bias in the $\hat{v}_0^2$ of equation. Notice that the true variance of $\bar{y}_1 - \bar{y}_2$ is given by the v^2 in equation. The bias in $\hat{v}_0^2$ is given by

$$b = E(\hat{v}_0^2) - v^2 = \frac{(n_1 + n_2 - 1)}{(n_1 + n_2 - 2)\, n_1 n_2}(n_2 - n_1)(\sigma_2^2 - \sigma_1^2).$$

When $b = 0$, the expectation of $\hat{v}_0^2$ is larger than the true variance v^2, so the statistic st in equation tends to be smaller than a statistic following the distribution of $t(n_1 + n_2 - 2)$; and it tends to be greater when $b < 0$. These will be reflected in the Type I error.

- When $n_1 = n_2$, $b = 0$ and $\hat{v}_0^2 = \hat{v}^2 = (s_1^2 + s_2^2)/n$, and consequently, $t_s = t_w$. If $s_1^2 = s_2^2$ also holds, $df_s = df_w$ and the two tests lead to identical results. If $s_1^2 \neq s_2^2$ although the two tests are not identical, they still perform similarly and satisfactorily in practice because of both $\hat{v}_0^2$ and $\hat{v}^2$ being unbiased.
- When $n_1 \neq n_2$ while $\sigma_1^2 = \sigma_2^2$, $b=0$ and both $\hat{v}_0^2$ and $\hat{v}^2$ are unbiased estimators of v^2. But they are generally unequal because of the sampling error, and neither $t_s = t_w$ nor $df_s = df_w$ holds. However, the performances of both tests are still close to each other if s_1^2 and s_2^2 are not significantly different. When s_1^2 and s_2^2 are significantly different because of sampling errors, Welch's t-test is preferred.
- When $n_1 \neq n_2$ and $\sigma_1^2 \neq \sigma_2^2$, $\hat{v}_0^2$ is biased for v^2, as reflected by the b in Equation. The Student's t-test cannot control the Type I error α properly even when both n_1 and n_2 are large. Let α_s be the actual Type I error rate of the Student's t-test. When $b > 0$, α_s will be smaller than α because of a stochastically smaller t_s. When $b \quad 0$, α_s will be greater than α.

In conclusion, without knowing the value of σ_1^2 and σ_2^2, Welch's t-test performs satisfactorily in practice, with α_w being close to α. Actually, the degrees of freedom df_w in Equation (8) already takes $b \neq 0$ into consideration.

F-test and ANOVA

F-tests are named after its test statistic, F, which was named in honor of Sir Ronald Fisher. The

F-statistic is simply a ratio of two variances. Variances are a measure of dispersion, or how far the data are scattered from the mean. Larger values represent greater dispersion.

Variance is the square of the standard deviation. For us humans, standard deviations are easier to understand than variances because they're in the same units as the data rather than squared units. However, many analyses actually use variances in the calculations.

F-statistics are based on the ratio of mean squares. The term "mean squares" may sound confusing but it is simply an estimate of population variance that accounts for the degrees of freedom (DF) used to calculate that estimate.

Despite being a ratio of variances, you can use F-tests in a wide variety of situations. Unsurprisingly, the F-test can assess the equality of variances. However, by changing the variances that are included in the ratio, the F-test becomes a very flexible test. For example, you can use F-statistics and F-tests to test the overall significance for a regression model, to compare the fits of different models, to test specific regression terms, and to test the equality of means.

Using the F-test in One-Way ANOVA

To use the F-test to determine whether group means are equal, it's just a matter of including the correct variances in the ratio. In one-way ANOVA, the F-statistic is this ratio:

F = variation between sample means / variation within the samples

The best way to understand this ratio is to walk through a one-way ANOVA example.

We'll analyze four samples of plastic to determine whether they have different mean strengths.

Analysis of Variance

Source	DF	Adj SS	Adj MS	F-Value	P-Value
Factor	3	43.62	14.540	3.30	0.031
Error	36	158.47	4.402		
Total	39	202.09			

Model Summary

S	R-sq	R-sq(adj)	R-sq(pred)
2.09805	21.58%	15.05%	3.19%

Means

Factor	N	Mean	StDev	95% CI
1	10	11.203	1.995	(9.857, 12.548)
2	10	8.938	2.980	(7.592, 10.283)
3	10	10.683	1.102	(9.337, 12.028)
4	10	8.838	1.879	(7.492, 10.184)

Numerator: Variation Between Sample Means

One-way ANOVA has calculated a mean for each of the four samples of plastic. The group means are: 11.203, 8.938, 10.683, and 8.838. These group means are distributed around the overall mean for all 40 observations, which is 9.915. If the group means are clustered close to the overall mean, their variance is low. However, if the group means are spread out further from the overall mean, their variance is higher.

Clearly, if we want to show that the group means are different, it helps if the means are further apart from each other. In other words, we want higher variability among the means.

Imagine that we perform two different one-way ANOVAs where each analysis has four groups. The graph below shows the spread of the means. Each dot represents the mean of an entire group. The further the dots are spread out, the higher the value of the variability in the numerator of the F-statistic.

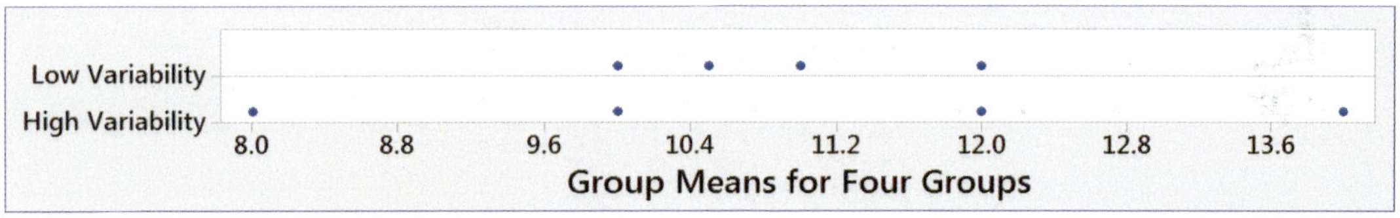

What value do we use to measure the variance between sample means for the plastic strength example? In the one-way ANOVA output, we'll use the adjusted mean square (Adj MS) for Factor, which is 14.540. Don't try to interpret this number because it won't make sense. It's the sum of the squared deviations divided by the factor DF. Just keep in mind that the further apart the group means are, the larger this number becomes.

Denominator: Variation within the Samples

We also need an estimate of the variability within each sample. To calculate this variance, we need to calculate how far each observation is from its group mean for all 40 observations. Technically, it is the sum of the squared deviations of each observation from its group mean divided by the error DF.

If the observations for each group are close to the group mean, the variance within the samples is low. However, if the observations for each group are further from the group mean, the variance within the samples is higher.

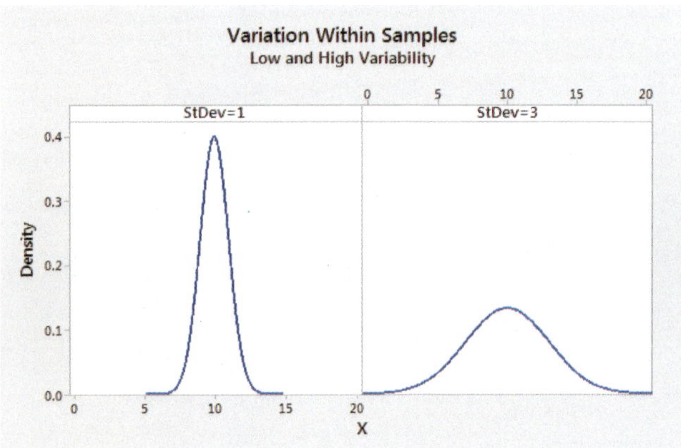

In the graph, the panel on the left shows low variation in the samples while the panel on the right shows high variation. The more spread out the observations are from their group mean, the higher the value in the denominator of the F-statistic.

If we're hoping to show that the means are different, it's good when the within-group variance is low. You can think of the within-group variance as the background noise that can obscure a difference between means.

For this one-way ANOVA example, the value that we'll use for the variance within samples is the Adj MS for Error, which is 4.402. It is considered "error" because it is the variability that is not explained by the factor.

The F-Statistic: Variation between Sample Means/Variation Within the Samples

The F-statistic is the test statistic for F-tests. In general, an F-statistic is a ratio of two quantities that are expected to be roughly equal under the null hypothesis, which produces an F-statistic of approximately 1.

The F-statistic incorporates both measures of variability discussed above. Let's take a look at how these measures can work together to produce low and high F-values. Look at the graphs below and compare the width of the spread of the group means to the width of the spread within each group.

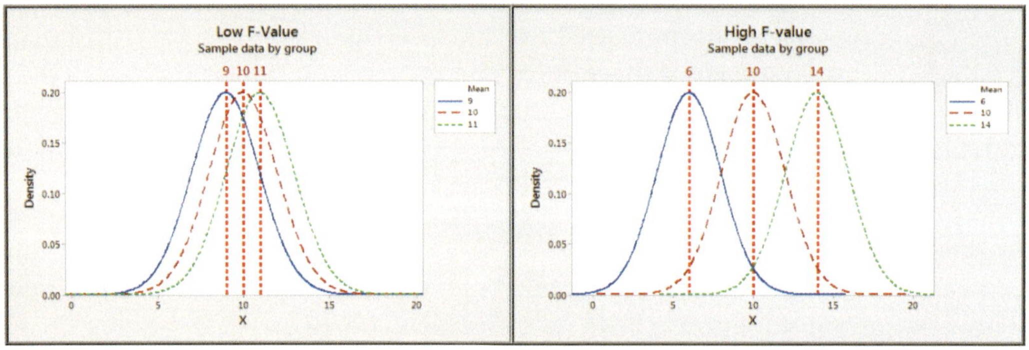

The low F-value graph shows a case where the group means are close together (low variability) relative to the variability within each group. The high F-value graph shows a case where the variability of group means is large relative to the within group variability. In order to reject the null hypothesis that the group means are equal, we need a high F-value.

For our plastic strength example, we'll use the Factor Adj MS for the numerator (14.540) and the Error Adj MS for the denominator (4.402), which gives us an F-value of 3.30.

Is our F-value high enough? A single F-value is hard to interpret on its own. We need to place our F-value into a larger context before we can interpret it. To do that, we'll use the F-distribution to calculate probabilities.

F-distributions and Hypothesis Testing

For one-way ANOVA, the ratio of the between-group variability to the within-group variability follows an F-distribution when the null hypothesis is true.

When you perform a one-way ANOVA for a single study, you obtain a single F-value. However, if we drew multiple random samples of the same size from the same population and performed the same one-way ANOVA, we would obtain many F-values and we could plot a distribution of all of them. This type of distribution is known as a sampling distribution.

Because the F-distribution assumes that the null hypothesis is true, we can place the F-value from our study in the F-distribution to determine how consistent our results are with the null hypothesis and to calculate probabilities.

The probability that we want to calculate is the probability of observing an F-statistic that is at least as high as the value that our study obtained. That probability allows us to determine how common or rare our F-value is under the assumption that the null hypothesis is true. If the probability is low enough, we can conclude that our data is inconsistent with the null hypothesis. The evidence in the sample data is strong enough to reject the null hypothesis for the entire population.

This probability that we're calculating is also known as the p-value!

In order to graph the F-distribution that is appropriate for our specific design and sample size, we'll need to specify the correct number of DF. Looking at our one-way ANOVA output, we can see that we have 3 DF for the numerator and 36 DF for the denominator.

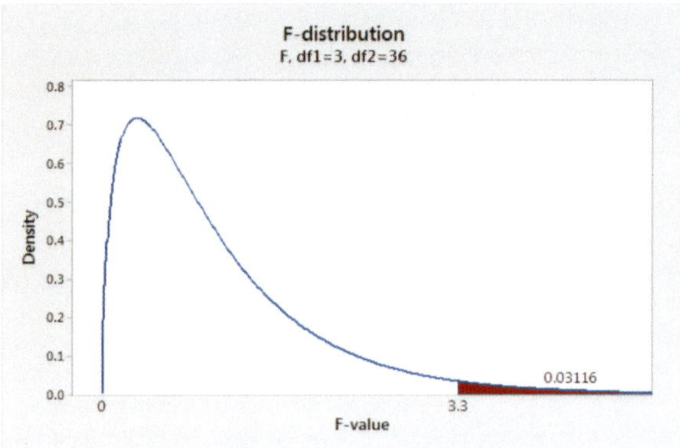

The graph displays the distribution of F-values that we'd obtain if the null hypothesis is true and we repeat our study many times. The shaded area represents the probability of observing an F-value that is at least as large as the F-value our study obtained. F-values fall within this shaded region about 3.1% of the time when the null hypothesis is true. This probability is low enough to reject the null hypothesis using the common significance level of 0.05. We can conclude that not all the group means are equal.

Assessing Means by Analyzing Variation

ANOVA uses the F-test to determine whether the variability between group means is larger than the variability of the observations within the groups. If that ratio is sufficiently large, you can conclude that not all the means are equal.

This brings us back to why we analyze variation to make judgments about means. Think about the question: "Are the group means different?" You are implicitly asking about the variability of the means. After all, if the group means *don't* vary, or don't vary by more than random chance allows, then you can't say the means are different. And that's why you use analysis of variance to test the means.

Type I and Type II Errors

Type I and Type II errors are two well-known concepts, which are related to hypothesis testing. Often engineers are confused by these two concepts simply because they have many different names. We list a few of them here.

Type I errors are also called:

1. Producer's risk
2. False alarm
3. α error

Type II errors are also called:

1. Consumer's risk
2. Misdetection
3. β error

Type I and Type II errors can be defined in terms of hypothesis testing.

- A Type I error (α) is the probability of rejecting a true null hypothesis.
- A Type II error (β) is the probability of failing to reject a false null hypothesis.

Or simply:

- A Type I error (α) is the probability of telling you things are wrong, given that things are correct.
- A Type II error (β) is the probability of telling you things are correct, given that things are wrong.

The above statements are summarized in table:

Table 1: Summary of Type I and Type II Errors

	when H0 is true	when H1 is true
Do not Reject H0	correct decision $p = 1 - \alpha$	Type II error $p = \beta$
Reject H0	Type I error $p = \alpha$	correct decision $p = 1 - \beta$

One concept related to Type II errors is "power." Power is the probability of rejecting H0 when H1 is true. The value of power is equal to 1-β. It is the power to detect the change.

Example - Application in Manufacturing

Assume an engineer is interested in controlling the diameter of a shaft. Under the normal (in control) manufacturing process, the diameter is normally distributed with mean of 10mm and standard deviation of 1mm. She records the difference between the measured value and the nominal value for each shaft. If the absolute value of the difference, $D = M - 10$ (M is the measurement), is beyond a critical value, she will check to see if the manufacturing process is out of control.

What is the probability that she will check the machine but the manufacturing process is, in fact, in control? Or, in other words, what is the probability that she will check the machine even though the process is in the normal state and the check is actually unnecessary?

Assume that there is no measurement error. Under normal manufacturing conditions, D is normally distributed with mean of 0 and standard deviation of 1. If the critical value is 1.649, the probability that the difference is beyond this value (that she will check the machine), given that the process is in control, is:

$$\Pr\left(|D| > 1.649\right) = \Pr(D > 1.649) + \Pr(D < -1.649)$$
$$= 0.049574 + 0.049574 = 0.1$$

So, the probability that she is going to check the machine but find the process is, in fact, in control is 0.1. This probability is the Type I error, which may also be called false alarm rate, α error, producer's risk, etc.

The engineer realizes that the probability of 10% is too high because checking the manufacturing process is not an easy task and is costly. She wants to reduce this number to 1% by adjusting the critical value. The new critical value is calculated as:

$$\Pr\left(|D| > \text{CriticaValue} \,|\, \text{process is in control}\right) = 0.01$$

Using the inverse normal distribution, the new critical value is 2.576. From the above equation, it can be seen that the larger the critical value, the smaller the Type I error.

By adjusting the critical line to a higher value, the Type I error is reduced. However, the engineer is now facing a new issue after the adjustment. Some customers complain that the diameters of their shafts are too big. Instead of having a mean value of 10, they have a mean value of 12, which means that the engineer didn't detect the mean shift and she needs to adjust the manufacturing process to its normal state.

What is the probability of failing to detect the mean shift under the current critical value, given that the process is indeed out of control? In this case, the mean of the diameter has shifted. The answer for this question is found by examining the Type II error.

The engineer asks a statistician for help. The statistician uses the following equation to calculate the Type II error:

$$\begin{aligned}
&\Pr\left(|D| < \text{CriticaValue} \middle| \text{Diameter Mean shift to 12}\right) \\
&= \Pr\left(|D| < \text{CriticalValue} \middle| \mu_D = 2, \sigma_D = 1\right) \\
&= \Pr(-2.576 < D < 2.576 | \mu_D = 2, \sigma_D = 1) \\
&= 0.7176
\end{aligned}$$

Here, μ_D is the mean of the difference between the measured and nominal shaft diameters and σ_D is the standard deviation. The mean value of the diameter shifting to 12 is the same as the mean of the difference changing to 2. From the above equation, we can see that the larger the critical value, the larger the Type II error.

The result tells us that there is a 71.76% probability that the engineer cannot detect the shift if the mean of the diameter has shifted to 12. This is the reason why oversized shafts have been sent to the customers, causing them to complain.

It seems that the engineer must find a balance point to reduce both Type I and Type II errors. If she increases the critical value to reduce the Type I error, the Type II error will increase. If she reduces the critical value to reduce the Type II error, the Type I error will increase. The engineer asks the statistician for additional help.

The statistician notices that the engineer makes her decision on whether the process needs to be checked after each measurement. This means the sample size for decision making is 1. The statistician suggests grouping a certain number of measurements together and making the decision based on the mean value of each group. By increasing the sample size of each group, both Type I and Type II errors will be reduced. However, a large sample size will delay the detection of a mean shift. The smallest sample size that can meet both Type I and Type II error requirements should be determined. The engineer provides her requirements to the statistician.

The engineer wants:

1. The Type I error to be 0.01.
2. The Type II error to be less than 0.1 if the mean value of the diameter shifts from 10 to 12 (i.e., if the difference shifts from 0 to 2).

Assume the sample size is n in each group. The mean value and the standard deviation of the mean value of the deviation (difference between measurement and nominal value) of each group is 0 and $1/\sqrt{n}$ under the normal manufacturing process. Based on the Type I error requirement, the critical value for the group mean can be calculated by the following equation:

$$\begin{aligned}
&\alpha = \Pr\left(|\bar{D}| > \text{CriticalValue} \middle| \mu_B = 0, \sigma_B = 1/\sqrt{n}\right) \\
&= 0.01
\end{aligned}$$

Under the abnormal manufacturing condition (assume the mean of the deviation shifts to 2 and the standard deviation is unchanged), the Type II error is:

$$\beta = \Pr\left(\left|\bar{D}\right| > \text{CriticalValue}\middle|\mu_B = 2, \sigma_B = 1/\sqrt{n}\right)$$
$$= \Pr(-\text{CriticalValue} < \bar{D} < \text{CriticalValue}|\mu_B = 2, \sigma_B = 1/\sqrt{n})$$
$$< 0.1$$

The smallest integer that satisfies the above two equations is the value of *n*.

Let's set *n* = 3 first. The critical value is 1.4872 when the sample size is 3. Using this critical value, we get the Type II error of 0.1872, which is greater than the required 0.1. So we increase the sample size to 4. The critical value becomes 1.2879. The corresponding Type II error is 0.0772, which is less than the required 0.1. Therefore, the final sample size is 4.

By using the mean value of every 4 measurements, the engineer can control the Type II error at 0.0772 and keep the Type I error at 0.01.

Sometimes, engineers are interested only in one-sided changes of their products or processes. For example, consider the case where the engineer in the previous example cares only whether the diameter is becoming larger. The hypothesis test becomes:

$$H0: \mu_D = 0$$
$$H1: \mu_D > 0$$

Assume the sample size is 1 and the Type I error is set to 0.05. The critical value will be 1.649. For detecting a shift of $\mu_D = 2$, the corresponding Type II error is $\beta = 0.3628$. The relation between the Type I and Type II errors is illustrated in figure:

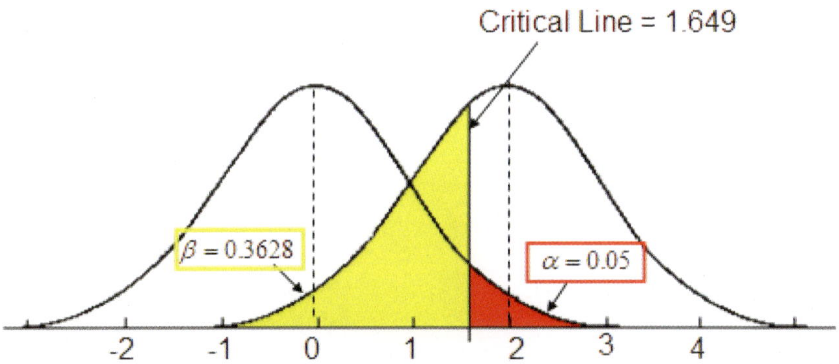

Figure: Illustration of Type I and Type II Errors

Example - Application in Reliability Engineering

Type I and Type II errors are also applied in reliability engineering. For example, in a reliability demonstration test, engineers usually choose sample size according to the Type II error.

A reliability engineer needs to demonstrate that the reliability of a product at a given time is higher than 0.9 at an 80% confidence level. She decides to perform a zero failure test. How many samples does she need to test in order to demonstrate the reliability with this test requirement?

The above problem can be expressed as a hypothesis test.

$$H0: R > R_t = 0.9$$

$$H1: R \leq R_t = 0.9$$

R_L is the lower bound of the reliability to be demonstrated. The engineer must determine the minimum sample size such that the probability of observing zero failures given that the product has at least a 0.9 reliability is less than 20%. In other words, the sample size is determined by controlling the Type II error. The percentage of time that no more than *f* failures are expected during a pass-fail test is described by the cumulative binomial equation:

$$\beta = 1 - CL \geq \sum_{i=0}^{f} \frac{n!}{i!(n-i)!}(1-R_L)^i R_L^{n-i}$$

or

$$0.2 \geq 0.9^n$$

The smallest integer that *n* can satisfy the above equation is the sample size.

Figure shows Weibull++'s test design folio, which demonstrates that the reliability is at least as high as the number entered in the required inputs. From this analysis, we can see that the engineer needs to test 16 samples.

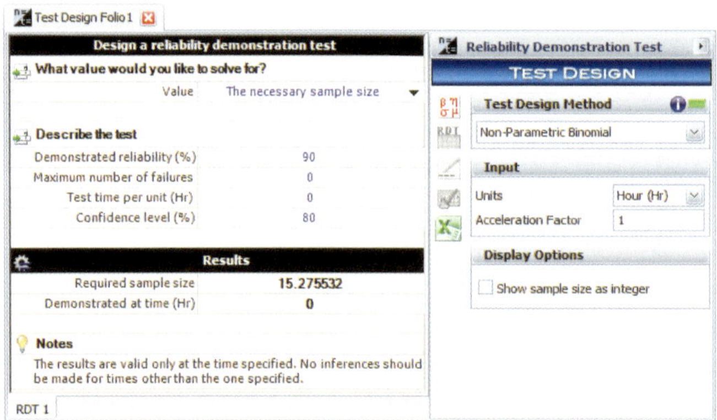

Figure: Determining Sample Size for Reliability Demonstration Testing

One might wonder what the Type I error would be if 16 samples were tested with a 0 failure requirement. In order to know this, the reliability value of this product should be known. Assume the engineer knows without doubt that the product reliability is 0.95. What is the Type I error if she uses the test plan given above? In other words, given a sample size of 16 units, each with a reliability of 95%, how often will one or more failures occur?

Using a sample size of 16 and the critical failure number of 0, the Type I error can be calculated as:

$$\alpha = 1 - \sum_{i=0}^{f} \frac{n!}{i!(n-i)!}(1-R)^i R^{n-i}$$

$$= 1 - 0.95^{16}$$

$$= 0.5599$$

Therefore, if the true reliability is 0.95, the probability of not passing the demonstration testing is 0.5599. In this case, the test plan is too strict and the producer might want to adjust the number of units to test to reduce the Type I error.

In conclusion a Type II error is very useful in sample size determination. In fact, power and sample size are important topics in statistics and are used widely in our daily lives. For example, these concepts can help a pharmaceutical company determine how many samples are necessary in order to prove that a medicine is useful at a given confidence level. So the next time a doctor tells you the effectiveness of a medicine is 99.9%, it is wise to ask how many patients were treated in the experiment and what the confidence level was.

Type III Error

A type III error is where you correctly reject the null hypothesis, but it's rejected for the wrong reason. This compares to a Type I error (incorrectly rejecting the null hypothesis) and a Type II error (not rejecting the null when you should). Type III errors are not considered serious, as they do mean you arrive at the correct decision. They usually happen because of random chance and are a rare occurrence.

You can also think of a Type III error as giving the right answer (i.e. correctly rejecting the null) to the wrong question. Either way, you're still arriving at the correct conclusion for the wrong reason. When we say the "wrong question", that normally means you've formulated your hypotheses incorrectly. In other words, both your null and alternate hypotheses may be poorly worded or completely incorrect.

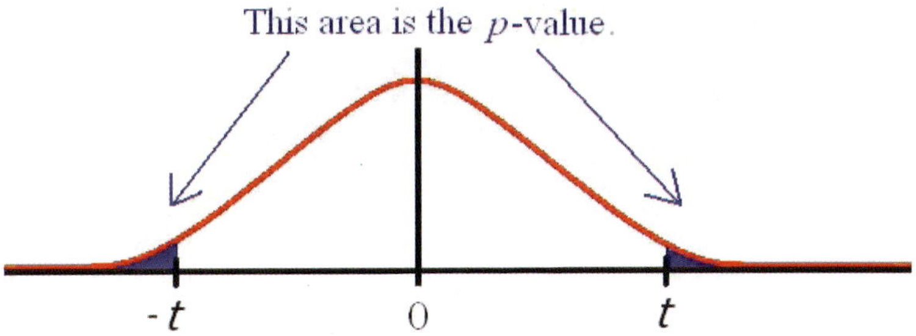

A two-tailed t-distribution.

Type III errors can generally be avoided by running a two-tailed test instead of a one-tailed test. A one-tailed test has a higher power if your hypothesized direction is correct. However, if your direction is wrong, the one-tailed test will return the probability of a Type III error (only you won't realize this!). For example, let's say you hypothesize that there is a difference between the means of two samples, and that the mean difference is lower. You test this theory by running a left-tailed test. The test returns a small p-value and you (correctly) reject the null hypothesis that the means are the same. However, unknown to you, the means *are* different: it's just that one set is *higher* (i.e. you should have run a right-tailed test), not lower.

Type III errors aren't limited to differences between means. The can happen in every type of statistical test (e.g., correlations, proportions, variances etc.).

Closed Testing Procedure

The closed test procedure introduced by Marcus, Peritz and Gabriel (1976) is one of the most general and efficient test procedures to control the experiment wise or multiple type I error rate when multiple hypotheses have to be tested.

The procedure is based on a set of hypotheses which is closed under intersection. This set can be ordered in a hierarchy of hypotheses with the elementary hypotheses at the bottom and global hypothesis at the top and in which every hypothesis is a subset of a hypothesis one level below. Using this hierarchy the closed test procedure is able to control the multiple a-level in an efficient way.

The Problem of Multiple Testing

The approach of testing simultaneously several hypotheses differs slightly from the concept of dealing with only one single hypothesis. Let us remember: A main idea of hypothesis testing is that every level α test for a single hypothesis controls the type I error rate in the sense that under the assumption that the null hypothesis is true the probability of rejecting it is less or equal α. Historically there has been a strong feeling that we need a similar concept also for handling multiple hypotheses and that simply applying individual tests at a given ('local') level a is not a good approach because then - under the assumption that all null hypotheses arc simultaneously true - the probability of falsely rejecting one of them would exceed the given level α. Especially, if all tests are independent the probability would be $1-(1-\alpha)^k$ where k is the number of hypotheses. One early solution for overcoming this problem has been the Bonferroni adjustment. That means that for testing k hypotheses the single tests should be performed at the level α / k. Another approach is Fisher's LSD test where the global (null-) hypothesis $H_{01} \cap ... \cap H_{0k}$ is tested at level α before and the single tests at level α are only performed if the global hypothesis could be rejected. This leads to the following definition of controlling the type I error rate in a multiple setup:

- A multiple test procedure is said to keep the global level α if the probability of rejecting at least one true null hypothesis is not larger than a when all null hypotheses are simultaneously true.
- It is clear that both the Bonferroni procedure and Fishers LSD test keep the global level. But problems still arise if only a subset of the set of null hypotheses is true. While false null should be rejected, any of the true null hypothesis should only be rejected with probability α. Then, the same argumentation as above restricted to this subset yields
- A multiple test procedure is said to keep the multiple level α if the probability of rejecting at least one true null hypothesis is not larger than α, independently of which subset of the set of null hypotheses actually is true.
- Note that by definition the global level is kept, too, if the multiple level is kept. It is also clear that the multiple level is the more adequate concept for transcripting the approach of significance tests to multiple hypotheses~ The Bonferroni procedure keeps the multiple level while Fisher's LSD test does not.

Some Examples

Main examples where multiple testing problems arise are problems comparing different groups within linear models. Let us assume the following one way design

$$X_{ij} = a_i + \varepsilon_{ij}, i = 1,\ldots,k, j = 1,\ldots,n_i$$

where ε_{ij} are independent, $N(0,\sigma^2)$ distributed random variables and $a_1,\ldots,a_k$ represent the different groups to be compared, i.e. the expectation of X within these groups. Then, one of the interesting problem is the pairwise problem, i.e. the problem of comparing each group with each other:

$$H_0^{ij} : a_i = a_j \text{ versus } H_0^{ij} : a_i \neq a_j, i, j = 1,\ldots,k$$

Let $X_j.$ be the mean of X in the i-th group, S^2 the usual estimate of the variance and v = k(k-1)/2. Then, general procedures for this problem are:

- Bonferroni
- Bonferroni, Holms .

Special procedures for pairwise comparison in linear models are, e.g.:

- Tukey
- Hochberg
- Tukey-Kramer
- Multiple stage tests

The Bonferroni procedure uses for testing the level α / v instead of α as mentioned above.

The Bonferroni-Holms procedure (Holms, 1979) is a further development of Bonferroni. It uses for testing the hypothesis with the I-largest p-value the level $\alpha / (v - I + 1)$. It starts with that hypothesis with the smallest· p:'value in ascending order and stops if for the first time the pvalue exceeds the given level.· Then, only those hypotheses already tested are rejected.

The Tukey test (Tukey, 1953) for equal sample sizes assumes that all $X_i.$ are iid. Then, the main idea is the following equivalence

$$\max_{1 \le i\, j \le k} |X_{i.} - X_{J.}| \le C_\alpha \Leftrightarrow \max_i X_i - \min_i X_i \le c_\alpha$$

With an appropriate standardization $s / \sqrt{n}$ the distribution of $\max_i x_i. - \min_i x_i$ is the studentized range distribution and, hence, tabulated. Thus, we get a test of the form

$$\Rightarrow \theta_{ij} = 1 \text{ if } \frac{|X_{i.} - X_{j.}|}{s / \sqrt{n}} \le q_{k,v,\alpha}$$

$$= 0 \text{ if } \frac{|X_{i.} - X_{j.}|}{s / \sqrt{n}} > q_{k,v,\alpha}$$

Variations of the Tukey test for unequal sample sizes are the GT2 (Hochberg) test (Hochberg, 1974), based on the Sidak inequality and the maximum modulus distribution, and the Tukey Kramer test (Kramer, 1956) which is similar to the Tukey test but uses another standardization according to the unequal sample sizes.

Finally, Multiple stage procedures look tirst at the homogeneity of all k means at level a α_k and, in the case of rejection, all subsets, i.e. all hypotheses comparing k-l means, are tested at level a α_{k-1} and so on. If on any stage one test for a set of means is not significant, all hypotheses corresponding to any subset of this set is considered also not to differ significantly and none of these subsets are tested. The different tests now differ in the levels $\alpha_1, \ldots, \alpha_k$ and in the test statistics used.

The test of Newman-Keuls uses a studentized range statistic and $\alpha_p \equiv \alpha$. But this procedure do not control the multiple level α. (An easy example to see this is: Assume live very different groups each consisting of two equal means, then, the probability of one false rejection is $\approx 1-(1-\alpha)^5$.)

The test of Ryan, Einot, Gabriel and Welsch uses a range- or F-test and the adjusted levels $\alpha_p = 1-(1-\alpha)^{p/k}$ if p < k-1 and $\alpha_p = \alpha$ if $p \geq k-1$.

With the exception of the test of Newman-Keuls all mentioned procedures keep the multiple level.

For the following discussion of the closed test procedure we use the pairwise problem for the one way design with k=4 groups. Using the notation (1,2) for the hypothesis $H_0^{12} = \{a_1 = a_2\}$ etc, the pairwise problem discussed above can be written as a set of different elementary hypotheses:

$$\{ (1,2), (1,3), (1,4), (2,3), (2,4), (3,4) \}.$$

Based on this set of elementary hypotheses a set that is closed under intersection may be constructed. The resulting closed set of hypotheses then includes the following single hypotheses

$$\{ (1,2,3,4),$$
$$(1,2,3),\ (1,2,4),\ (2,3,4),\ (1,2/3,4),\ (1,3/2,4),\ (1,4/2,3),$$
$$(1,2),\ (1,3),\ (1,4),\ (2,3),\ (2,4),\ (3,4) \}$$

where e.g. (1,2,4) denote the hypothesis $H_0^{12} \cap H_0^{14} = \{a_1 = a_2 = a_4\}$ and (1,2/3,4) $H_0^{12} \cap H_0^{34} = \{a_1 = a_2, = a_3 = a_4\}$.

In the closed test procedure every single hypothesis of this set is tested at level a using a suitable test. An elementary hypothesis is only rejected if its test is significant and the tests of all single hypotheses which are subsets of it. For example the hypothesis (3,4) is only rejected if all the tests. for the hypotheses (1,2,3,4), (1,2,4), (2,3,4), (1,2/3,4) and (3,4) are significant.

Let's assume that a single hypothesis is 'true'. The Closed Test procedure keeps the multiple level a, since every elementary hypothesis which is a superset of this 'true' hypothesis can only be rejected if the test of this 'true' hypothesis is significant.

A simple way to perform the closed test procedure is to build up a hierarchy within the set of single hypotheses where tests are connected which are direct sub- and supersets of each other:

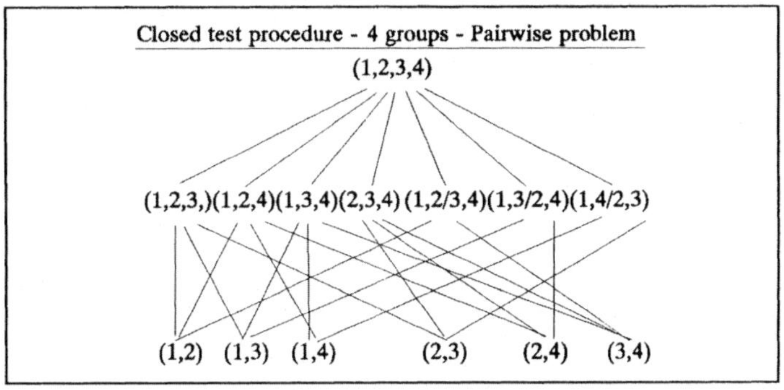

Then, the closed test procedure for this test problem can be performed in the following way: For every single hypothesis choose a suitable a-level test. The single hypotheses are tested in the order of the hierarchy starting with the hypothesis on the highest level. A single hypothesis will only be tested if all its supersets one level above are significant. Otherwise it will be not be tested and regarded as nonsignificant.

The Closed Test procedure has some special features:

- One can combine different a-level tests for testing the single hypotheses. The choice of those tests has an influence on the efficiency of the closed test procedure but not on keeping the type I error level. In a parametric setup like above, F-tests for linear hypotheses or contrasts could be used (with a nearly arbitrary model design like in Proc GLM of SAS) or non-parametric procedures like the Kruskal-Wallis test or Jonckheere's test could be applied.
- The principle of the closed test procedure does not depend on a special testing problem. It only assumes a closed set of hypotheses and uses the natural order therein.

Further examples are the neighborhood (trend) problem where only those groups side by side are compared. It is defined by the set of elementary hypotheses

{ (1,2), (2,3), (3,4) }.

Another example is the One to many problem, i.e. the comparison of one special group with all other, with the elementary hypotheses

{ (1,2), (1,3), (1,4) }.

The corresponding closed sets of hypotheses are:

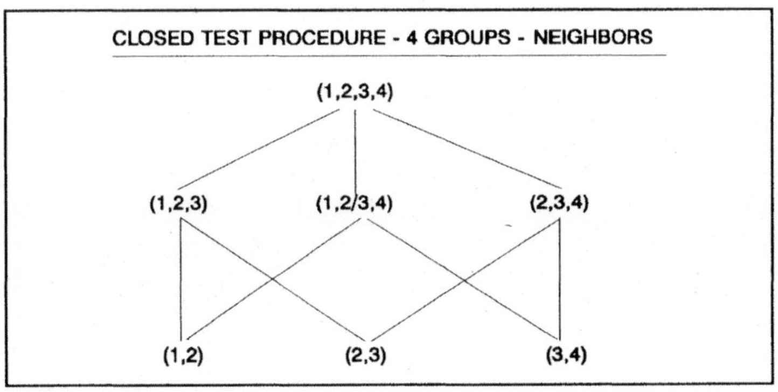

and

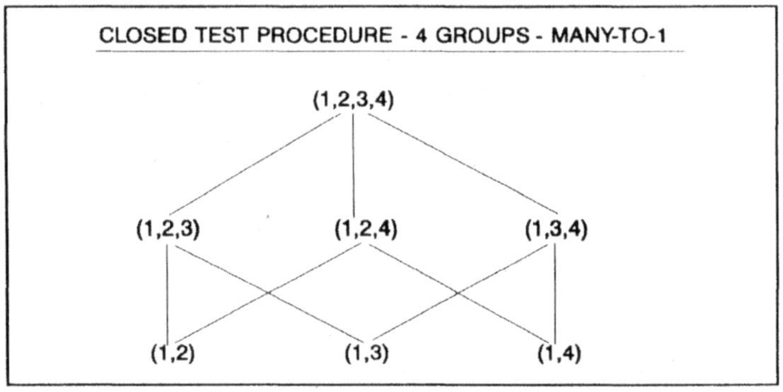

Again, known efficient procedures can be used for testing the single hypotheses within the closed test procedure.

Importance of Hypothesis in Business

Much of running a small business is a gamble, buoyed by boldness, intuition and guts. But wise business leaders also conduct formal and informal research to inform their business decisions. Good research starts with a good hypothesis, which is simply a statement making a prediction based on a set of observations. For example, if you're considering offering flexible work hours to your employees, you might hypothesize that this policy change will positively affect their productivity and contribute to your bottom line. The ultimate job of the hypothesis in business is to serve as a guidepost to your testing and research methods.

Essentially good hypotheses lead decision-makers like you to new and better ways to achieve your business goals. When you need to make decisions such as how much you should spend on advertising or what effect a price increase will have your customer base, it's easy to make wild assumptions or get lost in analysis paralysis. A business hypothesis solves this problem, because, at the start, it's based on some foundational information. In all of science, hypotheses are grounded in theory. Theory tells you what you can generally expect from a certain line of inquiry.

A hypothesis based on years of business research in a particular area, then, helps you focus, define and appropriately direct your research. You won't go on a wild goose chase to prove or disprove it. A hypothesis predicts the relationship between two variables. If you want to study pricing and customer loyalty, you won't waste your time and resources studying tangential areas.

Marketing Support

One of the most important hypotheses you'll make in growing your small business is the cost of acquiring a customer. Your viability as a business is founded on ensuring that your customers bring you more money than it costs you to get them in the door. Hypothesizing this number informs not only your pricing strategy but also your marketing efforts and the rest of your overhead expenses. You can also make predictions about the lifetime value of each customer to determine how much marketing you need to do. Businesses frequently attempt to guesstimate how long a customer will stick around and how much sales to each one will contribute to your profit.

In real life, hypotheses are honed and perfected over time through refining of your basic questions, assumptions and research methods. In addition, you may have more than one hypothesis to explain your observations, such as why your product failed or why morale is sinking in the office.

Hypothesize

To form a good hypothesis, you should ensure certain criteria are met when making your prediction statements. The hypothesis must be testable as a start. Don't make the mistake of trying to prove a tautology, or a hypothesis that is always true. For example, "Our social media strategy will succeed if it's social or it will fail." In addition, your hypothesis should be based on the most up-to-date research and knowledge on the subject matter.

Test It

The most important part of having a hypothesis is determining whether it's supported by the facts. The scope and formality of your research depend on your research and may simply involve examining the literature, polling your stakeholders or researching other areas. For example, in determining whether to locate your business in a pricey downtown or an exurb with no public transportation, you may look at commuting statistics of your general metropolitan area, the prevalence of carpooling, the socioeconomic status of most of your employees, as well as where your competitors are located.

References

- Everitt, Brian (1998). The Cambridge Dictionary of Statistics. Cambridge, UK New York: Cambridge University Press. ISBN 0521593468
- Using-hypothesis-testing-business, business-insights: quickbooks.intuit.com, Retrieved 29 March 2018
- Hurlbert, S. H.; Lombardi, C. M. (2009). "Final collapse of the Neyman-Pearson decision theoretic framework and rise of the neoFisherian". Ann. Zool. Fennici. 46: 311–349. doi:10.5735/086.046.0501. ISSN 1797-2450
- Business-ideas-null-hypothesis-1399: entrepreneurshipinabox.com, Retrieved 25 June 2018
- Aldrich, John. "Earliest Known Uses of Some of the Words of Probability & Statistics". Retrieved 30 June 2014. Last update 12 march 2003. From Jeff Miller
- Understanding-analysis-of-variance-anova-and-the-f-test, adventures-in-statistics-2: minitab.com, Retrieved 21 May 2018
- Burnham, K. P.; Anderson, D. R. (2002), Model Selection and Multimodel Inference: A Practical Information-Theoretic Approach (2nd ed.), Springer-Verlag, ISBN 0-387-95364-7
- Hypothesis-important-business-34382: smallbusiness.chron.com, Retrieved 29 April 2018
- Lehmann, E. L. (December 1993). "The Fisher, Neyman-Pearson Theories of Testing Hypotheses: One Theory or Two?". Journal of the American Statistical Association. 88(424): 1242–1249. doi:10.1080/01621459.1993.10476404
- Type-iii-error-in-statistical-tests: statisticshowto.com, Retrieved 31 April 2018

5

Econometrics

Econometrics is a branch of economics that applies statistical methods to economic data and ascribes empirical content to economic relations. All the diverse principles of econometrics have been carefully analyzed in this chapter, such as econometric model, endogeneity and panel data, for a comprehensive understanding of the subject.

Econometrics is the analysis and testing of economic theories to verify hypotheses and improve prediction of financial trends. Econometrics takes mathematical and statistical models proposed in economic theory and tests them. First, models are tested against statistical trials, followed by testing against real-world examples to support or disprove hypotheses.

Econometrics uses an important statistical method called regression analysis, which assesses the connection among variables. Economists use the regression method since they cannot usually carry out controlled experiments, choosing to instead gather information from natural experiments. The method typically includes the following steps:

1. Subject data is examined to attempt to understand the data set. In that examination, theories and hypotheses are formed as to why the data manifests the way it does to explain the variables being analyzed.
2. Models and statistical tools for testing the hypothesis are selected. The relationships between this step, the explanatory variable and the dependent variable are summarized.
3. Data is input into economic software and the selected statistical models are applied to estimate results from the supplied data.
4. Results are collected and portions are analyzed to obtain economic predictions. If the results are as expected, the hypothesis is generally considered validated. Otherwise, new hypotheses need to be found.

Real world applications of econometrics include the study of the income effect, defined as the change in demand for a product or service resulting from a change in income.

Probability Approach to Econometrics

The unifying methodology of modern econometrics was articulated by Trygve Haavelmo (1911-1999) of Norway, winner of the 1989 Nobel Memorial Prize in Economic Sciences, in his seminalpaper "The probability approach in econometrics" (1944). Haavelmo argued that quantitative economic models must necessarily be probability models (by which today we would mean stochastic). Deterministic models are blatently inconsistent with observed economic quantities, and it is incoherent to apply deterministic models to non-deterministic data. Economic models should be explicitly designed to incorporate randomness; stochastic errors should not be simply added to deterministic models to make them random. Once we acknowledge that an economic model is a probability model, it follows naturally that an appropriate tool way to quantify, estimate, and conduct inferences about the economy is through the powerful theory of mathematical statistics. The appropriate method for a quantitative economic analysis follows from the probabilistic construction of the economic model.

Haavelmo's probability approach was quickly embraced by the economics profession. Today no quantitative work in economics shuns its fundamental vision.

While all economists embrace the probability approach, there has been some evolution in its implementation.

The structural approach is the closest to Haavelmo's original idea. A probabilistic economic model is specified, and the quantitative analysis performed under the assumption that the economic model is correctly specified. Researchers often describe this as "taking their model seriously." The structural approach typically leads to likelihood-based analysis, including maximum likelihood and Bayesian estimation.

A criticism of the structural approach is that it is misleading to treat an economic model as correctly specified. Rather, it is more accurate to view a model as a useful abstraction or approximation. In this case, how should we interpret structural econometric analysis? The quasistructural approach to inference views a structural economic model as an approximation rather than the truth. This theory has led to the concepts of the pseudo-true value (the parameter value defined by the estimation problem), the quasi-likelihood function, quasi-MLE, and quasi-likelihood inference.

Closely related is the semiparametric approach. A probabilistic economic model is partially specified but some features are left unspecified. This approach typically leads to estimation methods such as least-squares and the Generalized Method of Moments. The semiparametric approach dominates contemporary econometrics, and is the main focus of this textbook.

Another branch of quantitative structural economics is the calibration approach. Similar to the quasi-structural approach, the calibration approach interprets structural models as approximations and hence inherently false. The difference is that the calibrationist literature rejects mathematical statistics (deeming classical theory as inappropriate for approximate models) and instead selects parameters by matching model and data moments using non-statistical ad hoc methods.

In a typical application, an econometrician has a set of repeated measurements on a set of variables. For example, in a labor application the variables could include weekly earnings, educational attainment, age, and other descriptive characteristics. We call this information the data, dataset, or sample.

We use the term observations to refer to the distinct repeated measurements on the variables. An individual observation often corresponds to a specific economic unit, such as a person, household, corporation, firm, organization, country, state, city or other geographical region. An individual observation could also be a measurement at a point in time, such as quarterly GDP or a daily interest rate.

Economists typically denote variables by the italicized roman characters y, x and/or z. The convention in econometrics is to use the character y to denote the variable to be explained, while the characters x and z are used to denote the conditioning (explaining) variables.

Following mathematical convention, real numbers (elements of the real line $\mathbb{R}$, also called scalars) are written using lower case italics such as y, and vectors (elements of R^k) by lower case bold italics such as x, e.g.

$$x = \begin{pmatrix} x_1 \\ x_2 \\ . \\ . \\ . \\ x_k \end{pmatrix}$$

Upper case bold italics such as X are used for matrices.

We denote the number of observations by the natural number n and subscript the variables by the index *i* to denote the individual observation, e.g. y_i, x_i and z_i. In some contexts we use indices other than i, such as in time-series applications where the index *t* is common and T is used to denote the number of observations. In panel studies we typically use the double index *t* to refer to individual *i* at a time period *t*.

The ith observation is the set (y_i x_i z_i). The sample is the set $\{(y_i, x_i, z_i) : i = 1,....,n\}$.

It is proper mathematical practice to use upper case X for random variables and lower case x for realizations or specific values. Since we use upper case to denote matrices, the distinction between random variables and their realizations is not rigorously followed in econometric notation. Thus the notation y_i will in some places refer to a random variable, and in other places a specific realization. This is undesirable but there is little to be done about it without terrifically complicating the notation. Hopefully there will be no confusion as the use should be evident from the context.

We typically use Greek letters such as β, θ and σ^2 to denote unknown parameters of an econometric model, and will use boldface, e.g. β or θ , when these are vector-valued. Estimates are typically denoted by putting a hat "^", tilde "~" or bar "-" over the corresponding letter, e.g. $\hat{\beta}$ and $\tilde{\beta}$ are estimates of β.

The covariance matrix of an econometric estimator will typically be written using the capital boldface V, often with a subscript to denote the estimator, e.g. $V_{\hat{\beta}} = \text{var}\left(\hat{\beta}\right)$ as the covariance matrix for $\hat{\beta}$.Hopefully without causing confusion, we will use the notation $V_{\hat{\beta}} = \text{avar}\left(\hat{\beta}\right)$ to denote the asymptotic covariance matrix of $\sqrt{n}\left(\hat{\beta}-\beta\right)$ (the variance of the asymptotic distribution). Estimates will be denoted by appending hats or tildes, e.g. $V_{\hat{\beta}}$ is an estimate of $V_{\hat{\beta}}$.

Econometric Model

A model is a simplified representation of a real world process. It should be representative in the sense that it should contain the salient features of the phenomena under study. In general, one of the objectives in modeling is to have a simple model to explain a complex phenomenon. Such an objective may sometimes lead to oversimplified model and sometimes the assumptions made are unrealistic. In practice, generally all the variables which the experimenter thinks are relevant to explain the phenomenon are included in the model. Rest of the variables are dumped in a basket called "disturbances" where the disturbances are random variables. This is the main difference between the economic modeling and econometric modeling. This is also the main difference between the mathematical modeling and statistical modeling. The mathematical modeling is exact in nature whereas the statistical modeling contains a stochastic term also.

An economic model is a set of assumptions that describes the behaviour of an economy, or more general, a phenomenon.

An econometric model consists of

- a set of equations describing the behaviour. These equations are derived from the economic model and have two parts – observed variables and disturbances.
- a statement about the errors in the observed values of variables.
- a specification of the probability distribution of disturbances.

Aims of Econometrics

The three main aims econometrics are as follows:

1. Formulation and Specification of Econometric Models

The economic models are formulated in an empirically testable form. Several econometric models can be derived from an economic model. Such models differ due to different choice of functional form, specification of stochastic structure of the variables etc.

2. Estimation and Testing of Models

The models are estimated on the basis of observed set of data and are tested for their suitability. This is the part of statistical inference of the modeling. Various estimation procedures are used to know the numerical values of the unknown parameters of the model. Based on various formulations of statistical models, a suitable and appropriate model is selected.

3. Use of Models

The obtained models are used for forecasting and policy formulation which is an essential part in any policy decision. Such forecasts help the policy makers to judge the goodness of fitted model and take necessary measures in order to re-adjust the relevant economic variables.

Econometrics and Statistics

Econometrics differs both from mathematical statistics and economic statistics. In economic statistics, the empirical data is collected recorded, tabulated and used in describing the pattern in their development over time. The economic statistics is a descriptive aspect of economics. It does not provide either the explanations of the development of various variables or measurement of the parameters of the relationships. Statistical methods describe the methods of measurement which are developed on the basis of controlled experiments. Such methods may not be suitable for economic phenomenon as they don't fit in the framework of controlled experiments. For example, in real world experiments, the variables usually change continuously and simultaneously and so the setup of controlled experiments are not suitable.

Econometrics uses statistical methods after adapting them to the problems of economic life. These adopted statistical methods are usually termed as econometric methods. Such methods are adjusted so that they become appropriate for the measurement of stochastic relationships. These adjustments basically attempts to specify attempts to the stochastic element which operate in real world data and enters into the determination of observed data. This enables the data to be called as random sample which is needed for the application of statistical tools.

The theoretical econometrics includes the development of appropriate methods for the measurement of economic relationships which are not meant for controlled experiments conducted inside the laboratories. The econometric methods are generally developed for the analysis of non-experimental data.

The applied econometrics includes the application of econometric methods to specific branches of econometric theory and problems like demand, supply, production, investment, consumption etc. The applied econometrics involves the application of the tools of econometric theory for the analysis of economic phenomenon and forecasting the economic behaviour.

Aggregation Problem

The aggregation problems arise when aggregative variables are used in functions. Such aggregative variables may involve:

- Aggregation over individuals

  For example the total income may comprise the sum of individual incomes.

- Aggregation over commodities

  The quantity of various commodities may be aggregated over e.g., price or group of commodities. This is done by using suitable index.

- Aggregation over time periods

  Sometimes the data is available for shorter or longer time periods than required to be used in the functional form of economic relationship. In such cases, the data needs to be aggregated over time period. For example, the production of most of the manufacturing commodities is completed in a period shorter than a year. If annual figures are to be used in the model then there may be some error in the production function.

- Spatial aggregation

  Sometimes the aggregation is related to spatial issues. For example, the population of towns, countries, or the production in a city or region etc.

  Such sources of aggregation introduces "aggregation bias" in the estimates of the coefficients. It is important to examine the possibility of such errors before estimating the model.

Econometrics and Regression Analysis

One of the very important role of econometrics is to provide the tools for modeling on the basis of given data. The regression modeling technique helps a lot in this task. The regression models can be either linear or non-linear based on which we have linear regression analysis and non-linear regression analysis. We will consider only the tools of linear regression analysis and our main interest will be the fitting of linear regression model to a given set of data.

Linear Regression Model

Suppose the outcome of any process is denoted by a random variable y , called as dependent (or study) variable, depends on k independent (or explanatory) variables denoted by $X_1, X_2, \ldots, X_K$. Suppose the behaviour of y can be explained by a relationship given by

$$Y = f(X_1, X_2, \ldots, X_K, \beta_1, \beta_2, \ldots, \beta_K) + \varepsilon$$

where *f* is some well defined function and $\beta_1, \beta_2, \ldots, \beta_K$ are the parameters which characterize the role and contribution of $X_1, X_2, \ldots, X_K$, respectively. The term ε reflects the stochastic nature of the relationship between y and $X_1, X_2, \ldots, X_K$, and indicates that such a relationship is not exact in nature. When $\varepsilon = 0$, then the relationship is called the mathematical model otherwise the statistical model. The term "model" is broadly used to represent any phenomenon in a mathematical frame work.

A model or relationship is termed as linear if it is linear in parameters and nonlinear, if it is not linear in parameters. In other words, if all the partial derivatives of y with respect to each of the parameters $\beta_1, \beta_2, \ldots, \beta_K$ are independent of the parameters, then the model is called as a linear model. If any of the partial derivatives of y with respect to any of the $\beta_1, \beta_2, \ldots, \beta_K$ is not independent of the parameters, the model is called as nonlinear. Note that the linearity or non-linearity of the model is not described by the linearity or nonlinearity of explanatory variables in the model.

For example

$$y = \beta_1 X_1^2 + \beta_2 \sqrt{X_2} + \beta_3 \log X_3 + \varepsilon$$

is a linear model because $\partial y / \partial \beta_i, (i = 1, 2, 3)$ are independent of the parameters $\beta_i, (i = 1, 2, 3)$. On the other hand,

$$y = \beta_1^2 X_1 + \beta_2 X_2 + \beta_3 \log X + \varepsilon$$

is a nonlinear model because $\partial y / \partial \beta_1 = 2\beta_1 X_1$ depends on β_1 although $\partial_y / \partial \beta_2$ and $\partial_y / \partial \beta_3$ are independent of any of the β_1, β_2 or β_3.

When the function f is linear in parameters, then $y = f(X_1, X_2, \ldots, X_K, \beta_1, \beta_2, \ldots, \beta_K) + \varepsilon$ is called a linear model and when the function f is nonlinear in parameters, then it is called a nonlinear model. In general, the function f is chosen as

$$f(X_1, X_2, \ldots, X_K, \beta_1, \beta_2, \ldots, \beta_K) = \beta_1 X_1 + \beta_2 X_2 + \ldots + \beta_k X_k$$

to describe a linear model. Since $X_1, X_2, ..., X_K$ are pre-determined variables and y is the outcome, so both are known. Thus the knowledge of the model depends on the knowledge of the parameters $\beta_1, \beta_2, ..., \beta_K$.

The statistical linear modeling essentially consists of developing approaches and tools to determine $\beta_1, \beta_2, ..., \beta_K$ in the linear model

$$y = \beta_1 X_1 + \beta_2 X_2 + ... + \beta_k X_K + \varepsilon$$

given the observations on y and $X_1, X_2, ..., X_K$.

Different statistical estimation procedures, e.g., method of maximum likelihood, principle of least squares, method of moments etc. can be employed to estimate the parameters of the model. The method of maximum likelihood needs further knowledge of the distribution of y whereas the method of moments and the principle of least squares do not need any knowledge about the distribution of y.

The regression analysis is a tool to determine the values of the parameters given the data on y and $X_1, X_2, ..., X_K$. The literal meaning of regression is "to move in the backward direction". Before discussing and understanding the meaning of "backward direction", let us find which of the following statements is correct:

S1: model generates data or

S2 : data generates model.

Obviously, S1 is correct. It can be broadly thought that the model exists in nature but is unknown to the experimenter. When some values to the explanatory variables are provided, then the values for the output or study variable are generated accordingly, depending on the form of the function f and the nature of phenomenon. So ideally, the pre-existing model gives rise to the data. Our objective is to determine the functional form of this model. Now we move in the backward direction. We propose to first collect the data on study and explanatory variables. Then we employ some statistical techniques and use this data to know the form of function f . Equivalently, the data from the model is recorded first and then used to determine the parameters of the model. The regression analysis is a technique which helps in determining the statistical model by using the data on study and explanatory variables. The classification of linear and nonlinear regression analysis is based on the determination of linear and nonlinear models, respectively.

Consider a simple example to understand the meaning of "regression". Suppose the yield of crop (y) depends linearly on two explanatory variables, viz., the quantity of a fertilizer X_1 and level of irrigation X_2 as

$$y = \beta_1 X_1 + \beta_2 X_2 + \varepsilon$$

There exist the true values of β_1 and β_2 in nature but are unknown to the experimenter. Some values on y are recorded by providing different values to X_1 and X_2 . There exists some relationship between y and X_1, X_2, which gives rise to a systematically behaved data on y , X_1 and X_2 . Such relationship is unknown to the experimenter. To determine the model, we move in the backward direction in the sense that the collected data is used to determine the unknown parameters β_1 and β_2 of the model. In this sense such an approach is termed as regression analysis.

The theory and fundamentals of linear models lay the foundation for developing the tools for regression analysis that are based on valid statistical theory and concepts.

Statement of the Problem Under Consideration

The first important step in conducting any regression analysis is to specify the problem and the objectives to be addressed by the regression analysis. The wrong formulation or the wrong understanding of the problem will give the wrong statistical inferences. The choice of variables depends upon the objectives of study and understanding of the problem. For example, height and weight of children are related. Now there can be two issues to be addressed:

(i) Determination of height for given weight, or

(ii) determination of weight for given height.

In this case, the height is response variable whereas weight is response variable in case 2. The role of explanatory variables are also interchanged in the cases 1 and 2.

Choice of Relevant Variables

Once the problem is carefully formulated and objectives have been decided, the next question is to choose the relevant variables. It has to kept in mind that the correct choice of variables will determine the statistical inferences correctly. For example, in any agricultural experiment, the yield depends on explanatory variables like quantity of fertilizer, rainfall, irrigation, temperature etc. These variables are denoted by $X_1, X_2, ..., X_K$ as a set of k explanatory variables.

Collection of Data on Relevant Variables

Once the objective of study is clearly stated and the variables are chosen, the next question arises is to collect data on such relevant variables. The data is essentially the measurement on these variables. For example, suppose we want to collect the data on age. For this, it is important to know how to record the data on age. Then either the date of birth can be recorded which will provide the exact age on any specific date or the age in terms of completed years as on specific date can be recorded. Moreover, it is also important to decide that whether the data has to be collected on variables as quantitative variables or qualitative variables. For example, if the ages (in years) are 15, 17,19,21,23, then these are quantitative values. If the ages are defined by a variable that takes value 1 if ages are less than 18 years and 0 if the ages are more than 18 years, then the earlier recorded data is converted to 1,1,0,0,0. Note that there is a loss of information in converting the quantitative data into qualitative data. The methods and approaches for qualitative and quantitative data are also different. If the study variable is binary, then logistic and probit regressions etc. are used. If all explanatory variables are qualitative, then analysis of variance technique is used. If some explanatory variables are qualitative and others are quantitative, then analysis of covariance technique is used. The techniques of analysis of variance and analysis of covariance are the special cases of regression analysis.

Generally, the data is collected on n subjects, then y on data, then y denotes the response or study variable and 1 2 , ,..., n yy y are the n values. If there are k explanatory variables $X_1, X_2, ..., X_K$ then x_{ij} denotes the ith value of jth variable $i = 1, 2, ..., n; j = 1, 2, ..., k$. The observation can be presented in the following table:

Notation for the data used in regression analysis

Observation number	Response y	Explanatory variables			
		X_1	X_2	$\cdots$	X_k
1	y_1	x_{11}	x_{12}	$\cdots$	x_{1k}
2	y_2	x_{21}	x_{22}	$\cdots$	x_{2k}
3	y_3	x_{31}	x_{32}	$\cdots$	x_{3k}
$\vdots$	$\vdots$	$\vdots$	$\vdots$	$\ddots$	$\vdots$
n	y_n	x_{n1}	x_{n2}	$\cdots$	x_{nk}

Specification of Model

The experimenter or the person working in the subject usually help in determining the form of the model. Only the form of the tentative model can be ascertained and it will depend on some unknown parameters. For example, a general form will be like

$$y = f(X_1, X_2, ..., X_k; \beta_1, \beta_2, ..., \beta_K) + \varepsilon$$

where ε is the random error reflecting mainly the difference in the observed value of y and the value of y obtained through the model. The form of $f(X_1, X_2, ..., X_k; \beta_1, \beta_2, ..., \beta_K)$ can be linear as well as nonlinear depending on the form of parameters $\beta_1, \beta_2, ..., \beta_3$. A model is said to be linear if it is linear in parameters. For example,

$$y = \beta_1 X_1 + \beta_2 X_1^2 + \beta_3 X_2 + \varepsilon$$

$$y = \beta_1 + \beta_2 \text{In } X_2 + \varepsilon$$

are linear models where as

$$y = \beta_1 X_1 + \beta_2^2 X_2 + \beta_3 X_2 + \varepsilon$$

$$y = (\text{In } \beta_1) X_1 + \beta_2 X_2 + \varepsilon$$

are non-linear models. Many times, the nonlinear models can be converted into linear models through some transformations. So the class of linear models is wider than what it appears initially.

If a model contains only one explanatory variable, then it is called as simple regression model. When there are more than one independent variables, then it is called as multiple regression model. When there is only one study variable, the regression is termed as univariate regression. When there are more than one study variables, the regression is termed as multivariate regression. Note that the simple and multiple regressions are not same as univariate and multivariate regressions.

The simple and multiple regression are determined by the number of explanatory variables whereas univariate and multivariate regressions are determined by the number of study variables.

Choice of Method for Fitting the Data

After the model has been defined and the data have been collected, the next task is to estimate the parameters of the model based on the collected data. This is also referred to as parameter estimation or model fitting. The most commonly used method of estimation is the least squares method. Under certain assumptions, the least squares method produces estimators with desirable properties. The other estimation methods are the maximum likelihood method, ridge method, principal components method etc.

Fitting of Model

The estimation of unknown parameters using appropriate method provides the values of the parameter. Substituting these values in the equation gives us a usable model. This is termed as model fitting. The estimates of parameters $\beta_1, \beta_2, ..., \beta_K$ in the model

$$y = f(X_1, X_2, ..., X_k, \beta_1, \beta_2, ..., \beta_K) + \varepsilon$$

are denoted by $\hat{\beta}_1, \hat{\beta}_2, ..., \hat{\beta}_K$ which gives the fitted model as

$$y = f(X_1, X_2, ..., X_k, \hat{\beta}_1, \hat{\beta}_2, ..., \hat{\beta}_K)$$

When the value of y is obtained for the given values of $X_1, X_2, ..., X_k$ it is denoted as $\hat{y}$ and called as fitted value.

The fitted equation is used for prediction. In this case, $\hat{y}$ is termed as predicted value. Note that the fitted value is where the values used for explanatory variables correspond to one of the n observations in the data whereas predicted value is the one obtained for any set of values of explanatory variables. It is not generally recommended to predict the y -values for the set of those values of explanatory variables which lie outside the range of data. When the values of explanatory variables are the future values of explanatory variables, the predicted values are called forecasted values.

Model Criticism and Selection

The validity of statistical method to be used for regression analysis depends on various assumptions. These assumptions become essentially the assumptions for the model and the data. The quality of statistical inferences heavily depends on whether these assumptions are satisfied or not. For making these assumptions to be valid and to be satisfied, care is needed from beginning of the experiment. One has to be careful in choosing the required assumptions and to decide as well to determine if the assumptions are valid for the given experimental conditions or not? It is also important to decide that the situations is which the assumptions may not meet.

The validation of the assumptions must be made before drawing any statistical conclusion. Any departure from validity of assumptions will be reflected in the statistical inferences. In fact, the regression analysis is an iterative process where the outputs are used to diagnose, validate, criticize and modify the inputs. The iterative process is illustrated in the following figure.

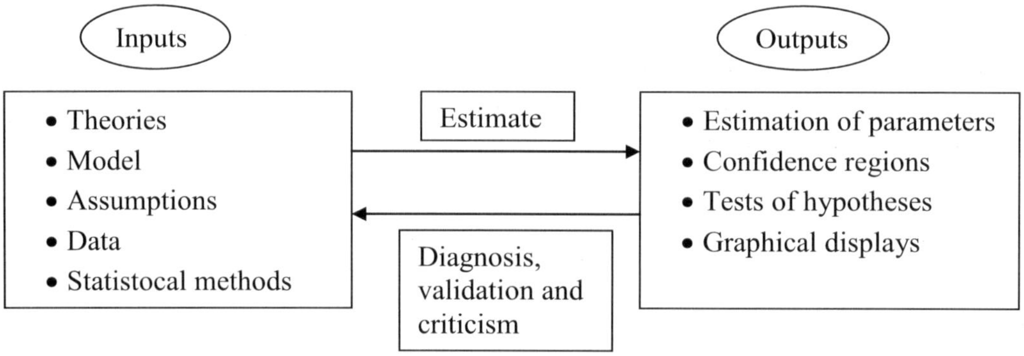

Objectives of Regression Analysis

The determination of explicit form of regression equation is the ultimate objective of regression analysis. It is finally a good and valid relationship between study variable and explanatory variables. The regression equation helps is understanding the interrelationships of variables among them. Such regression equation can be used for several purposes. For example, to determine the role of any explanatory variable in the joint relationship in any policy formulation, to forecast the values of response variable for given set of values of explanatory variables.

Generalized Linear Models

First, let's clear up some potential misunderstandings about terminology. The term *general linear model* (GLM) usually refers to conventional linear regression models for a continuous response variable given continuous and/or categorical predictors. It includes multiple linear regression, as well as ANOVA and ANCOVA (with fixed effects only). The form is $y_i \sim N(x_i^T\beta, \sigma^2)$, where χ_i contains known covariates and β contains the coefficients to be estimated. These models are fit by least squares and weighted least squares using, for example: SAS Proc GLM or R functions lsfit() (older, uses matrices) and lm() (newer, uses data frames).

The term *generalized linear model* (GLIM or GLM) refers to a larger class of models popularized by McCullagh and Nelder (1982, 2nd edition 1989). In these models, the response variable y_i is assumed to follow an exponential family distribution with mean μ_i, which is assumed to be some (often nonlinear) function of $x_i^T\beta$. Some would call these "nonlinear" because μ_i is often a nonlinear function of the covariates, but McCullagh and Nelder consider them to be linear, because the covariates affect the distribution of yiyionly through the linear combination $x_i^T\beta$. The first widely used software package for fitting these models was called GLIM. Because of this program, "GLIM" became a well-accepted abbreviation for generalized linear models, as opposed to "GLM" which often is used for general linear models. Today, GLIM's are fit by many packages, including SAS Proc Genmod and R function glm(). Notice, however, that Agresti uses GLM instead of GLIM short-hand, and we will use GLM.

The generalized linear models (GLMs) are a broad class of models that include linear regression, ANOVA, Poisson regression, log-linear models etc. The table below provides a good summary of GLMs.

Model	Random	Link	Systematic
Linear Regression	Normal	Identity	Continuous
ANOVA	Normal	Identity	Categorical
ANCOVA	Normal	Identity	Mixed
Logistic Regression	Binomial	Logit	Mixed
Loglinear	Poisson	Log	Categorical
Poisson Regression	Poisson	Log	Mixed
Multinomial response	Multinomial	Generalized Logit	Mixed

There are three components to any GLM:

- *Random Component* – refers to the probability distribution of the response variable (Y); e.g. normal distribution for *Y* in the linear regression, or binomial distribution for *Y* in the binary logistic regression. Also called a noise model or error model. How is random error added to the prediction that comes out of the link function?
- *Systematic Component* - specifies the explanatory variables $X_1, X_2, ..., X_k$ in the model, more specifically their linear combination in creating the so called *linear predictor*; e.g., $\beta_0 + \beta_1 x_1 + \beta_2 x_2$ as we have seen in a linear regression, or as we will see in a logistic regression in this lesson.
- *Link Function, η or $g(\mu)$* - specifies the link between random and systematic components. It says how the expected value of the response relates to the linear predictor of explanatory variables; e.g., $\eta = g(E(Y_i)) = E(Y_i)$ for linear regression, or $\eta = logit(\pi)$ for logistic regression.

Assumptions

- The data $Y_1, Y_2, ..., Y_n$ are independently distributed, i.e., cases are independent.
- The dependent variable Y_i does NOT need to be normally distributed, but it typically assumes a distribution from an exponential family (e.g. binomial, Poisson, multinomial, normal).
- GLM does NOT assume a linear relationship between the dependent variable and the independent variables, but it does assume linear relationship between the transformed response in terms of the link function and the explanatory variables; e.g., for binary logistic regression $\text{logit}(\pi) = \beta_0 + \beta X$.
- Independent (explanatory) variables can be even the power terms or some other nonlinear transformations of the original independent variables.
- The homogeneity of variance does NOT need to be satisfied. In fact, it is not even possible in many cases given the model structure, and *overdispersion* (when the observed variance is larger than what the model assumes) maybe present.
- Errors need to be independent but NOT normally distributed.
- It uses maximum likelihood estimation (MLE) rather than ordinary least squares (OLS) to estimate the parameters, and thus relies on large-sample approximations.

- Goodness-of-fit measures rely on sufficiently large samples, where a heuristic rule is that not more than 20% of the expected cells counts are less than 5.

Advantages of GLMs over Traditional (OLS) Regression

- We do not need to transform the response *Y* to have a normal distribution.
- The choice of link is separate from the choice of random component thus we have more flexibility in modeling.
- If the link produces additive effects, then we do not need constant variance.
- The models are fitted via Maximum Likelihood estimation; thus optimal properties of the estimators.
- All the inference tools and model checking that we will discuss for log-linear and logistic regression models apply for other GLMs too; e.g., Wald and Likelihood ratio tests, Deviance, Residuals, Confidence intervals, Overdispersion.
- There is often one procedure in a software package to capture all the models listed above, e.g. *PROC GENMOD in SAS* or *glm() in R*, etc... with options to vary the three components.

But there are some limitations of GLMs too, such as,

- Linear function, e.g. can have only a linear predictor in the systematic component.
- Responses must be independent.

Logit

Logistic regression is standard mathematical-statistic method for decades. It is applied almost in cases that explaining, dependent variable is not is not continuous but binary – dichotomous or alternative (if the explaining variable is continuous we use classical linear regression), so it means it can take only two values. Variable y that we try to explain using ratio (explanatory variables), it takes discrete value. If the company prospers it is the value 1 and if the company declared bankrupt it is the value 0. For this reason, we cannot use "classic" regression but adjusted regression analysis, called Logit and Probit models.

Logit analysis is characterized by prediction of probability of the event that either occur or not. Calculated probability is thus equal to either 1 or 0. It is necessary to realize logit transformation within the logistic regression to establish this condition. This logit transformation is based on "ratio of chances and hopes". Given transformation allows the ideal relationship between dependent variable y and a vector of independent variables x. If values of independent variable are very low the probability of the variable y close to zero and if the values of independent are high the probability of y close to one. Logistic regression uses categorically explained variable.

We meet in literature with different types of classification variables. According to one of approaches it is distinguished variables, where the main criterion is the type of relationship between values:

- Nominal variable is classified only quantitative. This means that its value either belongs or does not belong into certain category and we do not know determine the order of these categories. Individual values of nominal variable are expressed by words or numerical codes (so it make easier further computer processing). A typical example is marital status (single, married, divorced, widowed), place of birth (Bratislava, Rome, Wien, and so on), nationality (Slovak, Czech) and so on. A special case of nominal variable is dichotomous variable which acquiring only two possible values (gender, smoker and non-smoker, etc.).

- Ordinal variable meet all conditions that are required from nominal variable and in addition we can determine the order of its values. It is not possible to determine how much do one value higher or lower. We classify here for example the level of education (primary, secondary without graduation, secondary with graduation, and so on), the degree of customer satisfaction with certain product, etc.
- Interval variable allows to find out not only the order but also quantifies difference between of its two values. It does not allow to determine their ratio because it does not have "rational zero" in its scale of values. An example is the monthly income of household or level of blood cholesterol. In literature commonly reported example is temperature in Celsius (or Fahrenheit), where 0°C does not mean the absence of the temperature (temperature 30°C is higher about 15°C than 15°C but not two times higher).
- Ratios variable have defined "rational zero" and therefore it make sense to talk about how many times is one value higher (lower) than the other. If we measure the temperature on the Kelvin scale, so we can determine not only the fact that the temperature 100 degrees is about 50 higher than 50 degrees, but also the fact that the temperature is exactly two times higher. Another example is weight, number of household members, age, etc.

Nominal and ordinal variables are complexly marked as qualitative, interval and ratio variables and known as quantitative (cardinal, numerical). Quantitative variables can take form of discrete values so it means only integer values, or continuous values so it means discretionary value from certain interval.

The aim of logistic regression (it is similar to the linear regression) is expressed dependence of magnitude Y on the variable xk. It does not use a linear dependence. Observed data are interleaved by logistic curve instead of line and its prescript is:

$$\Pi = \frac{e^{\beta+\beta_1 x_1+\ldots+\beta_k x_k}}{1+e^{\beta+\beta_1 x_1+\ldots+\beta_k x_k}} = \frac{1}{1+e^{-(\beta+\beta_1 x_1+\ldots+\beta_k x_k)}}$$

where:

Π - probability of default,

x_k - the value of k-th financial indicator.

β_k - coefficients of individual indicator.

Variables of this logistic function X_k are chosen financial indicators while coefficients β_k is necessary to estimate – these coefficients are estimated by using of the method maximal likelihood. In this case it cannot to stated that these coefficients are weights of individual financial indicators and their finally interpretation is then more complicated than the linear models. For determine the probability of default it is not necessary to use calibration of model, it is sufficient to calculate median of known probabilities of all subjects (observed companies) which are in individual group. Logistic function may be increasing and also decreasing but its value is always between zero and one.

Logistic regression eliminates disadvantages of discriminant analysis – does not assume normal distribution of independent variables and homogeneity of variation-covariance matrices.

We can see in following table that we can use not only generalized logit model. Starting with the simple binary logit model, research progressed during the 1960s and 1970s to the multinomial logit (MNL) and nested logit models, the latter becoming the most popular of the generalized logit models. Also mixed logit models and its variants have now supplanted simpler models in many areas of economics, marketing, management, transportation, health, housing, energy, research and environmental science.

Table: Different logit models and their strengths and challenges

	Classical MNL	Nested Logit	Mixed Logit	Latent Class-MNL
Major Strenght	Closed-form solution	Closed-form solution	Allows for complete relaxation of IID condition	Clossed-form solution Semi-parametric specification
	Provides one set of globally optimal parameter estimates	Provides one set of globally optimal parameters	Avoids violation of the IIA condition	
	Simple calculation	Relatively easy to interpret	High level of behavioural definition and richness allowed in model specification	Like mixed logit, this model form is free form many limiting statstical assumptions, such as homogeneity in variances and normality assumptions
	Widely understood and used in practise	Relatively easy to calculate probability outcomes	Includes additional estimates for random parameters, heterogeity in means and decompositions in variances (these influences are effectively treated as "while noise" in basic models)	Incorporates firm-specific observed and unobserved heterogeneity through "latent class" constructs Incorporates firm-specific observed and unobserved heterogeneity through "latent class" constructs Less complex interpretation than mixed logit
	Easy to interpret parameter estimates	Only Prartially corrects fo IID condition		Lacks flexibility in specification of firm-specific unobserved

	Easy to calculate probability outcomes	Incorporates firm-specific observed and unobserved heterogeneity to some extent (especially the covariance extension)	Open-form solution (requires analytical integration and use of simalted maximum likelihood to estimate model parameters)	
	Less demanding data quality requirements			

	Classical MNL	Nested Logit	Mixed Logit	Latent Class-MNL
Major Challenges	Highly restrictive error assumptions(IID condition)	Only partially corrects for IID condition		
	Violates the IIA Assupmption	Analytically very closely related to basic MNL model (thus shares many of the limitations of MNL)		Model estimation can be time consuming due to computational intensity
	Ignores firm-specific observed and unobserved heterogeneity which can lead to inferior model specification and spurious interpretation of model outputs	Does not capture potential sources of correlation across nests	Lack of a single set of globally optimal parameter estimates (i.e. due to the requirement for simalted maximum likelihood)	Assumption that manifest variables within latent classes are independent can be unrealistic
	Parameters are point estimates with little behavioural definition	Judgement required in determining which alternatives can be appropriately partitioned into nests (nested logit requires well separated nests to reflect their correlation)	Assumptions must be imposed for the distribution of unobserved influences Complex interpretation Model estimation can be time consuming due to computational intensity	High quality data constraints
	Often provide good aggregate fits but can be misleading given simple form of the model		High quality data contraints	
	Tends to be less behaviourally resposive to changes in attribute levels			

Probit

Probit analysis is alternative of logit method. The main difference is that assume normal distribution of random variables (independent variables in model). The difference lies in fact that logistic function has harder "fat tails". There are no significant differences in practise, only in the case that sample contains numerous observations with extreme values. Parameters estimates obtained by logit and probit models cannot be compared directly because the logarithmic distribution has variance equal $\pi^2/3$, therefore the estimates obtained by logit model have to be multiplied by $3^{1/2}/\pi$ in order to be comparable with estimates obtained in the probit model.

In conclusion Logit and probit models are very similar to each other. Distribution function in the logit model on the contrary of probit model has "flatter tails" (distribution has more observations appearing at the end of the distribution function). Distribution function of probit model has steeper slope so we can see on the figure . Both distribution function are almost linear between $\pi = 0{,}2$ and $\pi = 0{,}8$.

Parameter estimation in logit and probit models vary significantly. Logarithmic distribution has variance equal to π2/3, β estimations comes from logit model have to be multiplied by 31/2/π in order to be comparable with estimations acquired from probit model which has variance equal to one.

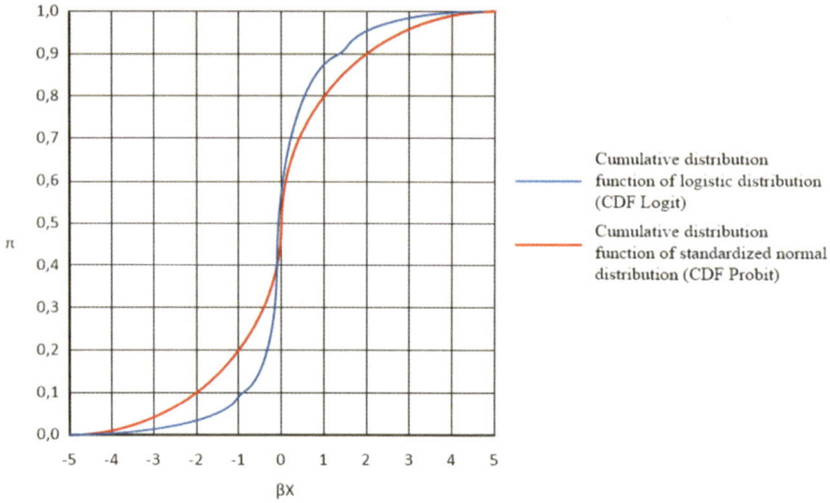

Compare distribution function of Logit and Probit models

Estimation of probability of default in these models is dependent variable which variance is independent variable. Independent variables are expressed by various financial indicators or other indicators which representing external variables reflected financial environment.

Logit model has two practical advantages on the contrary of probit model, despite their mutual similarity:

- Simplicity – equation of logistic distribution function is very simply while normal cumulative distribution function contains unquantified integral.
- Interpretability – inverse linear transformation of logit model can be interpreted directly as logarithm of chances, while inverse transformation of probit has not direct interpretation.

Tobit

21st century has brought a revolution in the business. For instance, a diverse change has been observed in increasing products availability for consumers. Customers were the centric to the business growth but now customers have an influential power and number of options of their own interest to decide what they wish to buy.

Retaining with your old customers and building a strong relationship and interaction over time builds customer loyalty, which ultimately leads to the growth of the organization. The relationship with customers focuses on cost & profitability for the life-time value of customers. The ultimate goals of the firms are to get maximum sales/revenues and for the purpose different marketing tools, mix, communication channels, strategic plans are deployed. If the customer are satisfied and delighted and purchase again and again then the firms shifts towards the prospering zone and can further extend their business venture.

Since the data of amount of revenue generation is supposed to be censored as there are the wind falls which also increase the amount of revenue generation and may obdurate and hamper the actual impact of various outlined marketing strategies on the amount of revenue generations, therefore, the data for the amount of revenue generation is made censored for the period when there was a wind fall. Keeping in mind the nature of dependent variable/ censored variable (amount of revenue generation) the tobit model is proposed to interrogate the data and the associations. The regression model based on censoring the distribution of dependent variable is referred to as the censored regression model or the Tobit model (Tobin, 1958). The regression is obtained by making the mean in the preceding correspond to a classical regression model. The general formulation is usually given in terms of an index function,

$$y_i^* = x_i'\beta + \varepsilon_i$$

$$y_i = 0 \text{ if } y_i^* \leq 0,$$

$$y_i = y_i^* \text{ if } y_i^* \leq 0.$$

Since the data of revenue generation is censored therefore, there are potentially two conditional mean functions we considered, which reflects the purpose of the study. While, for the index variable, sometimes called the latent variable, $E\left[y_i^* I x_i\right]$ is $x_i'\beta$.

For an observation randomly drawn from the population, which may or may not be censored, the following equation can be used for computing latent variable.

$$E\left[y_i^* I x_i\right] = \Phi\left(\frac{x_i'\beta}{\sigma}\right)\left(x_i'\beta + \sigma\lambda_i\right),$$

Where,

$$\lambda = \frac{\phi\left[\left(0 - x_i'\beta\right)/\sigma\right]}{1 - \Phi\left[\left(0 - x_i'\beta\right)/\sigma\right]} = \frac{\phi\left(0 - x_i'\beta\right)/\sigma}{\Phi\left(0 - x_i'\beta\right)/\sigma}.$$

As we are intending to confine our attention to censored observations, then the results for the truncated regression model may not apply, because the truncated regression model is no more amenable to least squares than the censored data model. It is an unresolved question which of these functions should be used for computing predicted values from this model. Intuition suggests that $E\left[y_i^* I x_i\right]$ is correct, for predicting the amount of revenue generation, say, to plan for an up-coming event via using outlined multiple marketing strategies, as the censored mean is obviously the relevant quantity. On the other hand, if the objective is to study the need for a new facility, then the mean of the latent variable y_i^* would be more interesting.

Findings and Results

Table: Tobit Estimates for amount of revenue generation due to various marketing strategies

Predictors	**Revenue Generation**		**Scaled OLS**	**Ordinary Least Squares**
	Coefficient (T-Value)	Slope		
Constant	1502.44			
	(9.13)			
Single Segment Strategy	1741.15	421.27	676.72	329.74
	(20.11)			
Differentiated Strategy	49.09	217.00	22.02	16.79
	(1.81)			
Un Differentiated	299.03	90.90	307.17	102.11
Strategy	(4.93)			
Product Development	184.17	70.05	43.35	26.14
	(2.89)			
Establishing The Brand	3.99.48	123.06	367.28	309.63
	(7.77)			
Innovation strategy	585.98	183.81	400.03	265.78
	(9..67)			
Market Growth Shares	851.87	331.45	666.16	349.69
	(12.64)			
Porter Cost Leadership	34.37	13.72	44.01	36.05
	(2.05)			
Market Expansion	342.76	29.52	765.70	321.91
	(6.92)			
Pricing	27.73	25.71	31.32	23.87
	(1.85)			

Diversification	349.26	285.03	479.08	199.15
	(14.01)			
σ	2231			
Sample size	5095			
Proportion working	0.490			

It is found that all of the marketing strategies in relevance to the varieties of products / services are objectively designed and implemented with the clear a intent to just make and grab money from each pocket which comes to market, concisely all outlined marketing strategies paves the clear and straight way to generate overwhelming amount of money as the betas for all outlined constructs of marketing strategies are found vigorously thick and significant at $t > 1.5$. While, the Tobit model/ censored regression is revealed as the robust model in comparison of the results of ordinary least square model, to investigate the effects of all outlined marketing strategies on the censored variables i.e. amount of revenue generation.

To conclude marketing strategies no matters to which category they belong, all are constituted for one similar reason which is not anything else except of making money for the respective organization. In fact and in short these strategies are formulated and implemented to achieve the excepted outlined target of revenue generation which every company desires. It is also notable that the single segment strategy and market growth share strategy are found to have the highest impacts on the amount of revenue generation but all other marketing strategies are also significantly involved in making money in relevance to the products/ services for which they are aimed. In support to the above stated concluding thoughts Rust (1997) found that the various marketing strategies are purposely designed and operationally implemented to meet the one common objective of revenue generation and its maximization.

Autoregressive Integrated Moving Average (ARIMA)

An autoregressive integrated moving average, or ARIMA, is a statistical analysis model that uses time series data to either better understand the data set or to predict future trends.

An autoregressive integrated moving average model is a form of regression analysis that gauges the strength of one dependent variable relative to other changing variables. The model's goal is to predict future securities or financial market moves by examining the differences between values in the series instead of through actual values.

An ARIMA model can be understood by outlining each of its components as follows:

- *Autoregression (AR)* refers to a model that shows a changing variable that regresses on its own lagged, or prior, values.
- *Integrated (I)* represents the differencing of raw observations to allow for the time series to become stationary, i.e., data values are replaced by the difference between the data values and the previous values.
- *Moving average (MA)* incorporates the dependency between an observation and a residual error from a moving average model applied to lagged observations.

Each component functions as a parameter with a standard notation. For ARIMA models, a standard notation would be ARIMA with p, d, and q, where integer values substitute for the parameters to indicate the type of ARIMA model used. The parameters can be defined as:

- *p*: the number of lag observations in the model; also known as the lag order.
- *d*: the number of times that the raw observations are differenced; also known as the degree of differencing.
- q: the size of the moving average window; also known as the order of the moving average.

In a linear regression model, for example, the number and type of terms are included. A 0 value, which can be used as a parameter, would mean that particular component should not be used in the model. This way, the ARIMA model can be constructed to perform the function of an ARMA model, or even simple AR, I, or MA models.

Autoregressive Integrated Moving Average and Stationarity

In an autoregressive integrated moving average model, the data are differenced in order to make it stationary. A model that shows stationarity is one that shows there is constancy to the data over time. Most economic and market data show trends, so the purpose of differencing is to remove any trends or seasonal structures.

Seasonality, or when data show regular and predictable patterns that repeat over a calendar year, could negatively affect the regression model. If a trend appears and stationarity is not evident, many of the computations throughout the process cannot be made with great efficacy.

Case Study of ARIMA

ARIMA can be defined as the combination of two autoregressive (AR) model that is integrated with the Moving Average (MA) model. Writing the notation Autoregressive Integrated Moving Average is an ARIMA (p, d, q). P is the degree of process of AR, d is the order of differencing and q is the degree of MA process.

Autoregressive model with the ordo of the AR (p) model of ARIMA (p,0,0) is stated as follows:

$$Y_t = \theta_0 + \theta_1 Y_{t-1} + \theta_2 Y_{t-2} + \ldots + \theta_p Y_{t-p} + e_t$$

Where:

Y_t =Stationary time series

θ_0 =Constant

θ_p =Parameter of autoregressive model

e_t =Residual time (t)

Moving Average model with the or do of the MA (q) or ARIMA (0,0, q) is stated as follows:

$$Y_t = \phi_0 + \phi_1 Y_{t-1} - \phi_2 Y_{t-2} - \ldots - \phi_q Y_{t-q} + e_t$$

Where:

Y_t =Stationary time series

ϕ_0 = Constant

ϕ_q = Coefficient of the model which shows the moving average weights

e_t = Residual tense used

To ensure the results obtainable right from ARIMA has accurate and reduce the level of error can be used with four models-selection criteria include root mean square error (RMSE), mean absolute error (MAE), mean absolute percentage error (MAPE) and Theil Inequality Coefficient.

TABLE: Model – accurancy metrics

Criteria	Formula
Root Mean Squared Error (RMSE)	$\sqrt{\sum_{t=T+1}^{T+h}(\widehat{y}-y_t)^2/h}$
Mean Absolute Error (MAE)	$\sum_{t=T+1}^{T+h}\lvert\widehat{y}-y_t\rvert/h$
Mean Absolute Percentage Error (MAPE)	$100\sum_{t=T+1}^{T+h}\left\lvert\frac{\widehat{y}-y_t}{y_t}\right\rvert/h$
Theil Inequality Coefficient	$\frac{\sqrt{\sum_{t=T+1}^{T+h}(\widehat{y}_t-y_t)^2/h}}{\sqrt{\sum_{t=T+1}^{T+h}\widehat{y}_t^{\,2}/h}-\sqrt{\sum_{t=T+1}^{T+h}\widehat{y}_t^{\,2}/h}}$

The first assessment criterion, RMSE is preserves the units of the estimation variable. This approach is more sensitive and minimizes large errors. Nevertheless, the ability to compare different time series is limited with this criterion. Conversely, MAE, the second criterion, determines the error magnitude for a precise set of forecasts. MAE defines how close forecasts are to the actual outcomes. This metric does not consider the direction of the forecasts. Moreover, these criteria determine the precisions of continuous variables. The third criteria is Theil Inequality Coefficient (U_1 and U_2), respectively. The former enables different predictions to be compared, which implies that actual values are compared with predicted values. U_1 provides a range of values on a zero-to-one scale. The nearer U_1 is to zero, the more accurate the prediction is. When faced with alternative predictions, the forecast with the smallest value of U_1 is regarded as the best and is thus selected. Conversely, U_2 performs relative comparisons based on random walk models and prediction models (naïve model). The naïve model may be described as the actual predetermined forecast model applied based on an indiscriminate-walk process. When U_2 levels off at unity, the naïve method is considered to be equally useful for forecasting. $U_2 < 1$ indicates that the forecasting model would work better than the naïve approach. MAPE, the fourth criterion, enables comparison of distinct time-series data without defining the relation or percent error. This metric is significant in instances in which the measured variables are very large. In this research using MAPE because of data availability.

This is a case study of estimation, model, and predicted sales of the newspaper. The data used is historical data obtained from the company in the form of the number newspaper sales from January 2016 to March 2017. Aim to get more accurate data and can be accounted from an object.

Analysis of the behavior data consists test and non-test stationary use the ADF test, after that analysis model used Box-Jenkins method and software Eviews 9. Box Jenkins method used for estimation model equations mean. At this stage the data verification and validation problems analysis in order to time-series and estimation parameter from newspaper sales index data so obtained the best model to suit the actual circumstances.

Data sample for this study are the data obtained from industries newspaper in solo. Plot of the time series original data demand newspaper is given in the figure below.

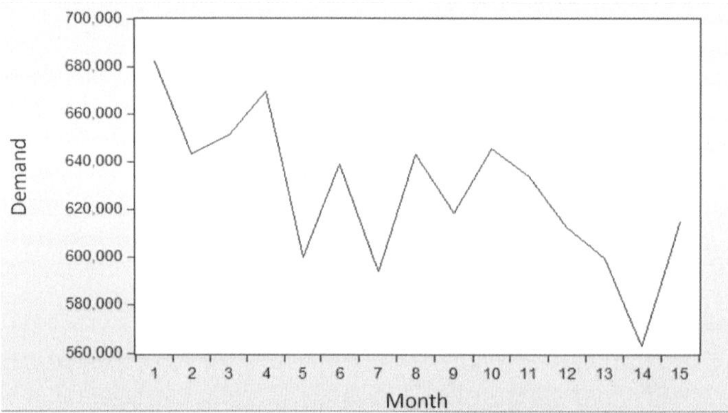

The Plot Of The Original Newspaper Sales Data

From the above data plots can be noted that the number of sales is very fluctuating that tends to decline. Based on the plot of the data indicate that the data has not been stationer against mean and variation. In particular needs to be done to test the Augmented Dickey-Fuller (ADF) so that known sales data newspaper has stationary. The result of the ADF test looks like table.

ADF test

		t-Statistic	Prob.*
Augmented Dickey-Fuller test statistic		-0.738086	0.7921
Test critical values:	1% level	-4.297073	
	5% level	-3.212696	
	10% level	-2.747676	

*MacKinnon (1996) one-sided p-values.

The value of the t-statistic in output is – 0.738086, still smaller than the value in table t McKinon at trust level 1%, 5%, or 10%. As well as the value of the Probability of 0.7921 is still greater than the value of the critique of $\alpha = 0.05$ ($0.7921 > 0.05$). The results of the output indicates that the data are not stationary. This data indicates need for differentiation and transformation. So that the data becomes stationary. ADF test done first with differentiation results done as in table.

ADF Test with 1st difference

		t-Statistic	Prob.*
Augmented Dickey-Fuller test statistic		-3.939905	0.0169
Test critical values:	1% level	-4.297073	
	5% level	-3.212696	
	10% level	-2.747676	

*MacKinnon (1996) one-sided p-values.

The value of the t-statistic in output is -3.939905 is already greater than the value in table t McKinon at trust level 5% and 10%. As well as the value of the probability of 0.0169 is already smaller than the value of the critique of 0.05 (0.0169 < 0.05). Thus the data has been stationary on the differentiation of the first stage (1st difference) and the null hypothesis can be rejected. After that, the next process is to do an analysis of the time series model with ARIMA.

ACF and PACF plot made to identify a suitable data for means of data. The results of the correlogram with the first differentiation will show ACF and PACF graph like figure.

Autocorrelation	Partial Correlation		AC	PAC	Q-Stat	Prob
		1	-0.626	-0.626	6.7573	0.009
		2	0.354	-0.063	9.0948	0.011
		3	-0.258	-0.102	10.448	0.015
		4	0.001	-0.316	10.448	0.034
		5	0.106	-0.045	10.728	0.057
		6	-0.227	-0.257	12.166	0.058
		7	0.325	0.016	15.555	0.030
		8	-0.256	-0.001	18.010	0.021
		9	0.238	0.045	20.555	0.015
		10	-0.215	-0.051	23.143	0.010
		11	0.065	-0.103	23.454	0.015
		12	0.099	0.153	24.548	0.017

ACF and PACF

From the above graph model, it can be predicted that the model of ARIMA is used for proper ARIMA (1, 1, 0), ARIMA (0, 1, 1), ARIMA (1, 1.1) without constant. Next do the estimation of the value of C, probability, and AIC on each model.

Model of ARIMA (1, 1, 0)

Variable	Coefficient	Std. Error	t-Statistic	Prob.
C	628259.3	9373.630	67.02412	0.0000
AR(1)	0.226804	0.363252	0.624373	0.5441
SIGMASQ	8.61E+08	4.43E+08	1.941980	0.0760

R-squared	0.046002	Mean dependent var	627452.2
Adjusted R-squared	-0.112998	S.D. dependent var	31099.19
S.E. of regression	32809.24	Akaike info criterion	23.81519
Sum squared resid	1.29E+10	Schwarz criterion	23.95680
Log likelihood	-175.6139	Hannan-Quinn criter.	23.81368
F-statistic	0.289322	Durbin-Watson stat	1.992774
Prob(F-statistic)	0.753850		
Inverted AR Roots	.23		

Model of ARIMA (0, 1, 1)

TABLE 5. Models of ARIMA (0, 1, 1)

Variable	Coefficient	Std. Error	t-Statistic	Prob.
C	627862.0	8507.323	73.80253	0.0000
MA(1)	0.127373	0.402339	0.316582	0.7570
SIGMASQ	8.80E+08	4.33E+08	2.032180	0.0649

R-squared	0.025116	Mean dependent var	627452.2
Adjusted R-squared	-0.137365	S.D. dependent var	31099.19
S.E. of regression	33166.45	Akaike info criterion	23.83441
Sum squared resid	1.32E+10	Schwarz criterion	23.97602
Log likelihood	-175.7581	Hannan-Quinn criter.	23.83290
F-statistic	0.154577	Durbin-Watson stat	1.729068
Prob(F-statistic)	0.858456		
Inverted MA Roots	-.13		

Model of ARIMA (1, 1, 1)

Variable	Coefficient	Std. Error	t-Statistic	Prob.
C	628580.8	18621.67	33.75533	0.0000
AR(1)	0.730270	1.290236	0.565998	0.5828
MA(1)	-0.464509	1.736313	-0.267526	0.7940
SIGMASQ	8.18E+08	5.06E+08	1.614447	0.1347

R-squared	0.094349	Mean dependent var	627452.2
Adjusted R-squared	-0.152647	S.D. dependent var	31099.19
S.E. of regression	33388.53	Akaike info criterion	23.90475
Sum squared resid	1.23E+10	Schwarz criterion	24.09357
Log likelihood	-175.2857	Hannan-Quinn criter.	23.90274
F-statistic	0.381985	Durbin-Watson stat	2.089046
Prob(F-statistic)	0.768040		
Inverted AR Roots	.73		
Inverted MA Roots	.46		

To determine the best model is to compare to the four models who are looking for a model with a value of AIC and Schwarz criterion to the smallest. From the results above, it is well known that the best model is the ARIMA (1, 1,0) without constant. Next is doing a diagnostic check to perform a test of normality residue. The results can be seen in figure.

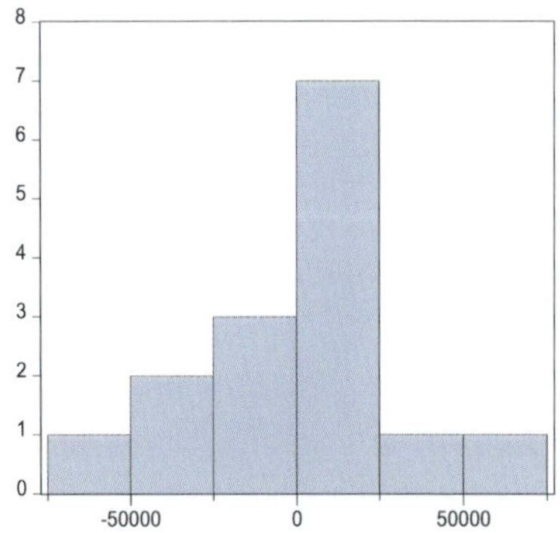

Series: Residuals	
Sample 2016M01 2017M03	
Observations 15	
Mean	-908.9233
Median	2179.237
Maximum	52512.60
Minimum	-58911.79
Std. Dev.	30360.88
Skewness	-0.181219
Kurtosis	2.332213
Jarque-Bera	0.360813
Probability	0.834931

The results of the diagnostic check

Based on the above, it can be seen that the output value of probability > alpha i.e. 0.913103 > 0.05 means that the data are normal and has been stationary against the variation. This means that these data have a relatively stable fluctuations from time to time. To prove that data are already normal can use assumptions autocorrelation test and assumptions heteroscedasticity test.

Autocorrelation	Partial Correlation		AC	PAC	Q-Stat	Prob
		1	-0.108	-0.108	0.2136	
		2	0.327	0.319	2.3164	0.128
		3	-0.102	-0.049	2.5395	0.281
		4	-0.176	-0.329	3.2609	0.353
		5	0.074	0.115	3.4021	0.493
		6	-0.175	0.011	4.2684	0.511
		7	0.311	0.234	7.3607	0.289
		8	-0.109	-0.075	7.7952	0.351
		9	0.158	-0.041	8.8564	0.355
		10	-0.207	-0.202	11.040	0.273
		11	-0.156	-0.130	12.601	0.247
		12	-0.110	-0.046	13.633	0.254

Test Correlation Assumptions

Autocorrelation	Partial Correlation		AC	PAC	Q-Stat	Prob
		1	-0.210	-0.210	0.7997	0.371
		2	-0.113	-0.164	1.0515	0.591
		3	-0.006	-0.073	1.0521	0.789
		4	0.029	-0.009	1.0719	0.899
		5	-0.197	-0.217	2.0570	0.841
		6	0.049	-0.056	2.1251	0.908
		7	0.076	0.016	2.3075	0.941
		8	-0.182	-0.201	3.5127	0.898
		9	0.122	0.048	4.1470	0.901
		10	-0.020	-0.082	4.1683	0.939
		11	-0.166	-0.223	5.9347	0.878
		12	-0.151	-0.290	7.8769	0.795

Test Assumptions Heteroscedasticity

After that it can be determined the sales forecast for short periods of time. The results of the forecast as shown in figure. From the result MSE is 27028, 18; MAE is 21855,49; and MAPE is 3,52.

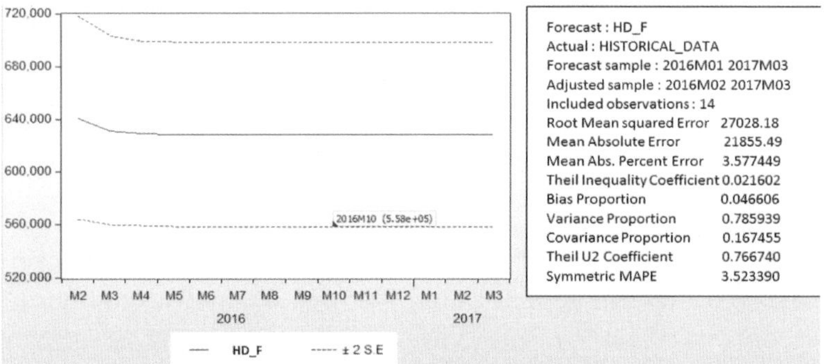

The Results of the Forecast

Forecasting should be reference of the customer order cycle to improve accuracy and lower returned. In order that sustainable improvement it needs to be stated in SOP as done by the large companies, include GMF, Pedro Neves Company, Hearst Company, and newspaper industries of UK & Netherland in improving its performance on an on going basis. In general the contributions of forecasting is to improve the relationship between the manufacturers and the consumers. Obtained ARIMA models that enable the following:

$$\Delta Y_t = \theta_0 + \theta_1 \Delta Y_{t-1} + e_{t-1}$$

$$\Delta Y_t = C + 0.226804 \Delta Y_{t-1} + e_{t-1}$$

$$\Delta Y_t = 628,259.3 + 0.226804 + 3.52$$

$$\Delta Y_t = 628,263.046804$$

$$\Delta Y_t = \pm 628.264$$

From the result, the production of newspaper for each month are ± 628.264.

In conclusion the number of newspaper sales data are not stationary and indicates instability the residual variation, then the fluctuating data need ADF test for get the stationary. To perform the demand forecast to be done stationary data with the first differentiation. Based on the selection of the best models of ARIMA model is obtained (1, 1, 0). $\Delta Y_t = C + 0.226804 \Delta Y_{t-1} + e_{t-1}$ and the results for the next 3 months of ± 628.264. ARIMA models can be used to predict the short-term forecast in good, it is supported with a level MAPE 3.52%. Circulation managers can use the results of this forecasting for planning determines the production master plan.

Endogeneity

Even a cursory glance at real world data indicates that firms do not emerge randomly or uniformly around the world. Similarly, individuals are not randomly assigned postings nor do they uniformly develop managerial expertise. As such, it is difficult to interpret the cross-sectional tests that we commonly employ in IB because our analysis violates the necessary conditions to make them a valid test (Roberts & Whited, 2011). Of course we are all familiar with this potential issue, which is often known under the broad title of "endogeneity." A common misconception is that ruling out reverse causality solves the endogeneity problem. Unfortunately, the problem is more pervasive, and reverse causality is only one distinct case of the non-random treatment effect. Statisticians and econometricians have been discussing the issue for decades, and over the past several years their remedies have become quite common in empirical business research.

The most successful studies in IB use the intuition and insights behind these methods in developing their research design to facilitate causal inference from their observational data. In IB research the objective usually centers on providing evidence about the causal effects of some particular IB phenomenon. Because this research usually involves observational data, rather than random trials, the relevant goal in IB research design centers on the development of a test that best approximates a controlled experiment (Angrist & Krueger, 2001). As a result, studies that explicitly identify the source of variability in the dependent variable can develop appropriate tests that improve the researcher's ability to make causal inferences (Angrist & Pischke, 2008). Research on the determinants of multinationality or studies that use data items such as individual patents also face this same endogeneity problem. Brenner (2011) exemplifies this approach to careful research design at JIBS in his study determining if resource advantages cause managers in firms with illegal international activity to cooperate with government prosecutions.

Technically, in a statistical model you have an endogeneity problem when there is a correlation between your X variable and the error term in your model. What does this mean? Well remember that the error term in your model is due to all of the stuff in your dependent variable that is not due to the variables you have in your model.

So in the broadest sense an endogeneity problem arises when there is something that is related to your Y variable that is also related to your X variable, and you do not have that something in your model. Call that something Z, although notice that I have not claimed that Z is a variable – it is just a "something."

What this broad meaning of endogeneity suggests is that there are a wide variety of sources of endogeneity problems. In fact one of the problems with the use of the term is that people use it to cover many different things, yet the solutions to those different things can be quite different.

For example, endogeneity in this broad sense can be caused by omitted variables, or unobserved heterogeneity. In this case, the endogeneity complaint is a complaint that you left a variable (or two) out of your model.

Exogeneity versus Endogeneity

In a stochastic model, the notion of the *usual exogeneity*, *sequential exogeneity*, *strong/strict exogeneity* can be defined. Exogeneity is articulated in such a way that a variable or variables is exogenous for parameter $\acute{a}$. Even if a variable is exogenous for parameter $\acute{a}$, it might be endogenous for parameter β.

When the explanatory variables are not stochastic, then they are strong exogenous for all the parameters.

If the independent variable is correlated with the error term in a regression model then the estimate of the regression coefficient in an ordinary least squares (OLS) regression is biased; however if the correlation is not contemporaneous, then the coefficient estimate may still be consistent. There are many methods of correcting the bias, including instrumental variable regression and Heckman selection correction.

Static Models

The following are some common sources of endogeneity:

1. Omitted Variable

In this case, the endogeneity comes from an uncontrolled confounding variable. A variable is correlated with both an independent variable in the model, and with the error term. (Equivalently, the omitted variable both affects the independent variable and separately affects the dependent variable.) Assume that the "true" model to be estimated is,

$$y_i = \alpha + \beta x_i + \gamma z_i + u_i$$

but we omit z_i (perhaps because we don't have a measure for it) when we run our regression. z_i will get absorbed by the error term and we will actually estimate,

$$y_i = \alpha + \beta x_i + \varepsilon_i \quad \text{(where } \varepsilon_i = \gamma z_i + u_i\text{)}$$

If the correlation of x and z is not 0 and z separately affects y (meaning $\gamma \neq 0$), then x is correlated with the error term ε.

Here, x and 1 are not exogenous for α and β, since, given x and 1, the distribution of y depends not only on α and β, but also on z and gamma.

2. Measurement Error

Suppose that we do not get a perfect measure of one of our independent variables. Imagine that instead of observing x_i^* we observe $x_i = x_i^* + v_i$ where $\acute{\imath}_i$ is the measurement "noise". In this case, a model given by

$$y_i = \alpha + \beta x_i^* + \varepsilon_i$$

is written in terms of observables and error terms as

$$y_i = \alpha + \beta(x_i - v_i) + \varepsilon_i$$

$$y_i = \alpha + \beta x_i + (\varepsilon_i - \beta v_i)$$

$$y_i = \alpha + \beta x_i + u_i \quad \text{(where } u_i = \varepsilon_i - \beta v_i\text{)}$$

Since both x_i and u_i depend on v_i, they are correlated, so the OLS estimation of β will be biased downward. Measurement error in the dependent variable, however, does not cause endogeneity (though it does increase the variance of the error term).

3. Simultaneity

Suppose that two variables are codetermined, with each affecting the other. Suppose that there are two "structural" equations,

$$y_i = \beta_1 x_i + \gamma_1 z_i + u_i$$

$$z_i = \beta_2 x_i + \gamma_2 y_i + v_i$$

Estimating either equation by itself results in endogeneity. In the case of the first structural equation, $E(z_i u_i) \neq 0$. Solving for z_i we get (assuming that $1 - \gamma_1\gamma_2 \neq 0$),

$$z_i = \frac{\beta_2 + \gamma_2\beta_1}{1-\gamma_1\gamma_2} x_i + \frac{1}{1-\gamma_1\gamma_2} v_i + \frac{\gamma_2}{1-\gamma_1\gamma_2} u_i$$

Assuming that x_i and v_i are uncorrelated with u_i, we have that,

$$E(z_i u_i) = \frac{\gamma_2}{1-\gamma_1\gamma_2} E(u_i u_i) \neq 0$$

Therefore, attempts at estimating either structural equation will be hampered by endogeneity.

Dynamic Models

The endogeneity problem is particularly relevant in the context of time series analysis of causal processes. It is common for some factors within a causal system to be dependent for their value in period *t* on the values of other factors in the causal system in period *t* – 1. Suppose that the level of pest infestation is independent of all other factors within a given period, but is influenced by the level of rainfall and fertilizer in the preceding period. In this instance it would be correct to say that infestation is exogenous within the period, but endogenous over time.

Let the model be $y = f(x, z) + u$. If the variable x is sequential exogenous for parameter α, and y does not cause x in Granger sense, then the variable x is strong/strict exogenous for the parameter α.

Simultaneity

Generally speaking, simultaneity occurs in the dynamic model just like in the example of static simultaneity above.

Panel Data

Panel data analysis is a method of studying an exacting subject within multiple sites, periodically observed over a defined time frame. Within the social sciences, panel data analysis has enabled researchers to undertake longitudinal analyses in a large variety of fields. In economics, panel data analysis is used to study the behavior of firms and wages of people over time. In political science, it is used to study political behavior of parties and organizations over time. It is used in psychology, sociology, and health research to study characteristics of groups of people followed over time. In educational research, researchers study classes of students or graduates over time. With repeated observations of enough cross-sections, panel analysis permits the researcher to study the dynamics of change with short time series. The combination of time series with cross-section can enhance the quality and quantity of data in ways that would be impossible using only one of these two dimensions (Gujarati, 2003; 638-640). Panel data analysis can provide a rich and powerful study of a set of people, if one is willing to consider both the space and time dimension of the data.

Reasons to use Panel Data

Using panel data have some benefits and some limitation. We can list several benefits and limitations of using panel data analysis. They are as follow:

Panel Data Analysis' Benefits

1. Controlling for individual heterogeneity: Panel data suggest that individuals, firms, states or countries are heterogeneous. Time series and crosssection studies not controlling for this heterogeneity run the risk of obtaining biased results. For example, we point to Baltagi and Levin study (1986, 1987). They consider cigarette demand across 46 American States for the years 1963-1988.

Consumption is modeled as a function of lagged consumption, price and income. These variables vary with states and time. However, many other variables may be state invariant or time invariant that may affect consumption.

Let us call these Z_i and W_t, respectively. Examples of Z_i are religion and education. For the religion variable, one may not be able to get the percentage of the population that is, say, Mormon in each state for every year ,nor does one expect that to change much across time. The same holds true for the percentage of the population completing high school or a college degree. Examples of W_t include advertising on TV and radio. This advertising is nationwide and does not vary across states. In addition, some of these variables are difficult to measure or hard to obtain so that not all the Z_i or W_t variables are available for inclusion in the consumption equation. Omission of these variables leads to bias in the resulting estimates. Panel data are able to control for these state and timeinvariant variables whereas a time series study or a cross section study cannot. In fact, from the data one observes that Utah has less than half the average per capita consumption of cigarettes in the US because it is mostly a Mormon state a religion that prohibits smoking. Controlling for Utah in a cross-section regression may be done with a dummy variable, which has the effect of removing that state's observation from the regression. This would not be the case for panel data, as we will shortly discover. In fact, with panel data, one might first difference the data to get rid of all Z_i type variables and hence effectively control for all state-specific characteristics. This holds whether the Z_i are observable or not. Alternatively, the dummy variable for Utah Controls for every state-specific effect that is distinctive of Utah without omitting the observations for Utah.

2. Panel data give more informative data, more variability, less co-linearity among the variables, more degrees of freedom and more efficiency: Timeseries studies are plagued with multicollinearity; for example, in the case of demand for cigarettes above, there is high collinearity between price and income taken together time series for the US. This is less likely with a panel across American states since the cross-section dimension adds a lot of variability, adding more informative data on price and income. In fact, the variation in the data can be decomposed into variation between states of different sizes and data can be decomposed into variation between states of different sizes and characteristics and variation within states. The former variation is usually bigger. With additional, more informative data one can product more reliable parameter estimates. Of course, the same relationship has to hold for each state, i.e. the data have to be this is a testable assumption and one that we will tackle in due course.

3. Panel data are better able to study the dynamics of adjustment: Crosssectional distributions that look relatively stable hide a multitude of changes. Spells of unemployment, job turnover, residential and income mobility are better studied with panels. Panel data are also well suited to study the duration of economic states like unemployment and poverty, and if these panels are long enough, they can shed light on the speed of adjustments to economic policy changes, For example in mea-

suring unemployed at a point in time. Only panel data can estimate what proportion of those who are unemployed in one period remain unemployed in another period.

4. Panel data are better able to identify and measure effects that are simply not detectable in pure cross-sections or pure time-series data: Ben-Porath (1973) gives an example. Suppose that we have a cross-section of women with a 50 per cent average yearly labor force participation rate. This might be due to (a) each woman having a 50 per cent chance of being in the labor force, in any given year, or (b) 50 per cent of the women work all the time and 50 per cent do not. Case (a) has high turnover, while case (b) has no turnover. Only panel data could discriminate between these cases.

5. Panel data models allow us to construct and test more complicated behavioral models than purely cross-section or time-series data: For example, technical efficiency is better studied and modeled with panel data models. In addition, fewer restrictions can be imposed in panels on a distributed lag model than in a purely time-series study.

Types of Panel Analytic Models

There are several types of panel data analytic models. There are constant coefficients models, fixed effects models, and random effects models. Among these types of models are dynamic panel, robust, and covariance structure models. Solutions to problems of heteroskedasticity and autocorrelation are of interest here. We will try to summarize some of the prominent aspects of this kind of methodology. For this, first we need to consider the data structure

The Constant Coefficients Model

One type of panel model has constant coefficients referring to both intercepts and slopes. In the event that there is neither significant country nor significant temporal effects, we could pool all the data and run an ordinary least squares regression model. Although most of the time there are either country or temporal effects, there are occasions when neither of these is statistically significant. This model is sometimes called the pooled regression model.

The Fixed Effects Model (Least Squares Dummy Variable Model)

Another type of panel model would have constant slopes but intercepts that differ according to the cross-sectional (group) unit. for example, the country. Although there are no significant temporal effects, there are significant differences among countries in this type of model. While the intercept is cross- section (group) specific and in this case differs from country to country, it may or may not differ over time.

These models are called fixed effects models. After we discuss types of fixed effects models, we proceed to show how to test for the presence of statistically significant group and/or time effects. Finally, we discuss the advantages and disadvantages of the fixed effects models before entertaining alternatives. Because i-1 dummy variables are used to designate the particular country, this same model is sometimes called the Least Squares Dummy Variable model.

$$y_{it} = a_1 + a_2 group_1 + a_2 group_2 + \beta_2 x_{2it} + \beta_3 x_{3it} + e_{it}$$

Another type of fixed effects model could have constant slopes but intercepts that differ according to time. In this case, the model would have no significant country differences but might have auto-correlation owing to time-lagged temporal effects.

The residuals of this kind of model may have autocorrelation in the process. In this case, the variables are homogenous across the countries. They could be similar in region or area of focus. For example, technological changes or national policies would lead to group specific characteristics that may effect temporal changes in the variables being analyzed. We could account for the time effect over the t years with t-1 dummy variables on the right-hand side of the equation. In equation the dummy variables are named according to the year they represent.

$$y_{it} = a_1 + \lambda_1 + \beta_1 x_{it} + e_{it}$$

Fixed Effects Model

Fixed effects models are not without their drawbacks. The fixed effects models may frequently have too many cross-sectional units of observations requiring too many dummy variables for their specification. Too many dummy variables may sap the model of sufficient number of degrees of freedom for adequately powerful statistical tests. Moreover, a model with many such variables may be plagued with multicollinearity, which increases the standard errors and thereby drains the model of statistical power to test parameters. If these models contain variables that do not vary within the groups, parameter estimation may be precluded. Although the model residuals are assumed to be normally distributed and homogeneous, there could easily be country-specific (group wise) heteroskedasticity or autocorrelation over time that would further plague estimation. The one big advantage of the fixed effects model is that the error terms may be correlated with the individual effects. If group effects are uncorrelated with the group means of the regressors, it would probably be better to employ a more parsimonious parameterization of the panel model.

The Random Effects Model

William H. Greene calls the random effects model a regression with a random constant term (Greene, 2003). One way to handle the ignorance or error is to assume that the intercept is a random outcome variable. The random outcome is a function of a mean value plus a random error. But this crosss-ectional specific error term vi, which indicates the deviation from the constant of the cross-sectional unit (in this example, country) must be uncorrelated with the errors of the variables if this is to be modeled. The time series cross-sectional regression model is one with an intercept that is a random effect.

$$y_{1t} = \beta_i + \beta_1 x_{1t} + \beta_2 x_{2t} + e_{it}$$

$$\beta_{0i} = \beta_1 + v_1$$

$$\therefore y_{1t} = \beta_1 + \beta_1 x_{1t} + \beta_2 x_{2t} + e_{it} + v_1$$

Under these circumstances, the random error vi is heterogeneity specific to a cross-sectional unit, in this case, country. This random error vi is constant over time. Therefore, the random error e_{it} is specific to a particular observation. For vi to be properly specified, it must be orthogonal to the individual effects. Because of the separate cross-sectional error term, these models are sometimes called one-way random effects models. Owing to this intra-panel variation, the random effects model has the distinct advantage of allowing time-invariant variables to be included among the regressors.

Error Components Models

If, however, the random effects model depends on both the cross-section and the time series within it, the error components (sometimes referred to as variance components) models are referred to as a two-way random effects model. In that case, the error term should be uncorrelated with the time series component and the cross-sectional (group) error. The orthogonality of these components allows the general error to be decomposed into cross-sectional specific, temporal, and individual error components.

$$e_{1t} = v_1 + e_1 + n_{it}$$

The component, *vi*, is the cross-section specific error. It affects only the observations in that panel. Another, *et*, is the time-specific component. This error component is peculiar to all observations for that time period, *t*. The third hit affects only the particular observation. These models are sometimes referred to as two-way random effects models (Sas, 1999).

The Random Parameters Model

According to Robert Yaffee, in some random coefficient models like Hildreth, Houck, and Swamy, the parameters are allowed to vary over the cross-sectional units. This model allows both random intercept and slope parameters that vary around common means. The random parameters can be considered outcomes of a common mean plus an error term, representing a mean deviation for each individual. This model assumes neither heteroskedasticity nor autocorrelation within the panels to avoid complicating the covariance matrix. In multilevel models pertaining to students, schools, and cities, there can be individual student, school, and city random error terms as well. There can also be cross-level interactions within these hierarchical models.

Dynamic Panel Models

If there is autocorrelation in the model, it is necessary to deal with it. One can apply one or more of the several tests for residual autocorrelation. The Durbin-Watson test for first-order autocorrelation in the residuals was modified by Bhargava et al. to handle balanced panel data. Baltagi and Wu (1999) modified it further to handle unbalanced panel and equally spaced data (Stata, 2003). There may be panel specific autocorrelation or there may be common autocorrelation across all panels.

There are provisions for specifying the type of autocorrelation. Alternatively, an autoregression on lags of the residuals may indicate the presence or absence of autocorrelation and the need for dynamic panel analysis. If there is autocorrelation from one temporal period to another, it is possible to analyze the "differences in differences" of these observations, using the first or last as a baseline (Wooldridge, 2002). If autocorrelation inheres across these observations, the model may be first partial differenced to control for the autocorrelation effects on the residuals (Greene, 2002). Arellano and Bond introduced lagged dependent variables into their model to account for dynamic effects. The lagged dependent variables can be introduced to either fixed or random effects models. Their inclusion assumes that the number of temporal observations is greater than the number of regressors in the model. Even if one assumes no autocorrelation, problems from the correlation of the lagged endogenous and the disturbance term may plague the analysis. Bias can result especially when the sample is finite or small. If one uses General Methods of Moments(GMM), with instrumental variables, the use of the proxy variables or instruments may circumvent problems with correlations of errors. Moreover, there are a large number of instruments provided by lagged variables. GMM with these instruments and larger orders of moments can be used to obtain additional efficiency gains. Another approach to deal with autocorrelation in the random errors is the Parks method. The model assumes an autoregressive error structure of the first order along with contemporaneous correlation among the cross-sections and this model is estimated by a two-state generalized least squares procedure.

$$e_{1t} = \rho_1 e_{2t-1} + \eta_{1t}$$

Panel data models with generalized estimating equations can handle higher order panel data analysis.

Robust Panel Models

There are number of problems that plague panel data models. Outliers can bias regression slopes, particularly if they have bad leverage. These outliers can be down weighted with the use of M-estimators in the model. Heteroskedasticity problems arise from group wise differences, and often taking group means can remove heteroskedasticity. The use of a White heteroskedasticity consistent covariance estimator with ordinary least squares estimation in fixed effects models can yield standard errors robust to unequal variance along the predicted line (Greene, 2002; Wooldridge, 2002). Sometimes autocorrelation inheres within the panels from one period to another. Some problems with dynamic panels that contain autocorrelation in the residuals are handled with a Prais-Winston transformation or a Cochrane-Orcutt transformation that amounts to a first partial differencing to remove the bias from the autocorrelation. Arellano, Bond, and Bover developed one and two step General Methods of Moments (GMM) estimators for panel data analysis. GMM is usually robust to deviations of the underlying data generation process to violations of heteroskedasticity and normality, insofar as they are asymptotically normal but they are not always the most efficient estimators. If there is autocorrelation in the models, one can obtain a weight-adjusted combination of the White and Newey - West estimator to handle both the heteroskedasticity and the autocorrelation in the model.

References

- Wooldridge, Jeffrey M. (2009). Introductory Econometrics: A Modern Approach (Fourth ed.). Australia: South-Western. p. 88. ISBN 978-0-324-66054-8
- Logit-and-Probit-Model-used-for-Prediction-of-Financial-Health-of-Company-281169370: researchgate.net, Retrieved 31 March 2018
- Econometrics: whatis.techtarget.com, Retrieved 15 May 2018
- Johnston, John (1972). Econometric Methods (Second ed.). New York: McGraw-Hill. pp. 267–291. ISBN 0-07-032679-7
- Autoregressive-integrated-moving-average-arima.asp: investopedia.com, Retrieved 03 July 2018

Permissions

All chapters in this book are published with permission under the Creative Commons Attribution Share Alike License or equivalent. Every chapter published in this book has been scrutinized by our experts. Their significance has been extensively debated. The topics covered herein carry significant information for a comprehensive understanding. They may even be implemented as practical applications or may be referred to as a beginning point for further studies.

We would like to thank the editorial team for lending their expertise to make the book truly unique. They have played a crucial role in the development of this book. Without their invaluable contributions this book wouldn't have been possible. They have made vital efforts to compile up to date information on the varied aspects of this subject to make this book a valuable addition to the collection of many professionals and students.

This book was conceptualized with the vision of imparting up-to-date and integrated information in this field. To ensure the same, a matchless editorial board was set up. Every individual on the board went through rigorous rounds of assessment to prove their worth. After which they invested a large part of their time researching and compiling the most relevant data for our readers.

The editorial board has been involved in producing this book since its inception. They have spent rigorous hours researching and exploring the diverse topics which have resulted in the successful publishing of this book. They have passed on their knowledge of decades through this book. To expedite this challenging task, the publisher supported the team at every step. A small team of assistant editors was also appointed to further simplify the editing procedure and attain best results for the readers.

Apart from the editorial board, the designing team has also invested a significant amount of their time in understanding the subject and creating the most relevant covers. They scrutinized every image to scout for the most suitable representation of the subject and create an appropriate cover for the book.

The publishing team has been an ardent support to the editorial, designing and production team. Their endless efforts to recruit the best for this project, has resulted in the accomplishment of this book. They are a veteran in the field of academics and their pool of knowledge is as vast as their experience in printing. Their expertise and guidance has proved useful at every step. Their uncompromising quality standards have made this book an exceptional effort. Their encouragement from time to time has been an inspiration for everyone.

The publisher and the editorial board hope that this book will prove to be a valuable piece of knowledge for students, practitioners and scholars across the globe.

Index